FOUR SEASONS
NORTH

FOUR SEASONS NORTH

Billie Wright

HARPER & ROW, PUBLISHERS
New York, Evanston, San Francisco, London

Designed by C. Linda Dingler

Library of Congress Cataloging in Publication Data

Wright, Billie.
    Four seasons north.
    1. Wright, Billie. 2. Brooks Range, Alaska.
3. Alaska—Description and travel—1959-
I. Title.
F912.B75W74   1973   917.98'7'045   79-138774
ISBN 0-06-014756-3

CONTENTS

Illustrations follow page 86 and page 182

INTRODUCTION

One hundred miles north of the Arctic Circle in northern Alaska, there is a mountain range called the Brooks Range. These craggy, snow-crested peaks sweep across the top of the world, west and east, for some six hundred miles, from the western arctic coast to the northern end of the Canadian Rockies. Many believe them to be the most beautiful, the most dramatic and the wildest mountains in North America.

For centuries, this remote range was inhabited only by small bands of nomadic Eskimo hunters and wild animals such as caribou herds, wolf packs and roaming grizzly bears. Then the 1890 gold strikes brought in the white men, in numbers enough to swell the native population a hundredfold. Most of the gold-seekers left after one arctic winter; some died of exposure, starvation or gunshot wounds. A few remained in isolated cabins along staked-out creeks nestled in the deep canyons of the range. All who stayed were part of a roughly bound community shaped more by a shared life style influenced by environmental necessity than by circumscribed territory. But as these old-timers—the prospectors, trappers, the native nomadic hunters and fishermen —died off or joined the country's migration to urban centers, they were not replaced. Today, despite the developmental view which sees Alaska, including its most northerly reaches, only as the potential great dollar bonanza of our century, when winter settles upon the arctic lands of the Koyukuk regions of the Brooks Range, only the caribou, wolves, grizzlies, one small native village and a handful of isolated settlers remain.

In this, our home territory, it is difficult to do a population count over a roadless, telephoneless isolated area of some twelve thousand square miles. The mountainous area of the upper Koyukuk district, which covers the central portion of the Brooks Range, includes in its present population the Eskimo village of Anaktuvuk Pass, with about 110 to 120 men, women and children plus the non-native schoolteacher couple; six or seven single white men, most of whom live in the remnants of what was once a thriving gold-mining town—and four or five families and couples living in widely separated, isolated places in the mountains.

My husband and I are one of the latter. We live in the Brooks Range one hundred miles north of the Arctic Circle, on the shore of one of the few large lakes in these mountains—two hundred miles from the nearest pavement, thirty miles from our nearest neighbor. Our home is a twelve-by-twelve-foot log cabin we built with only the simplest of hand tools, on a mountain slope above the lake.

The life we lead here is much like that of the hunting life of the Nunamiut Eskimos. Learning to live this life, which, through climate and environment, is shaped more by necessity than by choice, has nevertheless called for deliberate choices to be made. These, curiously enough, are in the realm of values.

We came to this Alaskan wilderness as part of my husband Sam's sabbatical-year study on value formation. We came to look at the shifting value systems of cultures in rapid transition among peoples still remote from urban centers and technological in-fluences.

Two years before, Sam had been landed by float plane on a small unnamed lake in the central Brooks Range, and had back-packed with a photographer friend into this wilderness in search of plots where spruce tree seeds had been planted north of timber line. They hiked a hundred miles in to the mountain village of Anaktuvuk Pass, the home of the Nunamiut Eskimos. His experience with these caribou-hunting people helped to crystallize the framework of his value-formation study.

I was able to join him as wilderness companion in the Arctic as observer, recorder and photographer. We backpacked and filmed through the mountain wilds of the Brooks Range; planted spruce seedlings beyond the northernmost timber line to carry on the tree-growth experiment begun in 1930 by Robert Marshall, arctic explorer–author–forester; and went again to visit the people of Anaktuvuk Pass.

It became increasingly clear that while many of the values present in the changing culture of these inland Eskimos had already become similar to those of the white urban culture, there were other values still primary in this so-called more primitive society which were indecipherable viewed from a non-native perspective. These elusive values were most striking in that special relationship to the environment which is the basis of the Eskimo's rare and remarkable selfhood.

We became keenly aware of this relationship, sensing its life-sustaining importance in the Nunamiut hierarchy of values. But we knew, too, the difficulty of translating, without loss or distortion, concepts which are so lacking in our own technologized culture.

An old Eskimo woman gave us the key. She said, "How you understand Eskimo unless you live like Eskimo, early days ago? Not like he live now—he pretend to be white man now. White man don't know what it like to live alone in Arctic—hunt—trap—catch fish through hole in ice. What you know about Eskimo, go look and talk to him? He tell what he think you like to hear. Go live like Eskimo early days ago. Then *you* know."

It has been said that "truth is a hard deer to hunt." Once the quarry is sighted, what hunter will turn away? The sabbatical year of study immediately underwent a major transformation. Before we "studied" any more so-called primitive cultures, we would ourselves live, as far as possible, like the Eskimos, "early days ago." We moved into the Arctic, just in time to begin to prepare for the long, frozen winter.

This journal of my first year in the wilderness is in the tradition of personal diaries and accounts kept by isolated dwellers of the Arctic since before the turn of the century. It is my view of a way of life shaped and dominated by a dramatic cycle of seasons, a record of lessons learned and attitudes unlearned, of insights gained in coming to know, intimately, and to trust, implicitly, the teachings of the land and the natural world. This is my personal record of the dailiness that makes up an arctic year— or lifetime.

While all the people here are very real, some of their names have been changed. The far north still lives by a frontier code of respect for the privacy of the individual.

My arctic mountain lake can be located on some maps of Alaska, but not by the name of Koviashuvik. Why is that? It seems obvious, if only from the above comment. In addition it is because I don't wish my world to be invaded by people seeking an "instant" wilderness experience in ten or twenty easy lessons. It doesn't work. One cannot grasp the eternal "instantly."

I like our timelessness, serenity, solitude. We—and the wolf packs and caribou bands and grizzlies—need our "living room." So I wish you well and say to you: Go, seek, find your own lake or creek, marsh or mountain or garden—your own "Koviashuvik" —place and time of joy. It may still be there, if you hurry . . . if you hurry. . . .

Koviashuvik
Brooks Range
Alaska

Winter, 1972

AUTUMN

TO KOVIASHUVIK

Our bush pilot starts a circling descent, bringing the details of the arctic landscape into ever-sharpening focus. On the far shore of the lake below, a bull moose stands in the shallows, the afternoon light striking glints off his white rack. Now, over the larger of the two islands, a sudden streak of white motion below becomes a caribou buck on the run. As we level off for the smooth-as-silk landing and glide in toward the shore, another moose, this one a cow, breaks into an awkward slow-motion gallop away from a little sand beach, up onto the tundra and out of sight.

The small cove our pilot has aimed for seems to be directly below the mountain cabin we have sighted from the air. Aware now of the darkening day, having left the last light of early evening in the skies high above the lake, we hurriedly wade ashore with our gear. Daryl, with a wave and a promise to bring in a load of our supplies on Saturday, turns the small Super Cub into the wind and takes off. A hundred feet from us, a late-migrating band of five merganser ducks, disturbed by the roar and backwash, take off in the opposite direction.

Here at the bottom of the bowl, a thousand feet below the crest, the sun has disappeared and a chill evening wind come up. While I watch Daryl's plane vanish into infinite space, Sam loads the 30/06 rifle. We are in the land of unpredictable grizzlies and feisty moose. They are as likely to be spooked by us as are the wolves, wolverines and caribou—but more dangerous in an unexpected encounter.

3

Turning, I scan the steep mountainside we are obviously going to climb, searching for a path or trail through the thick tussocks and lichens of its tundra cover—but I see none. Patches of melt shine whitely with early ice among the tundra browns. A split packboard Sam cached in a rotting hulk of a derelict boat when he checked out our winter home weeks earlier is loaded and roped with our cartons. Sam leads the way, straight up, moving as if he is following an exact trail, but I still see no evidence in the mossy duff that anyone has ever walked here before.

We climb steadily for a half mile, zigzagging briefly to avoid particularly high growths of tussocks and outcroppings of rocks, pausing once or twice to puff and to stare, almost disbelieving, at the wild panorama all around us. Just as we reach the edge of the gently sloping plateau and see above us, still a quarter of a mile off, the cabin—a dark, small silhouette against the last remnants of a crimson sunset sky—we pause again. Behind us, out over the now black-water lake, the moon begins its rise from behind a white peak across the water and shimmers with a halo in the deepening blue. There is nothing to say in the face of this incredible beauty. We nod and hurry on.

The nearness of the cabin speeds us along. Even in the twilight, with the first stars of evening overhead, it looks sturdy, arctic-winter-proof, inviting. No time to explore or investigate when we reach it; chores to be done before nightfall have top priority. The two windows unboarded of their anti-grizzly shutters, a roaring fire made, buckets of sparkling icy water brought up from the creek I'd spotted from the air. Fortunately, the cabin contains a few staples and some trail foods Sam left on his earlier exploratory trip in mid-August. One carton we've carried with us all this day is a box of fresh vegetables, picked this morning in the garden of Fairbanks friends. With these riches, we are soon hungrily devouring a remarkably good dinner of instant soup, mashed potatoes, raw carrots and fresh coffee—and beginning, in the fragrant warmth of our Yukon stove, to unwind from this long day's journey. . . .

FIRST DAYS

Awakened to sunrise filling the cabin, the rich morning aroma of perking coffee and an eagerness to rush into this day, making it seem either our last or our first on this planet! Stepping outside the heavy Dutch door of our new home, I find a morning sky which looks like a realistic painting of the old "buckeye" style, as a gold-red-salmon sunrise reflects pink on the white mountain spires opposite, then fades off into a misty, low-hanging silver cloud hung in a blazing arctic sky above the western peaks. Ringed by mountains, covered by a vast turquoise-blue roof.

We are just below timber line here. The highest reaches of the sparse thickets of spruce forests end only a few hundred feet above where I stand.

Back inside for a good breakfast of oatmeal with raisins and brown sugar and coffee—and talk of the chores we must get to. It is mid-September. All that we see is a reminder that winter will move in swiftly and that we are far from ready for it. Eight cords of wood is a minimum winter supply, we've been told by Fairbanks friends who have wintered in the bush. And Sam says we must "get in" our winter meat. This does not mean mailing off an order for meat to be flown in the two hundred miles from a Fairbanks supermarket, but that we will hunt and dress our own game. I remember the moose and caribou sighted as we flew in and wonder how I will feel about converting those creatures into my "winter meat." The Yukon stove needs repairs—the cabin must be chinked—cracked lights (panes of glass) replaced. The territory explored. What is the order of priorities when all these chores must be done at once?

Breakfast over, priorities settle themselves when Sam examines the stove closely and finds that there are gaps in the already repaired metal sides where sparks can fall through. To arctic bush dwellers, fire is a greater threat than freezing to death. The first may guarantee the second if it occurs on a midwinter night! As soon as all our supplies have arrived, I'll see that we have emergency food, clothes and medicines cached somewhere away from the cabin, just in case.

Sam sets off with his packboard to Jim Pup, a mile up the creek, where two derelict old cabins are all that remain of a three-man gold-mining operation during the 1930s and '40s. He remembers from his earlier reconnoiterings that he has seen a piece of asbestos on one of the ·broken-down shelves.

I watch him disappear to an infinitesimal speck on the sloping tundra, then turn to my own chores. Make an inventory of all the food supplies. No need to worry. In these various varmint-proof cans and storage containers is enough food to last a year, if one can take a year's diet of beans, dried peas, cornmeal-mush makings and oatmeal.

Something nags at me, a distraction from these chores. I listen, very carefully, then realize that the distraction is that I *have* been listening. But to what? Silence? I stop work altogether, listening very hard—and hear nothing. I can feel some slight, strange readjustment taking place inside my ears as I hear the immense sound of—no sound. Only after I have heard and acknowledged this clearly do my ears begin to pick out the myriad sounds within silence. One at a time they emerge: The even rhythm of my breath. A whisper of the Yukon stove's dying fire consuming air. A gray jay's wings slicing through the air outside the open cabin door. And somewhere distantly, two flies buzz a kind of counterpoint. I feel as well as hear a very slight momentary tremor in the spruce floorboards as the permafrost underneath them melts and shifts. And somewhere in the background of these fragments of sound is a larger humming from far off—noise inside my own head? I think it may be the wind roaring round canyons and peaks far in the distance. Or perhaps it is the sound of the northern lights. The Eskimos say you can *hear* the aurora borealis. If that is true, the sound must continue during the day even though the lights are of course visible only at night.

Perhaps our ears stay filled with remembered sounds, with the screeching, whirring, humming clamor of "civilization," long after we've left them behind. If true, here in this "silent" wild place, there may be other dimly remembered sounds, predating those learned in civilization. I feel I've gone through some kind of metamorphosis, discovered a new—or lost—sense, and in so doing come more alive. Still, I do not hear Sam's footsteps on the tundra until he is less than twenty-five feet from the cabin. But then Sam walks like a forest Indian.

He returns with the asbestos and forces it into the gaps of the metal sheet wrapped round the sides of the Yukon stove. While the stove is cool, he also replaces the rusting stovepipe with the new one we've brought with us. We must remember the warning from our Eskimo friend Dishu that the stovepipe must be tapped hard now and then to shake down the accumulation of spruce pitch inside it. She also says that we should climb up on the roof periodically and, with a long pole poked down inside the stovepipe, knock off the flammable deposits of pitch charcoal.

For lunch we open a small tin of franks, with more carrots and coffee. We have no bread until I take time to bake some, but that is for the future.

With packboards and rifle, we set off after lunch for the lake shore, taking a different trail. This narrow path through the woods is clearly visible, recognizable as an old trail, though willows, alder and sturdy spruce seedlings have already begun to reclaim it. This is the old dog sled trail, a more gradual climb than yesterday's direct route straight up the mountainside, but half again as long. Still there are some very steep places, and finding the going on foot a bit treacherous where the melt has already frozen to a slippery crust, I wonder at how easily even a dog team could navigate these sharp declines.

At the bottom of the trail, twenty feet from the shore, are the derelict remains of a small, one-room log cabin which belongs to Dishu. The turf roof has collapsed into a frozen mass of dirt inside the cabin, leaving the interior wide open to snow and sun. A side wall has also given way, log by log, and buckled the three remaining walls to crazy tilting angles. The whole thing looks as if it might best be used for firewood. But on closer inspection, some of the lower logs look salvageable, though most are rotten. Tundra roofs are excellent insulation, especially with the winter snows on top of them, but only if the cabin is being lived in. Without cabin heat, in a very few years the snow-melt- and rain-soaked turf will rot the ceiling logs on which the tundra rests, as well as the big beams which support everything —and an open-roofed, earth-filled shell is the result.

Along the shore, fresh wolf tracks, a pair, one set small, the other large—mother and pup? Moose tracks, very fresh, too— but no game in sight. We launch the sturdy old rowboat which belongs to the miner who has loaned us our winter home and try for some trout, using the ivory hook Dishu gave Sam. But the wind is too stiff, and we have not the feeling of time and relaxation needed for good fishing. Winter is too close, and fish are not adequate "winter meat"—not enough fat! We soon go back to shore, tie the five-gallon Blazo gasoline fuel can on one pack-board, a carton on the other, and head straight up the mountain. Today I discover that there *is* a faint impression of a foot trail. Less seen than sensed, it is the only logical route to follow from the bottom of the mountain to the top. Miners and game must have used this shortcut for years. Today I puff a little less!

At the cabin, Sam makes a roaring fire while I cut up a batch of our fresh vegetables to be cooked in bouillon-cube broth for a vegetable stew, then quickly mix a batch of biscuits. The small camp oven looks ancient and battered, but efficient, warming on the stove—and supper is on the way. But some surprise! When the biscuits come out of the oven, they have collapsed into a soft, flat tortilla! My vanity is shaken until I discover that the unmarked "flour" tin holds not flour but instant milk. We eat the biscuits with a spoon. They have an interesting cheesy flavor.

Sam is edgy about that "winter meat." After dinner, he hikes over the mountain to an old cache still standing on the lake-shore, where he has seen fresh evidence of a moose in the vicinity. While he's gone, I make another batch of biscuits, having now found some flour in an old twenty-five-pound tin under the table, and put them on to bake.

Although it is not quite dusk outside, inside the cabin the light is very dim. Dishes are washed by candlelight. Then I blow out the candle and sit in the twilight by the window to wait for Sam, and to look, to see, for really seeing takes time. I get caught in trying to translate what my eye sees into film images, for I plan to photograph this coming year with both sixteen-millimeter movie camera and thirty-five-millimeter stills. But not yet. At this point, still a stranger in this land, photographing would be nothing more than snapshooting. I will take the time to come to know this world before I try to capture it on film. This is not the "instant" world of "outside." Here it is timeless, eternal.

Something moves way off below on the tundra—a dark, slow-moving, shapeless mass. A grizzly? Sam has the binoculars with him. I glance up at the beam where the 30/06 has been hung. Sam, of course, has taken it with him, and our other two rifles have not yet arrived. But at least the camera is here. I will get a grizzly on film! The dark moving shape is still unrecognizable and its outline looks like nothing I can imagine. It comes closer and closer, and finally I can see that it is Sam, balancing three long spruce logs on his shoulders and, at closer view, looking like a drunken windmill. He has not found the moose but has brought back the beginnings of our woodpile.

After the wood is cut and stacked, we sit again, here in the bright circle of light, drinking our coffee and smoking our roll-your-own cigarettes (to roll one that doesn't spill burning ash and tobacco into my lap, all I need is a little more practice!). We make our journal notes, even though we are both weary. This feeling of contentment and well-being is even stronger today. This will be a fine home, I think. . . .

Today, brilliant sun—then clouds moving in with the feel of snow to them. Sam off early this morning to look for that moose. Later he rowed out to the island and tramped across it, looking for the caribou buck that was there the day we flew in. But no luck.

After lunch, we go out to the woods west of camp, and wood

gathering begins in earnest. We take only the dead trees. Sam axes them. I knock off their brittle branches, many of which are covered with a black, velvety mosslike growth, working with the back side of a hatchet blade. Then we drag the logs down the mountain to the edge of the woods, and stand them in a tripod, tepee shape, so that later they can be found easily in the snow and sledded down to the cabin for sawing and splitting. Hard work! Even in the chill wind, I feel like I'm moving about in a portable steam bath, but the sight of that towering collection of thirteen or fourteen logs for firewood brings its own rewards. These arctic white spruce, the farthest-north-growing trees of this species, are incredibly sturdy to survive this land's subzero temperatures. From a distance of twenty feet, some of them look completely dead, their trunks and branches silver black and bare, not a green needle visible anywhere. Yet one must look very carefully before swinging the ax, for somewhere among that tangle of dead branches there may be, on close inspection, one single branch with a thriving new growth of green—still a sturdy purchase on life.

This is the day Daryl said he'd try to bring in our supplies and so, midafternoon, we hike down to the lake to wait for him. Rowing out to the middle of the lake, we troll for trout, but again no luck. Rowing back to shore, we follow the arc of a rainbow—iridescent colors, bright and close overhead.

On shore, we amble along to the derelict cabin and decide that the logs will make a good portable blind once the lake has frozen over. We can use the blind in filming animals, or as a wind-break for ice fishing. The overcast is thickening, and the wind carries a hint of the ice at the tops of the peaks it has swept across. There are more fresh moose tracks in the sand, and Sam follows them along the shore a little way while I build a small fire on the beach and huddle over it to await his return. By now it is getting too late for Daryl to come in and then get back to Bettles before dusk. When Sam returns, still mooseless, we decide to go on up the mountain via the dog sled trail. But in the willows just behind the old cabin, Sam discovers the dog sleds we have been told we might use. They need repair before they can haul a load. Sam decides to pack the smaller one up the mountain to the cabin, where he has his few tools. While he is considering how he will fit a five-foot-long, three-foot-high sled onto a fourteen-by-twenty-inch packboard, I wander about over the giant tussocks, which would be boggy and wet were the tundra not already semifrozen.

I am looking for berries, and soon find a small patch of low-bush cranberries under a thick cluster of willows. These tart, crimson little berries, the size of large green peas, make commercially grown cranberries taste pallid. Though these are called cranberries, they are lingonberries—very rich in vitamin C, and the only year-round source of anything resembling "fresh" fruit, for their high acidity makes it possible to store them through the winter. No elaborate preservation methods are needed beyond freezing, or storing in jars or crocks, uncooked or cooked, with a little sugar added if they taste too tart. Whether they are raw or cooked, the tartness is an excellent complement to game meat of all kinds.

Perhaps it's an atavistic food-gathering instinct that makes most women unable to pass by a wild berry patch. Certainly some compulsion takes over when I see this lush, scarlet carpet. I don't notice near-numb fingers, chilled to the bone from the frozen berries, nor cold, aching knees, frigid from kneeling in the frosty tundra. Everything waits while this wild crop is harvested. I stop reluctantly, only after noting suddenly that Sam has hitched sled, packboard and himself together in some miraculous fashion and—having apparently called several times that he was going on—is already disappearing up the trail. He has the 30/06; I hurry after him. I have a quart of plump, tart wild cranberries!

Several days later. Not sure of the date. We have no calendar. I forget to wind my watch, too; but neither calendar nor clock has much meaning here anyway. The sun is the only timepiece to decide the day's activities. And who needs a calendar to know "when" it is? It is the beginning of winter! The snows have begun. Each storm leaves the tundra under a slightly deeper, whiter coverlet, but so far the intermittent days of bright sun continue. Although the trails are slippery in our rubber-soled pacs, snowshoes still stand unused in the cabin corner. A reminder to add to the chore list: sandpaper and varnish the snowshoes and repair the tears in their rawhide webbing.

It must be the weekend, for today we have visitors! The sound of any aircraft over Anaktuvuk Pass brought the villagers tumbling out of their tents to scan the skies with shouts of "*Air-plan! Air-plan!*" Here it is the same. With the same excited curiosity, we watch a small, strange plane circle the lake. Only when the little amphibian craft lands and cruises into the shallows do we recognize three of our friends from Fairbanks. After so little time in our isolated wilderness, we've not yet begun to "miss" people—yet this unexpected arrival of friends who have flown two hundred miles to get here for a brief visit is an event to be celebrated.

We invite them to the cabin, with just enough time to share some good talk and biscuits and coffee before they have to take off to get back and relieve their baby-sitter at 5 P.M. Only in Alaska, where one out of every eight or nine residents is a licensed pilot, is a four-hundred-mile round trip by plane the equivalent of a Sunday afternoon's drive!

Now that Daryl has ferried in the last of our winter supplies, we expect no further contact with "outside" until after freeze-up, when the lake will be iced over. This may mean several months, for though Daryl hopes to supply us with mail service on some basis, we are not on his regular twice-a-month bush mail route. After the lake ice is at least five inches thick, we will mark off a "runway" on it a thousand feet long, to indicate a landing surface free of thin ice or overflow, for any plane wishing or needing to stop here.

CARIBOU HUNT

We have not as yet been able to hunt very seriously, not wanting to go too far from camp until the arrival of our supplies. Now the hunting takes top priority.

In past years, Koviashuvik has often been a main migration route, spring and fall, for the caribou herds that summer on the tundra between the north slope of the Brooks Range and the Arctic Ocean, and winter to the south in the interior mountains. Caribou may pass in herds of thousands, and even when the main migrations pass some miles distant, small bands and strays pass through Koviashuvik.

A good hunter can take most of his winter meat in a single day's hunt from one large herd migrating through his territory. While the entire state of Alaska is covered by game control and management laws and regulations, there are few restrictions on caribou hunting for residents of the range, for trophy hunting, as such, is unknown among the Eskimo and white bush settlers. Caribou is hunted for meat and fat, the staples of the inland arctic diet. And although mail-order "store-bought" parkas and boots have become commonplace in native dress in the last few years, caribou skins are still used by many natives and some whites for parkas, mukluks (boots) and bedding.

Moose, even in the range, must be taken in season, usually late August to late September. After that, the bulls go into rut, stop feeding and live off their accumulated fat, which turns the flavor of the meat strong and gamy. The Anaktuvuk hunters figure the meat of one moose to be equivalent to that of five caribou, with caribou considered far superior in taste and tenderness. Whites who live in the range also prefer caribou, but in other sections, most non-native Alaskans who hunt for their meat express a preference for the taste of moose.

Today we rise early and start down the mountain, stopping at various points to glass the shore and slopes, but no game is to be seen in the vicinity. Until winter has covered the landscape with white, the arctic tundra provides a near-perfect camouflage for most game. Even through binoculars, at a distance of a mile or more a creature as large as a moose will look deceptively like a large mound of willow and tussocks until he moves or the sun glints off a white antler. Still glassing the areas, we row across the lake to a small, shallow, sedge-rimmed bay, good browsing ground for moose, with its thick underwater beds of mosses. As we round the point and drift silently into the bay, a family of seven merganser ducks eye us curiously, then turn serenely back to their bottoms-up feeding near the shore.

We go ashore, and while scouting for fresh signs of game, cross a huge crimson patch of thickly growing lowbush cranberries. Reluctantly moving on, I carefully note the location for future reference. The game signs are not promising. Back in the boat, we row across the channel between the mainland and the eastern end of the large island, then slowly along its mile length to the western tip. Nothing moves but the wind-stirred branches of the tallest spruce. No sound but the oars quietly cutting through the water, and the faraway cries of a pair of loons. At the far end of the island we go ashore and sit on the sunny, moss-covered bank to have our lunch. We eat quickly, speaking very little, still glassing and scanning the shore and slopes. Our mood is strangely tense, as if, having shifted into high gear for the hunt, we cannot now slow down or relax even in this tranquil place. Minutes later, we get up and move without speaking along the island shore. A few hundred feet along, Sam suddenly pauses, then turns abruptly into the interior of the island, which is thickly overgrown with willow and spruce. I can tell that he has seen—heard—sensed something. This moment always spells out the difference between a fine hunter and an ordinary one; it happens out of something akin to magic, something that goes far beyond anything like experience or competence. The good hunter himself can't explain—or teach—it, for it's a thing of instinct, I suspect. Most of the native hunters are such hunters—and Sam is this kind of hunter. But many whites rely on their small "cannon" firearms to try to substitute for these skills.

At the top of the bank rising up from the sandy shore, Sam stops, a hand outstretched to warn me. Behind him I freeze in my tracks, even before I see the great caribou buck a hundred yards in front of us. His head with its huge arching white rack is lowered as he browses on the white reindeer moss on a high tussock. He is still unaware of us. Sam raises the 30/06, but though he can easily wound the buck at this farily short range, the head-high tangle of willows and young spruce between him and the caribou prevents a sure, clean shot. Hunting has its own ethics. Injured game must be tracked down, for any fair chance of survival from other predators—wolves and wolverines in the case of caribou—has been removed by the careless or luckless shot. Sam lowers the rifle slightly, and moves cautiously around toward the clear side of the thicket. But even at the barely perceptible movement, the buck's head jerks instantly upward. In one great bound, he turns and disappears into the spruce woods, headed toward the other end of the island. We follow, running, but at the far end he is still out of sight. He has not swum across to the mainland—there is not a ripple in the water. Therefore, he must have rounded the island shore and be traveling back along the beach to where we first sighted him. We, too, cross the island and at once pick up his fresh tracks on the narrow sandy beach.

Midway, a narrow spit of land connects the two main parts of the island. I remain here, hoping this time to head the buck off, while Sam continues on and disappears in the brush. I wait, listening to silence broken only by my own loud, excited breathing. Then hoofbeats are pounding right toward me, it seems; but just as suddenly the sound veers off. The buck bounds out of the brush and into the water parallel to the spit, only a hundred feet away. He swims with surprising speed, only his head and antlers visible above the water. Reaching land, he again vanishes among the scrub. I begin to have a disheartening vision of spending the next week in a kind of island ring-around-a-rosy with this caribou, but Sam, as he joins me, with an expression that is at the same time alert and patient, only matter-of-factly signals me not to move in the direction of the buck but to stay this time in the center of the island. He moves swiftly toward the right-hand shore and again disappears like a silent wraith.

Once more the silence beyond my own thumping heart and rasping breath is absolute, all sound absorbed by the soft, thick tundra. I can neither hear nor see any movement anywhere. Then—a single shot explodes the stillness. Nothing more. I wait, listening, and thinking that were *I* the hunter in this instance, I'd much prefer to be alone with my quarry in this boxed-in space. My parky, I note, is much the same color as the caribou's coat. I crouch low, waiting for the second shot. Instead, ten seconds later, the shout, "O.K. Got him!"

Sam reappears for a second, headed toward the left-hand shore, then drops again from sight. Scrambling over the tussocks, in and out of the tundra's sunken hollows, dodging around the spruce, I reach him just as he finishes cutting the jugular for the animal to bleed.

I find it difficult to describe this moment of the hunt. Food hunters, as compared to trophy hunters, rarely speak of it. The moment itself is paradoxical, and all hunting peoples have ritualized it in forms of acknowledgment and forgiveness to the spirit of the animal. There is immediate remorse at the sight of a majestic creature, crimson staining the ground beneath it. Relief that the perfectly placed neck shot has brought instant death, with no suffering. Undeniable elation that the hunt has provided winter food. And a realization lurking somewhere in the back of the mind that the pristine antiseptic package of meat purchased at the supermarket, if not the equivalent of a lie, is then only one of many plastic-wrapped fantasies in our consumer world of "instant" manna.

We manage to drag the three-hundred-pound carcass into a better position for skinning, and while Sam begins the long vertical opening down the caribou's belly, I walk slowly along the island shore, get the boat and row it back.

By late afternoon we have skinned, eviscerated and quartered our fat young buck and hauled it into the boat and back across the lake. Making a pole cache in a grove of cottonwoods at the foot of the shortcut trail up the mountain, we string up the quartered meat. Fresh, large wolf tracks in the grove are a worry, for the wolves, of course, will be after the fresh meat, and a determined one can and will leap high enough to reach the quarters, which are as high up as the tree height will allow. Sam brings over four traps he's cached earlier at Dishu's place and sets them beneath the meat. These number three traps are not powerful enough to hold a wolf, but their very presence will give the wolves pause!

The sun is gone now, the wind turned wintry. Filling a cloth flour sack with the caribou liver, heart, tongue and testicles, and extra fat from the thick deposit along the caribou's back and rump, we tie the bag onto a packboard and start the long climb home.

The days become shorter and shorter. Fairbanks radio reports the daily loss of light—six minutes yesterday, five today. Not the only sign of the coming cold. Already the mountains shut off all but four hours of direct sun, and when the sun disappears, the wind comes up, ice tinged, to chill the bones and fingers.

We've now gone from a meatless to almost an all-meat-and-fat diet. The difference has been immediately apparent. More than providing higher energy, better endurance, the fat provides fuel for body heat.

Arctic explorer Vilhjalmur Stefansson suggested that the major cause of disaster among early explorations by white men was in their failure to realize that the Eskimo diet of meat and fat, seal oil, muktuk (whale fat) was the primary key to arctic survival. Instead of adopting the diet natural to the environment, the whites relied on their "superior" tinned beef—and perished.

After years of carefully trimming away the fat on steaks and chops, I'm surprised at the relish with which we now devour fat. Lean browsing years can mean stringy, tough winter meat, but a fine, fat caribou, which is, after all, processed tundra, is superb eating; its white, dense, sweet-tasting fat surpassed only by bear fat.

Most of the meat still hangs down in the cottonwood grove, for it should "season" for about two weeks. But we haven't waited. We've been eating "unseasoned" meat as well as boiled heart and tongue, fried testicles and liver (finer than the finest calves' liver). Traditionally, the Eskimos eat not only the organs, but also the head, boiled. In earlier days, the contents of the second stomach, after "setting" for three days, were used as a green or salad, a welcome addition to the meat/fat winter fare. The caribou forelegs, though relatively meatless, contain large amounts of delicious marrow—and also supply excellent skins for making the upper parts of mukluks. Little of the caribou remains unused, as food and clothing, sinew and bedding—and, until fairly recent times, the caribou-skin tents of the nomad hunters. All that is left goes to the dogs and wolves.

AT THE CREEK

This morning when we went down to the creek for water, the cover ice was two inches thick. But water still runs beneath this crust. We clear away the snow, then chip through the ice to make a hole big enough to get the pails down into the stream. Our ice chipper is a simple device but a superb tool for the job: a rusted old rasp filed down to a sharp edge and wired tightly into a broom-handle-length spruce pole.

I find that it is not as easy to use as it looks, though. The trick is not to pound away at the ice with all one's strength, but to let the chipper's cutting edge fall downward, striking the ice with a sharp, firm blow. This cracks and splinters the ice. Some more blows, a few inches away from the first crack, and large chunks of ice give way.

By morning the hole is frozen over again. But we don't mind. It's a beautiful spot to be in. There are always fresh tracks and scats to check out—fox, ermine, shrews, wolves. The jays fly along with us, hoping we are going to uncache some food, and so the long haul over the tussocky trail with the noisy chatterers overhead is always pleasant, even with arms which feel near pulled out of sockets by the heavy pails. A pail in each hand is obviously better balance, with considerably less sloshing over of ice water into boots.

Soon we will be carrying up loads of ice, not ice water, for the water will be frozen solid down to the creek bed—and that lovely muted sound of water running under ice will be stilled.

A SURFEIT OF HEAT AND OATMEAL COOKIES

Every day, in addition to all our other chores, we continue to go to the forest to take down dead trees for our firewood.

By the time dinner is over, I'm usually too weary to think of anything but crawling stiffly into the sleeping bag on top of the caribou skins. (No wonder no one in the arctic bush minds the "long night" of winter. By then it must seem like a well-deserved vacation after the weeks of getting ready for it!)

But as a "wood gatherer," I've suddenly become painfully aware of how much wood is being consumed to keep that Yukon fire going. It seems almost a sin to waste the roaring fire that lingers on after dinner has been cooked. But I'm learning! Now in the evening a batch of cookies is rushed into the same oven to make use of that heat. Sam has made me two cookie sheets cut from an empty old five-gallon Blazo gas can. And I've just about mastered the art of stoking the fire so that it will hold at "medium" heat for baking. But even so, baking time takes twice as long if the cookies are not to scorch on the bottoms. While I was discovering this, Sam was very understanding, claiming that charcoal is good for digestion. By the time this year is up, I will be able to put out a cookbook on the numbers of ways to make oatmeal cookies! With plenty of oatmeal, raisins, dry chocolate, instant milk and brown sugar, they must be as nutritious as pemmican—but they don't last as long.

AT ROONEY'S GRAVE

Today we backpacked all the caribou from the cottonwood grove a quarter of a mile over to Dishu's collapsed old cabin. Far from animalproof, with its open-air roof and crumbling log walls, it is at least at the foot of the old dog sled trail on which, sans dogs, we will sled provisions up the mountain to the cabin. Wolves have been discouraged by the traps, although some tracks ringing the grove show that they have investigated the cached meat. But the jays are less fortunate. They have been after the fat, tearing great chunks off the caribou, and several jays unfortunately perched on the delicately balanced traps and sprung them. Now we've wrapped the meat in old flour sacks to protect suet and the camp robbers.

Still keeping an eye out for moose, we row over to the opposite shore of the lake, where, on the caribou hunt, I'd spotted a good patch of lowbush cranberries, which seem to grow most luxuriantly in semidry land, in the shelter of willows and alder.

In the middle of this lush growth of scarlet berries are two crude graves. On the crest of a slight knoll, a rough-hewn cross of spruce boards made from a miner's sluice box has fallen down on a mound of scattered rocks. In rough letters, scratched into the wood with a penknife, is the legend:

ROONEY—BORN 1873—DIED JUNE 17, 1941. RIP

Who buried him here, I wonder.

We stand up the cross, prop it upright with some of the stones. Rooney was one of the old-time prospectors, part of the small mining community here in the twenties and thirties. Dishu tells how she and her mother, dog-sledding over from Wiseman one winter, were met by old Rooney, tearing out of his cabin and bellowing a raucous welcome composed almost entirely of an endless string of four-letter words. Wise to the vocabularies of old sourdoughs, the ladies accepted the salutation as evidence of Rooney's enthusiastic delight at having visitors.

Near Rooney's cross on the knoll is a second grave, unmarked, where Nakuchluk, the wife of the Eskimo Big Jim, is buried. Big Jim and Nakuchluk were also a part of the Koviashuvik community, coming here frequently, winter and summer, from their permanent camp in Wiseman, to hunt, trap and fish— combining the old nomadic ways of the Eskimos with the new, "settled" ways of the white man.

Everywhere here on the knoll, the crimson berries grow. The family of seven merganser ducks passes by in a neat flotilla, and from off the island shore, a loon "laughs" and skims the water in a clattering splash of sound.

SOURDOUGH BREAD

Last night I began our sourdough pot.

Only in the Arctic does this ritual retain any of its original significance—a source of the "staff of life," and all that symbol implied in a simpler, supermarketless time. I brought with me a small packet of dried sourdough starter, given to me in Fairbanks by Dishu, whose own sourdough starter was begun, perhaps forty or more years ago, with starter given her by her mother, begun with starter from *her* mother . . . and so on. This starter of mine must be close to a century old, with its origins in the sourdough pots carried across the western plains by frontier mothers, who then sent it along in the packs of their own goldminer sons en route to the camps along the mighty Yukon and into the arctic north.

The starter—a small packet of dried yeast and flour—is dissolved in a half cup of warm water, then mixed in an enamel pot with two cups of flour and two cups of warm water and stirred with a wooden spoon. Metal containers and utensils have no place in the sourdough picture.

I set the pot overnight in a warm place—on a shelf up behind the stove. Water and warmth activate the yeast, which gives off a carbon dioxide gas as it grows, forming bubbles in the dough. Starch and sugar are changed by lactic acid bacteria to lactic acid, which gives the dough that sour, yeasty aroma. More gas is formed when soda is added later and it reacts with the acid, making the batter even lighter and "spongier."

This "sponge," next morning, is ready for use in making hotcakes, muffins, bread—even cakes.

In Alaska's early history of white settlers, lone prospectors and isolated homesteading families saw sourdough as one of their most prized possessions, for it guaranteed them a basic necessity in diets severely restricted by the hardships of getting in supplies from "outside." Supplies from the nearest town might be a year in transit, by boat, barge, canoe or river boat, backpack or dog sled. Ordinary yeast plants became deactivated en route and would not grow in the severe cold. But the wild native yeasts in the sourdough starter would thrive, if refreshed periodically by more flour and water.

Today, with supplies and freight delivered regularly by rail, truck or plane to all but the most isolated bush dwellers, sourdough is no longer the basic necessity it once was. However, many Alaskans still keep a sourdough pot going out of preference for the fresh, yeasty quality of hearty sourdough hotcakes and bread.

Few of the doughty old-timers once known as "sourdoughs" remain outside the confines of the Pioneer Homes or a few hotel/boardinghouses where they sit in lobby rocking chairs and watch the girls go by as they swap often-repeated yarns of the good old days of prospecting, trapping, feuding and freezing in the Arctic. But those few who still live the life of the old days, on remote creeks and rivers in the wilds, know the sourdough pot to be one of the most essential ingredients for the good life.

So this morning I make sourdough bread. For too many years I have spent such mornings in repetitious rounds of committee meetings, tied to desks and trilling telephones, immersed in data logging and issue arguing. Today is new. Today I bake bread.

ONE LOAF OF SOURDOUGH BREAD

4 cups sifted white flour (or less) or 3 cups white
   flour and 1 cup whole wheat
3 tablespoons sugar
1 teaspoon salt
2 to 3 tablespoons melted caribou or bear fat
2 cups sponge, set the night before
   Soda water (¼ teaspoon soda dissolved in 1 teaspoon liquid from sponge pot or warm water),
   added at *second kneading*

Sift dry ingredients into bowl. Add fat to sponge and mix well. Add to dry ingredients and mix. Knead dough on a floured canvas cloth until light and springy (10 to 15 minutes). Place in large greased pan or bowl, grease top of dough, cover with cloth and set near Yukon stove in warm place. Let rise until doubled in size (2 to 5 hours). Put back on canvas, add soda water to dough and knead thoroughly (5 minutes). Shape into loaf and place in greased bread pan. Let rise until doubled (1 to 2 hours).

Get the Yukon stove very hot with a roaring fire and bake loaf for 50 to 70 minutes or until done. Remove bread from pan and place on rack if available. Serve in thick slices as soon as it has cooled enough to cut, with tinned butter and jam or honey.

Keep the remainder of starter cool if not to be used for several days—a half cup of starter is a good amount to have in reserve. Or, if dried, the yeast remains in spore stage and will keep inert for years.

I've heard that commercial sourdough starter is available in some stores around the country, but it seems more rewarding to originate one's own: Dissolve 1 cake or packet of yeast in ½ cup warm water, add 2 cups flour and 1½ cups warm water, mix well, set in warm place overnight.

For the sourdough pot in frequent use, replenish remainder after the amount used for baking is taken out, with 2 cups warm water and 2 cups flour. Mix thoroughly, cover with lid. Never contaminate starter. It should contain only yeast, flour and water. Soda added to the starter will kill the yeast and should be added to the sponge just before baking.

All instructions are to be modified to meet the circumstances: humidity, cold, the thickness of the starter, the mood of the baker! For example, I find that here in an environment which is surprisingly desertlike in dryness, the dough may be too dry to hold together well for kneading, and may require even more sponge, diluted with warm water and mixed in slowly. Even so, to knead sourdough to a good pliable consistency can be a bit like wrestling a large boulder—but that may be only because the dough, once removed from the immediate vicinity of the Yukon stove to the table across the cabin, is too cool until my hands give it the warmth necessary for good elasticity.

At midnight, after a long day of wood gathering, sawing, splitting logs and stacking, I take the baked sourdough bread out of the little camp oven. In the warm light of the lantern, the cabin fragrant with burning spruce and yeasty dough, we set to with thick slices of hot, fresh-baked bread spread with melting tinned butter and heaped with strawberry jam. The world looks so very good right now that I have high hopes for it once again!

Today must be Sunday, for I awaken to Sam singing old-time hymns along with the radio. After a cup of coffee I join in— pretty good harmony! The acoustics are best right under two big pots hanging from the ceiling beam.

The sky a gray overcast this morning, the look of snow on its way. Sam spends the morning replacing cracked windowpanes in the two cabin windows. The six panes are double-glassed, providing insulating air space and making a great difference in cabin warmth. The original lights are of hand-blown glass. When the cabin was built, these pieces of glass must have traveled from Fairbanks to Bettles by river boat, from Bettles to Wiseman by mule train or dog sled, and another hazardous twenty-five to thirty miles through mountain divides and across creeks and cuts by dog sled to Koviashuvik.

The windows' wooden frames of whipsawed and adzed spruce boards, very carefully fitted together, have moss chinking packed tightly all around the sills.

SKIN SCRAPING AND A MOOSE

Today I work on the caribou skin. I could sit on the floor, legs straight out in front of me, Eskimo woman skin-scraping fashion. But whether this traditional position actually provides better leverage for working the skins or is only a carryover from the nomadic days without tables or chairs, I don't know. I prefer to work at the table. First, the bits of fat and meat that remain on the skin are removed with my hunting knife and an ulu (pronounced *ooloo*). The latter is the Eskimo woman's traditional all-purpose "knife," one of the most versatile and competent tools ever created. It is about the size and shape of a quarter piece of pie, the narrow end of the metal blade wedged tightly into a bone or antler handle which has been modeled to fit the hand of its owner. The razor-sharp wide end slices, chops, cuts, scrapes.

Once the skin is "clean," serious scraping begins. Different skins require different types of scrapers. Ermine, wolf and bear pelts are not the same as caribou. Even a caribou skin is not uniformly thick or thin, and will require several different kinds of scrapers. The best I've seen are made from varying lengths of shotgun barrel, sharpened at one end to a fine cutting edge—or of tin, shaped similarly—with bone or wooden handles carved exactly to fit the thumb and palm of the user's hand as it grasps the tool.

Three or four of these, of different lengths and sharpnesses, can scrape any skin to a clean and pliable softness. But all I have time for today is to remove the bits of fat and meat before rolling the skin up and tucking it under the bunk to work on later, for Sam comes in to have lunch. He has decided that *today* he is going to get a moose. He has tracked a couple this week, but darkness or distance made him decide not to continue on. Backpacking a thousand pounds of moose meat back to camp is a definite consideration in *where* you drop your moose!

Our one caribou will not see us through the winter; no bands or single bucks have moved into the vicinity. But there *are* moose around somewhere! Their fresh tracks, droppings and the high browsing on willow and alders show several to be in the territory. Even so, for such mammoth creatures, they manage to be incredibly elusive.

Sam takes off after lunch in a light snowfall, his snowshoes hung over his packboard, the 30/06 over his shoulder. Within an hour a full-scale blizzard has developed. The snow falls so thickly that I cannot see the lake. The world seems to drop off at the edge of the plateau into a white nothingness. Spruce and willow look like shrouded, ghostly shapes. I have planned to do any number of chores, but there is something hypnotic about the falling snow, the immensity of whiteness, and I cannot pull away from the window.

The whiteout is even more dense now. Visibility stops ten feet from the window, and darkness is very close at hand. I am not *really* concerned about Sam, less concerned than I would be for anyone else, probably, for Sam's survival skills and knowledge of wilderness are matchless in my experience. The only danger is from the unexpected. Bull moose are unpredictable and can be deadly in a charge. Or a slip, a fall, a broken limb . . . and no way to track Sam once the snow has obliterated his tracks. I leave the window and go to work.

Before finishing my first job of sugaring and mashing the raw cranberries picked yesterday, I hear the muffled crunch of snowshoes on the packed snow around the cabin.

One look and I know that Sam has got his moose. Though he is wet and a bit frozen, the "winter meat" edginess is gone. Except for a slight air of preoccupation with some worrisome mathematical problem, he is completely relaxed and joyful. He dropped the moose near the far end of the lake, with a single neck shot. We will be able to bring the meat to the foot of the trail by boat, saving ourselves several five- to six-mile round trips of packing it on our backs. Even with the blizzard's whited-out visibility, getting within rifle range was not the problem, Sam reports while stripping off his damp things and settling down next to the Yukon stove, near the pot of steaming coffee. The problem was that the big bull was feeding knee deep in the shallows—and that is no place to drop a moose if you have a choice. In this instance, if he spooked, he'd either head out into deep water or hit the shore and disappear into the blizzard. But the problem resolved itself quickly when the moose suddenly caught a fresh scent on the wind and, half veiled in a great splashing curtain of water, began moving off at a fast, rolling gallop. With our winter victuals swiftly vanishing, Sam fired and the moose dropped, only his huge head and rack and the curve of his great belly showing above the lake surface.

Now the question was—is—how to get it, all twelve hundred to fifteen hundred pounds of it, ashore, for skinning and butchering. By pushing, hauling, tugging, Sam from the boat managed to move the carcass a few feet closer to shore. But it is still thirty feet away from solid ground.

The sparse light of the snow-filled dusk had almost entirely vanished. The shallows were already covered with a thin sheet of ice. No spoilage overnight, however, with ice-water refrigeration, and predators probably won't go into the water. Sam came home.

We now have enough meat to last the winter. But tomorrow, first thing, we will have to finish up the moose business.

We set out at sunrise with freshly sharpened skinning knives, extra pairs of work gloves, lunch of caribouburgers on sourdough bread and oatmeal cookies, a slightly worn pulley and tackle found in the storage shed, rifle, cameras and packboards. We row the boat three miles to the north end of the lake where the moose lies huge and inert in a small inlet, just as Sam left it. The ice has thickened overnight and when the boat prow can no longer break through, we slam the oars down on the ice and chop our way through to the shore. On a line with the carcass is a shallow ledge of a sand-gravel beach, about five feet long, four feet deep, and backed by the tundra, which is three feet higher. This will be close quarters for us *and* the moose, providing we can get the moose out of the water, which is too deep to work in, too shallow to float the moose in, too cold to be in for more than a very few minutes. But the post-storm morning is crystalline clear, the temperature an exhilaratingly mild twenty-six degrees. A blazing blue sky and bright golden sun turn the snow-covered peaks and tundra a glittering amber—a day when the spirit dances and all challenges are to be met!

Sam anchors one end of the block-and-tackle rope to a sturdy spruce tree, the other end around the forelegs of the carcass. Together, we haul on the rope. Nothing happens. The moose is iced in, and Sam wades out to free it, each broken-off chunk of ice sending a long clear bell-like note reverberating out across the frozen surface. We haul some more. The moose forelegs move forward an inch. But the hind legs move backward an inch. We study the situation, then tie a second rope to the back legs to hold them in place. This time they do not slip back and we make some progress. Within an hour, by attaching the block and pulley rope alternately to front and back legs, we have moved the carcass all of ten feet closer to shore. Only twenty feet more to go. We pull harder, at times straining backward to within inches above the water, which is slippery from the floating ice around and under our feet.

Sam takes a purchase on the rope, next to the spruce tree, braking his feet on the tree itself until he is hauling back so hard on the rope that he is actually at a right angle to the tree, perpendicular to it. I suddenly let go of my anchor rope, for I see Sam flying up and out through space in a great catapulting arc backward which ends in a mighty splash and crack of exploding water and ice. Before I start breathing again, he is on his feet, shaking himself fiercely like a wet terrier. Fortunately, he has earlier removed his parky and sweater and now quickly strips off his wet flannel shirt and replaces it with his sweater. We have extra gloves; there is nothing to be done about the damp jeans, long johns and boots.

We check the old rope, weakened from many years' cycles of freezing and thawing, but it is the thick wire wrapped many times around the spruce that has snapped. We make repairs and continue. When the carcass is ten feet from the shore, the spruce tree itself, roots and all, comes exploding out of the tundra. We anchor onto a sturdy stump farther back from the shore. By early afternoon, our winter meat is finally up on the small ledge, or almost so—the back still extends out into the water a foot or more, but it is the best we can do. Besides, once the sun disappears behind the peaks, the temperature will take a sharp drop. A slight wind is already cutting through the sun's warmth.

We hurry through lunch, and back to work, which appears considerable as I try to hoist one immense moose leg in position to start skinning. The afternoon passes in silence except for the background music of temple bells being played by gusts of wind jangling sheets of ice. We are too busy for talk. I begin to think we will *never* finish with this job. The experience begins to take on a quality of the surrealistic—the very immensity of this creature, the incredible complexity and colors of its inner workings. To cut the latter free, Sam leans so far inside the stomach cavity that I have a premonition that, like Alice, he may disappear altogether. The bitter arctic wind comes up strongly as the sun vanishes behind the mountains, and in minutes the temperature drops fifteen to twenty degrees. By now, all our gloves are soaking wet. The carcass itself is beginning to freeze. Now the shore ice makes a long continuous jangle of sound as the wind-whipped water turns choppy and rising waves crash through.

Two trips will be needed to ferry all the meat back. Together we hoist the four mighty legs, the shoulders and a huge flour sack of heart, liver, kidneys, tongue, testicles and suet into the boat. The rest we leave where it is, pulled up on shore and wrapped in the hide, for the boat can carry no more without capsizing, and we are feeling the cold acutely. The boat is already locked in by ice; again we crack a path through it with the oars. Rowing against the icy wind, in the barely moving, heavy-laden boat, we ride so low in the water that every wave washes into it. Half sitting, half leaning against two of the frozen moose hams, I bail water clumsily with a rusty can held in fingers too numb to even feel the can. I am colder than I've ever been in my life. Halfway, we reach Big Jim's abandoned cache, still sturdy after many years of neglect. Sam unloads half the meat into the cache while I lope back and forth across the snow, beating myself with my arms as I have seen in movies of the far north. It doesn't help. Perhaps I have turned blue, for without a word, Sam finds a windbreak made by a stand of spruce, breaks off some dry twigs and branches close to the tree trunks and hurriedly builds a small but blazing fire in the snow. I huddle as close to it as I can without singeing eyebrows and lashes, and dully begin to philosophize over the miracle of fire as in a few minutes aching hands begin that painful stinging sensation of coming to life, and the shivering which has been jarring me begins to subside.

We continue on, moving faster against the wind now that the load is lightened. Our wet gloves freeze and stiffen on our hands. We have to remove them. We have planned to cache the rest of the meat at Dishu's, but after beaching the boat and tying the sack of vitals onto a packboard, we leave the meat in the boat and race up the mountain to home and fire. Never has this tiny log cabin looked more beautiful than tonight as I thaw out next to the crackling warm stove sipping cup after cup of steaming coffee. The winter meat is in!

MOOSE POSTSCRIPT

Midmorning, Sam calls me outside to listen to the wolves howling at the shore. He says their call means "M-e-e-a-a-t-t . . ."

Ours! And he is off down the mountain to debate the question and then to bring the rest of the carcass back to be cached. Yesterday we had only knives with us. Today he takes saw and hatchet to cut the rest of the frozen meat into more easily managed pieces.

At dusk, Sam returns carrying a hundred pounds of moose leg and shoulder on his packboard. The wolf chorus we heard this morning was indeed a song of joy—for Sam found one of the moose hams we'd left in the boat well gnawed, and wolf tracks all up and down the shore as well as circling around the old cabin.

This is the last time we shall use the boat until the spring thaw. In getting to the little inlet to pick up the rest of the carcass and the hide, the ice was too thick for the prow or the oars to break through. By standing in the back of the boat, Sam jockeyed the prow up on top of the ice, then ran forward and jumped with all his weight, which slammed the boat down on the ice and cracked a clear passage through. No signs of predators at the kill, but the meat was already frozen to the ground.

Now all of our meat supply is hanging from the beams in the open-roofed cabin at the foot of the trail. We will have to start bringing it up the mountain—probably by sled.

THE WOLVES

Today we snowshoe down to the shore to bring a sledload of meat up the mountain to the cabin. We are concerned about the wolves. Several packs are in the territory, and now we hear their singing every day. The fresh snow is crisscrossed with tracks of all kinds—and I understand why the Eskimos speak of winter as the "best" time in the Arctic. This land was designed for snow and ice, I think. Almost impossible to traverse comfortably in summer because of the muskegs, the swamps and the slippery, awkward tussocks, in winter the terrain is smoothed over, leveled off, filled in. On snowshoes one can glide across it, moving much more swiftly and easily. Game is lost among the browns and golds and greens of summer foliage—a perfect camouflage. But in winter, when foliage is gone, movement against the black-on-white vastness is immediately visible.

Experienced hunters and trappers can read animal spoor in all seasons, but on the fields of fresh-fallen snow, reading them becomes as easy as an ABC primer. As we start down the trail, we see that three wolves, in the last twenty-four hours, have come up the trail, leaving it about one hundred feet below the cabin to veer off and detour around the camp. At first glance, it appears there must be only a single wolf, for wolves walk in each other's tracks. But as we continue on down the mountain, we discover that not only are three traveling together, but that one is an exceptionally large male, another a smaller female, and that a third, about the same size as the female, is probably a year-old pup. But the wolves are only a small part of the busy flow of traffic wandering along our trail, or crossing it to bound off over the snowy tundra.

Weasels, voles, a single full-grown porcupine, one very large snowshoe hare, a lone bull moose, a small band of caribou of several adults and two calves, a track deceptively like that of a small bear but more likely that of a wolverine; even the infinitesimal prints of the tiny shrews clearly show their scurryings between the snowbanks to either side of the trail.

We check our meat and find that nothing has touched it even though wolf tracks are all around the old cabin. Open to the sky, our improvised cache nevertheless has a door, somewhat fragile and askew in its frame but still closable. A very large and particularly bold wolf has obviously come close enough to stand up on his hind feet, press his forepaws on the door and look through the broken glass at the meat hanging inside no more than two feet from him. From the size of his prints, it is miraculous that the door did not swing open at his first touch. We debate whether or not to set wolf traps around the place. Trapping has not been on our agenda, for a trap line can be a full-time job in itself, requiring frequent, regular visits. But "who gets the meat" *is* a prime question in these parts, and until we can haul ours up to a safer cache, the traps may help to dissuade the wolves.

After removing several huge chunks of caribou and moose to load onto the small sled, we wire the cabin door closed and set a trap just outside it. To the cabin's side, several collapsed logs make a perfect ramp for animals, from the ground up to the top of the side walls where we have stretched the already frozen moosehide as a partial snow cover until we have time to rig a better roof. At the base of the ramp we set another trap, and cover both over with a light sprinkling of snow. These traps are so finely set that even a sudden fall of snow can trigger them.

One final precaution before we go up the trail is to urinate at the four corners of the cabin. According to some naturalists, wolves mark their own territory in this fashion. According to the Eskimo hunters, the only way to outsmart a wolf is to think like a wolf. Sam marks *our* territory boundaries.

Authentic data on the wolf is still relatively sketchy. Unfortunately, even the few studies made by reliable observers result in conflicting interpretations. Yet these differences are minimal compared to the gap between the views held by these relatively unbiased naturalists in the field and those held by many arctic old-timers.

Among the latter, stories of the arctic wolf's cunning, treachery, savagery are corraled, savored and transmitted with all the enthusiastic bias of the avid collector and true believer. The best yarns are set against the most dramatic of arctic settings: stygian black nights of at least minus-forty-five-degree temperatures, raging blizzards and impenetrable whiteouts; a monstrously large wolf, stealthily stalking; or the snarling, vicious pack closing in for a savage attack—on man, moose or caribou. Yet somehow the stories are always secondhand.

Although near-connoisseurs of wolf yarns, we have yet to hear a tale told by anyone who has actually ever had a face-to-face encounter with a free wolf. That the wolves are extremely intelligent, almost impossible to trap and very difficult to track—that they are amazingly skillful hunters, working in pairs or packs to herd and cut out a caribou from the larger band, or surround and bring down a moose—is agreed to by all who have shared the territory with them. But while ecologists know that the caribou-wolf relationship is essential to the preservation of both species in the Arctic, many of the bush people and hunters still insist that the wolf is a threat to, and adversary of, both caribou and man.

Most bush dwellers are natural if untutored ecologists in all areas except this one, and in those related to their own immediate financial interests. The arctic miner, for example, may have a surprisingly erudite understanding of the complex food-chain relationships of all the living creatures in the territory, of the complex interrelationships of the botanical-biological world he lives in. And if he is a goldminer he will have an unerring grasp of the subtle interrelationships of geology, stream beds and mineral deposits. But he gives not a thought to stripping the land around his mine of every bit of its timber in order to keep his mining operation going. Selective harvesting of timber is suddenly something these "conservationist lunatics" fuss about. As is selective harvesting of wolves.

Well, we shall learn "firsthand" about the ecology of the wolves this winter—and about our own in the bargain—for we share a kinship made immediately and crystalline clear by this environment. We are fellow predators.

Today, according to the radio, it is September 25. And my old friend Alice's birthday. I'll acknowledge this special day of hers by writing a letter to her and her husband, our good friends, even though the mail plane may not land here for a month or more to take my letter out. They will be impatient to hear about our life here—what we are doing and seeing and thinking so far, in our year's sojourn in the Arctic. Underneath the surface of any "factual" report I can send them is an elusive quality more difficult to communicate. I'm not certain that I yet know what it is—this indefinable, mysterious quality that connects all of the myriad facets of dailiness here into something far beyond the events themselves.

Dear Alice:

. . . It is 2:30, the afternoon of your birthday—and as I send warm birthday-celebration thoughts, I pause and look toward one of our cabin's two double-glassed windows. In two hours, the sun will have gentled its way through gray-pink and white clouds, down behind the mountain which glistens now below it, blinding white-gold where the sun strikes full, deep shadowed blue in the sunless recesses. Between that distant mountain to the west and the cabin lies a limitless slope, divided in half by a creek bed. Already the creek ice is several inches thick. We use an ice chopper made from an old rasp and wired to a spruce pole to break through the ice, fill our buckets with freezing water and chunks of ice to carry up to the cabin and replenish our old-fashioned wash-boiler "water storage tank." The south slope of the creek is covered with straight dark-green spruce; the facing slope, stripped of timber for the fires built by miners on the creek for the last fifty years to speed the melting of the frozen earth, is barren except for a partial cover of low willow and alder brush, with here and there a lone young spruce accenting the whiteness. All is carpeted with snow. A half to three-quarters of a mile away, I can see the tepees of dead spruce we have axed and stacked at the edge of the woods. Until yesterday the tundra and tussocks still jutting above the layers of snow made it impossible to haul the heavy logs to camp. Now that another heavy snowfall has smoothed the way, we can haul them on the dog sled—crudely but efficiently crafted by the Eskimos who hunted here. Minus dogs, we pull the sleds ourselves.

Between me and my window, on the oilcloth-covered table where I write, an array of things tell of the activities around this surface: a kerosene lamp with its hand-blown glass chimney; a jar of delicately exotic fireweed honey given us in Fairbanks by friends who lived and prospected in the Range for many years . . . (while he gathered this honey, he fussed softly at his bees when they began to buzz irritatedly, brushing them gently off his face with his bare hands and shooing them back into the hive); beside the honey jar, another container, this one of scarlet cranberries picked on the Chena River flats for us by Dishu, one of the most delightfully feminine wilderness experts ever to be encountered . . . the berries added to from our own pickings of lowbush cranberries, here, across the lake near old Rooney's grave, after the first snowfall; a bright-red can of tobacco with scattered flakes and a pack of Zig-Zag papers next to my typewriter; Fannie Farmer's cookbook, open and much thumbed, still a classic for baking powder biscuits and cornbread that will come out near perfect though cooked twice as long as the recipe calls for when baked in a portable camp oven atop the Yukon stove; a handful of caribou tendons for sewing hides; an empty coffee can filled with pens and pencils and brushes, ready for a long winter of notes and journal writings; a skin-scraper with a few caribou hairs still embedded in fat and gristle, waiting for another session on the caribou skin; my hunting knife, just used to cut up frozen caribou heart for the eternal stewpot bubbling on the back of the stove. Now I look beyond the table to just outside the window and resume my puzzlement, for I can see wolf tracks alongside the cabin. They were not there at noontime when I looked carefully at that snow, for our alternative to chopping creek ice is to gather up buckets of fresh snow. When did he pass by?

I pause to wonder—and to watch a passing snow flurry, each crystal a falling brilliant because the sun is also shining down. I then go on to tell our friends about the caribou and moose we have taken, about the small cabin we live in, that the temperature this morning was eight degrees above zero, about Dishu's old cabin at the foot of the trail, and more about Dishu. . . .

She is the lady who gave us the cranberries *and* the most practicable, helpful advice we received on the arctic winter. Unlike many of the native village women of her generation, she speaks English easily, fluently. More, she seems able to think in both languages, not a simple accomplishment with two such disparate cultures. Before we met, we encountered her as a young woman in *Arctic Village,** Robert Marshall's study of Wiseman. At the time of Marshall's writing—1929–30—Wiseman had some one hundred inhabitants scattered in and around its general territory; most of the single white male residents were prospectors, most of the native families hunters and trappers.

As a young woman, Dishu, with her mother, regularly backpacked

* New York: Random House, 1933.

or dog-sledded across the mountains from Wiseman to Koviashuvik to trap and fish. After her marriage to the white storekeeper in the town, Dishu and her family often came to Koviashuvik to their small cabin on the shore of the lake. Here she could indulge her legendary enthusiasm for fishing.

Even today, any mention of this subject triggers in her an excitement that makes her eyes begin to flash. "Yessss . . ." she says, leaning forward in intense concentration, and nodding rapidly in perfect empathy. "Bigggg . . . and what kind fly you catch 'im with?" Though Sam, too, has that magical luck of all great fishermen, he listens eagerly to Dishu's animated recall of ice fishing at Koviashuvik, of "jigging" through a hole in the ice with a short willow pole fishline, curved to fit the arm—to her careful description of the best spots for taking lake trout or the mammoth fierce pike, the small tasty whitefish and the large ling cod or "lush," as they are often called by the natives. This intense dialogue ends with a gift from one fellow fisherman to another. One of Dishu's most cherished hand-carved ivory fishhooks has returned with Sam to Koviashuvik.

Like many of the Eskimo women we've met, this lithe, quick little woman possesses a life view that expresses itself vividly in laughter, hearty and frequent, but also in a completely unself-conscious acknowledgment of the infinite and tragic in the world. Watching our films on the Brooks Range wilderness and the people of Anaktuvuk Pass, her immediate and penetrating perception of every scene, every nuance of gesture and meaning, surpassed that of all the white viewers. But why not? This is Dishu's centuries-old homeland. Few non-natives can ever match the Eskimos' knowledge of, or at-homeness in, the Arctic.

As with so many of these older Eskimo women whose own hunting, trapping, survival skills are comparable to their husbands' even though the traditional role of male "hunter" is acknowledged as primary in the tribal group, Dishu communicates abundantly, along with her knowledgeability and skills, a piquant and total femininity. Perhaps this unabashed quality of "selfhood," with its obvious lack of confusion about sexual identity, seems so exceptional only in juxtaposition to the Freudian "overkill" of self-doubt which prevails in more "civilized" circles.

I look toward the cabin's other window, to the east, and see the chill blueness of the lake, backed by endless snow-topped spruce-

and tundra-covered mountains and Caribou Island, and the long slope down from our cabin, which rests on a plateau, and the end of that slope, which begins the steep descent straight down to the lake shore —and I see by the shadows on the mountains that the sky is still filled with clouds. It is enough for me right now that there are still mysteries, that this year is a time for discovery and for adventure, that the beauty and solitude are immense beyond comprehension— and that I do not know when the wolf passed by. . . .

This morning it is ten degrees above zero. The sun may soon bring the temperature up into the mid-twenties, but an overcast sky is in the offing, and a cold wind blows from the west.

The battle to protect our supplies from the varmints is an unending one! At breakfast time we catch a shrew in one of the several mousetraps set in the cabin corners. Sam, planning to skin and dissect it for anatomical study, casually places the small corpse next to his plate of sourdough hotcakes while he answers my questions about the arctic shrew, which I'd not seen before. It is not squeamishness, I tell myself, that makes me look askance at the body on the breakfast table, but as so many of the "niceties" accumulated as manners over the years seem completely irrelevant in this setting, I dismiss my reservations and concentrate instead on hotcakes.

Weasels and squirrels are getting into the screened-in meat cache behind the cabin, too. We repair the broken place in the wooden base, but an hour later find a weasel perched on one of the hanging caribou hams, gnawing away. The bright-eyed little creature gives us a raucous scolding before darting back up the rope to jump across to a screened wall, then race down it and out through a hole he has dug under the base and into a tunnel he has burrowed in the snow banked high around the cache bottom. Whether we like it or not, a trap is now set next to his hole on the floor of the meat cache.

As a precaution against the possibility of fire, I have finally taken some of our food supplies and cached them as emergency rations. Our backpacks with complete trail equipment—trail foods, down sleeping bags, a two-man mountain tent, as well as extra gloves and mukluks and a large jar of matches—have also been placed down in the food cache. (I would not have thought to store the matches in a varmintproof container unless I'd heard Sam say that animals like to eat the sulphur in match heads; another interesting fire hazard.)

We use the screened-in smaller cache for meat, and a larger, closed-in cache for foods. The latter, a required adjunct of all arctic residences, is a miniature log cabin. Ours is about four feet square and three feet high, built atop four tall spruce logs, each of which has been partially wrapped in Blazo tin or tin cans to keep small creatures from climbing up into the cache. A rough-hewn ladder is placed up to the small door, which is just barely big enough for a person to crawl through. The cache is usually built high enough off the ground to be beyond the reach of even a good-sized bear. But there is no foolproof cache for a determined bear.

One of the old sourdoughs in Wiseman had a cache full of moosemeat which a grizzly decided was to be his own special larder. Twice the big bear clambered up onto the cache, tore off the small door with a mighty paw, and fed hugely on moosemeat. After each visit, the old-timer barricaded the door more solidly, but still the bear got in. After the third raid, a powerful bear trap was set right inside the door. It was evaded, and more provisions cleaned out. On his next return, he got around an elaborately rigged "fall" or snare to gorge himself on still more meat.

By now the old prospector was in a state akin to apoplexy. The next time the grizzly made his way to the cache and lumbered his clumsy way up onto it to tear the door off its hinges, his first step inside the door was met with a head-on blast from a 30/06. The owner of the moosemeat had camped three freezing-cold nights inside the dark little cache, waiting for the thief!

Fortunately, our cache has stayed relatively free of marauders. Placed about fifty feet down the mountain from the cabin, it contains flour, sugar and assorted other staples, and now our protection in case of fire. Today I divide up the medicines and first-aid supplies in our medicine chest and store an emergency medical kit in the cache as well.

Speaking of fire hazards, something has happened that I never could have anticipated. Sam set fire to the outhouse. Absent-mindedly striking a broken-off match head he found in his pocket, he flipped it down the hole, stood up, smelled smoke and found the privy was afire! Enough snow to put out the flame in a hurry—but that's the way she goes!

Another emergency looms. I have run out of cigarette papers. Had hoped I might give up smoking this year, but I must now admit to a weak character. Instead I live with the illusion that I am actually only smoking half as much because I roll my own cigarettes, and they come out about half the thickness of "store-boughts." In any event, I think the present paper shortage is resolved at last, for I have found a substitute after much experimentation. I started with the onionskin typing paper on which my poetry has been typed over the years, and at first this seemed a close approximation of cigarette paper. But after cutting off and smoking all the margin paper around my poems, I found I don't care for the acrid taste. Next, remembering Mexican cigarettes I'd seen, I tried brown paper from a grocery bag. But it is not the same—won't draw. Toilet paper, single or double-sheeted, is the worst. When the rolled cigarette edge is licked and the cigarette lighted, the whole thing disintegrates in a cloud of soft, falling ash. Regular typing paper burns too fast and hot. But newspaper—newspaper is definitely the best answer, provided one does not smoke the photographs. It must be the concentration of ink that tastes so terrible, for the want ads, with the ink evenly and thinly distributed, are the best. So by fishing all the old newspaper want ads out of the box of fire-starter trash beside the stove and cutting them into "papers," I can continue this stupid habit until I run out of tobacco. *Then* I will *have* to give up smoking!

The snow continues off and on. Still less than knee deep, so we go about our work even in blizzards as if the sun were shining brightly.

Before going down for a sledload of meat, we check over the outside of the cabin very thoroughly for chinking repairs. Our borrowed home for the year was originally well built in that the logs were carefully matched and fitted and each log adzed top and bottom to fit more snugly and smoothly. Still, gaps between the logs are inevitable—and these spaces are "chinked" or filled in with moss and tundra. Rags are also sometimes stuffed into the cracks but these are harder to come by.

As the cabin weathers, the moss chinking dries and chunks may fall away—or shrews and squirrels work the moss loose so they can get through the cracks into the cabin. Built on permafrost, which melts and shifts with changing seasons and cabin heat, the cabin walls themselves continually shift and resettle, dislodging the dried chinking.

By now only a very few high tussocks remain visible above the snow, and even these are pretty well frozen. We should not delay in collecting our chinking material. Gathering the moss takes time, for the arctic tundra is fragile—it scars easily and heals slowly. The moss that we tear away in handfuls from the permafrost below will take years to regrow, so we do not take all we need from any one spot, but only one handful here, the next several feet distant.

After filling the holes between the cabin logs with the clumps of moss and tapping them firmly into place with a spruce stick, we mix a sealer to cover over the moss. Soon after we arrived, I found one place near the cabin where, two or three inches beneath the tundra surface, there is a deposit of clay. We dig out some clay and mix it with water and spruce ashes from the Yukon stove to a good mud consistency. With a flat spruce chip this is spread thickly over the chinking. The added sealer is primarily a windproofer. Our friend Erling, of many years' prospecting and bush living, has warned us that at sixty degrees below zero, you make sure that even the keyhole is well plugged!

Inside the cabin, the log walls are covered over with cardboard from flattened-out cartons in which supplies have arrived. Until the very cold winds of winter come, we will not be able to tell whether there are any serious leaks inside the cabin.

We may also find that we have to cover the outside walls with cardboard, but this, too, must wait. Snow is the best natural insulator and we will pile it high around the cabin once the drifts are deep enough.

By now our fingers, even in fleece-lined leather work gloves, are numb with cold, for the icy turf and clay have sapped all the heat from our hands. We come inside to warm up before our afternoon trek to the forest.

Overcast and snow flurries for several days. The sun is missed on these gray days.

Butchered a section of frozen caribou ribs with saw, hatchet and ulu—a half day's work in itself—but now we have a carton of ribs, ready for the roaster, in our outsized refrigerator, the cabin entryway, which we call the dogtrot.

The term "dogtrot" is one we inherited along with our borrowed home, but its origins could not be explained. This enclosed entryway or "porch," typical of arctic log cabin construction, contains all the overflow from the small confines of the cabin, items needed throughout the winter but likely to disappear in the deep snows if left outside—and frozen caribou and moose, bacon and cranberries. Built of spruce logs stood vertically, it is covered outside with scrap wind- and snowproofing materials of canvas, Blazo tins, cardboard.

Perhaps it is the white man's version of the earlier arctic igloos, the snow houses of the coastal Eskimos. The igloos were entered by way of a snow tunnel, which not only deflected the wind but also served as sleeping quarters for excess guests, and sheltered sled dogs in the worst of arctic blizzards and winds. We have neither guests nor dogs in our dogtrot; I suspect it will become a winter catchall for all kinds of paraphernalia and junk.

Last night, Sam winterized the rifles, wiping away all the lubrication, which would freeze if left in the guns, and then washing the bolts in gasoline. From now on the rifles will be left out in the dogtrot until spring. Bringing them into the warmth of the cabin will make moisture condense and form rust.

There is a large fly, only half alive, crawling around the table as I write. Probably the cabin heat has brought him out of frozen hibernation. I suppose he should be disposed of, but that kind of tenacious hold on aliveness deserves all the support it can get! He seems unable to fly, sluggish, feeble. Maybe he will revive, but there is a long winter ahead.

Yesterday, glanced out of the window and saw a dark round shape in the upper branches of a spruce tree fifty feet down from the cabin. Certain it was a black bear cub, with great excitement I rushed out to photograph it. Sam took the rifle on his way out, in case it was a cub with a nervous sow in the vicinity. But the cub turned out to be a full-grown porcupine, with gold-colored guard hairs making his spiky coat look blond. As we watched, he lumbered awkwardly down from his perch, and as Sam went close, spread his needle-sharp back quills into a fanlike shape, ready for defense. I backed away, forgetting for a minute that the old wives' tale heard in my youth—that porkys "throw" their quills—is a myth. Tried a few photographs, but the overcast light isn't promising.

Part of today spent in banking snow up around the cabin walls for added insulation. The coldest wind blows down the cut from the west. We flatten out some of the supply cartons we've been saving for just this purpose, and nail the cardboard in flat sheets on the west wall, covering all the logs above the line of banked snow. The short nails we use have been salvaged from derelict old cabins and sluice boxes. Many of the nails are rusty, some bent—but here nothing is wasted. We have brought some new nails in with us, but we save them and use these old ones instead. Even as we hurry to fit and cut and nail on the cardboard, fingers begin to burn from the cold. The temperature is only in the low twenties, but a blizzard is in progress, with a sharp, knifelike wind whipping round.

As we work, we hear above the wind, which is muffled by our parky hoods, a deep growling roar in the distance—the distant rush of winds moving through the far canyons, on their way toward us.

All night long the snow falls steadily, filling in all our snowshoed trails. This morning, fresh wolf tracks circle our woodpile before heading off and up the mountain behind the cabin.

The trap in the meat cache discouraged small predators for a few days, but today we find a weasel in the trap. His pelt is a beautiful, transitional beige-white, extraordinarily soft to the touch. As Sam skins the weasel at the kitchen table, a strong smell of musk, one of the sources of perfume base, pervades the cabin, but it is not too unpleasant a smell. I wonder why the weasel pelt has no value until winter has whitened the fur. Suddenly the weasel has economic value—it is now an ermine. He has the same coat, only a little denser and thicker for winter protection, but it is white. The transitional color is more beautiful.

Late today, down to the creek for ice. The water has been frozen solid for several days. Not a trickle runs, not even in the deepest holes. This will be our last haul of ice. Snow is deep enough now to supply our water needs. The freshly fallen snow here is so very dry that seven to eight pailfuls are necessary to make one pail of water. We take the wash boiler and pails down on the small sled and fill them with chunks of ice chipped out of the frozen stream. The chipping goes so well that we get a second sledload, storing the ice in a galvanized tin sarcophagus-shaped "bathtub" set next to the cabin's outside wall. This supply will be used up before we need the tub for a bath—a few more days, at least.

And the snow continues to fall. At one point, the wind drives the falling crystals so hard that they move horizontally. At sunset, a sudden break in the thick snowclouds reveals a patch of bright arctic blue sky looking like a jewel in its setting of gray overcast. Soon the sky rimming the solid white southern mountains turns lavender. Arctic painters of the realistic school would not be believed.

We think of the landscape as white, for in every direction the land is now snow-covered. But this vast whiteness is a reflector—golden when the sun is high, pale gray blending horizonless into gray sky when overcast—and most often, a spectrum of myriad blues reflecting back the immense canopy above. Most often, this is a blue world, the Arctic.

Snowing again, warm at eighteen degrees above zero. Will spend the day at the cabin catching up on small chores. Sam sets off early to snowshoe trails and reconnoiter the mountains to the south. I offer him one of my hairbands to keep his long hair out of his eyes. He wears it low on his forehead and looks like an Indian out of an old western movie as he takes off on snow-shoes with the .22 rifle.

A panful of caribou ribs on the stove to roast for supper. Another pan of dried apples on to cook. Cookies into the oven. I decide to wash my hair, an old and familiar ritual for which I shall have to find a new form as I learn how to "decivilize" my ways. Here there is no "dirt" as we know it in the city. Even perspiration seems of an entirely different chemistry, perhaps because of the almost exclusively meat diet we are on. More likely, it's clean air—a total absence of air pollution—that creates this feeling of cleanliness without constant use of soap and water. As with other chores, lack of running water is no inconvenience. A dishpan, two kettles of steaming hot water, some chunks of creek ice and a plastic tube of shampoo, and the job is done. A brush, two rubber bands; coiffure complete, guaranteed not to catch on logs when gathering firewood, nor to blow into eyes in snow and wind.

The day moves along, neither racing nor dawdling, but easy, pleasant—what might be idealized, usually after the fact, as the best kind of "average" day. Baking, mending, reading, the outside chores: eight buckets of snow inside to replenish the washtub "water storage" tank, the slops taken out, the daily two armloads of firewood brought in to be stacked behind the Yukon. Each task savored for itself, given meaning because it has unique value here. No pressure to hurry on to the next, meet deadlines or be defined by appointment books.

And always the long pauses, long moments of just looking. A landscape always new—in a state of constant flux as sky light moves and shifts, mountains emerge in sun, recede in shadow, colors change like a moving palette of pastel tints.

A tiny black dot appears at the far end of the plateau, a strange shape for Sam. As it nears, I see that it *is* Sam with the small sled filled with more meat from the shore cache—a terrible load for one person to struggle with up the steep trail. Throwing on my parky, I rush out to give him a hand up the last incline. Coming suddenly up to him, I find this grizzled figure startling in his turquoise hairband, hair and beard wild from the wind, jacket still spotted red from the day of the moose. He has seen three moose grazing near the cache, tracked a grizzly bear along the shore for a few miles and called a raven to light within ten feet. His eyes sparkle, cheeks flame red with the cold, and he looks like a man so filled with aliveness that my own good spirits soar even higher just at the look of him. Like winter, he seems designed for this wild land. We roar old Nelson Eddy–Jeanette MacDonald medleys, full voice, as we haul the sled up to our cabin. Even the jays are struck dumb!

PRESENCES

After many days of grayness, with daily snowstorms and temperatures skipping around from zero to twenty degrees above, with only occasional brief glimpses of sun, today is ablaze with brilliant sunlight. A soft Chinook breeze, touched with a glacial freshness, blows gently from the south.

Each of the nine clusters of mountains ringing us is sharply etched with spruce, willow, alder and shadow crevices. The lake with its thin translucent ice patches and wide ring of shore ice has never looked so blue—the entire spectrum of blue, from cobalt to azure to turquoise.

A sense that someone or something has come into the vicinity is so strong that I prepare letters and orders for "outside." Perhaps our nearest neighbors are hunting in our area or are going to pay us a call. These are the Johnsons, who live some thirty ground miles, ten air miles, away, over a few mountain passes, around a small unnamed lake, across a frozen river or two, up along a small creek where they have their gold mine and small airstrip. Mr. Johnson is white, Mrs. Johnson an Eskimo, and although their two-passenger Super Cub plane enables them to move freely about the territory, they apparently live most of the time in total isolation. They mine in summer and bounty-hunt for wolves in winter.

Or could one of the old-timers from Wiseman be trapping in this area? Not likely, for usually only the Eskimos wander this far afield from home base. And all the natives are gone from Wiseman. Or perhaps the young schoolteacher couple from the Athapascean Indian village a hundred miles from here may come by. When our paths crossed at Bettles this summer, they said they'd try to make it over for a visit.

No, no visitors today. No one is going to risk landing on a lake dotted with floating, drifting sheets of ice. This is the time of "freeze-up." Daryl said he'd try to land on the lake ice *after* freeze-up." No one seems to know just when freeze-up will come. The term apparently describes both the process and its conclusion, and refers less to the land than to the waters of the arctic tundra. Creeks, rivers, lakes—these have been the winter-summer "highways" of trappers, hunters, prospectors, traders, dog sled drivers, snowshoers, river boaters and canoeists. And today are the landing strips of float- and skiplane pilots. But during freeze-up and its springtime opposite, breakup, these wilderness "highways" become unnavigable and treacherous for travelers.

We will have no visitors this beautiful sunlit day. But the

sense of other presences is still very strong—as tangible as the sounds within silence have become. There must be a band of caribou passing through somewhere nearby. If the fragrance of glaciers mixed with south seas is sensed in the Chinook wind, why not the earthy odor of warm, moving caribou? Or is it our fellow sharers of the territory—the wolves? Are they out there, somewhere just beyond sighting, sensing our presence as well?

THE NEWS

Our portable radio on the high shelf at the back of the cabin is wrapped many times around with wire. From it an aerial wire leads out the small air vent cut into the logs of the back wall, up a thirty-foot spruce pole attached to the cabin, then runs a hundred feet across the snow to the top of a second tall spruce.

Reception is unpredictable. When we can get the news, we hear it with a somewhat different perspective at the top of the world. We are more aware of its sameness. If a few days are missed, when only the wild cacophonous wails and shrieks of the arctic static come through, nothing has changed but the smallest details: the affairs of men change little. Eternal themes —international crises, national politics, violence, disasters, wars. We "communicate" in numbers: numbers of war dead this week, numbers of protesters jailed, numbers of persons killed in the car crash, numbers of dollars needed or spent. I suppose if we were all not already suffering severe symptoms of depersonalization, we could not tolerate this language. I feel like a computer being programmed; *must* listen impersonally. To listen beyond the numbers, to translate them into meaning, would be to reach the conclusion that one of us, I or my world, is mad.

Shortwave brings in the whole world. Russia's English-speaking broadcasts also communicate in numbers. They are as obsessed with them as are we—numbers of Russian citizens now attending night schools, numbers of tractors on numbers of farms, numbers of women doctors, engineers, numbers of cars produced. London,

Havana, Tokyo, Johannesburg, Quito. Tomorrow morning's news tonight. In the news from the rest of the world, America is not the "center"—a power, perhaps, an ally, an enemy, a competitor, an absurdity, dream, but only a part of, one small piece of the planet.

From the arctic waters off the Alaskan coast, Russian-speaking fishermen bark terse messages back and forth between their ships; women singsong messages in Eskimo between remote villages; pilots carry on taut, one-sided monosyllabic conversations; a doctor gives someone step-by-step instructions for emergency treatment.

Alaskan stations carry evening programs of personal messages to the residents of the remote villages and bush. The Fairbanks program called "Tundra Topics." World community in miniature. From Sophie in Fairbanks: "Sophie in Fairbanks wants Annie in Minto to know that Mother is doing well in Tanana Native Hospital and Sophie will be back on Friday mail plane." From John in Fairbanks: "John wants Walter in Anaktuvuk Pass to send eighty dollars for snowmobile repair parts next plane. Everything O.K." "Mary Smith in Arctic Village wants Jonathan Smith in Barrow to send check at once or come get the children." "Mr. Allen in Fairbanks wants Charley Jones in Stevens Village to know that he should come to Fairbanks on Monday's plane, ticket arranged for. He has a job for you on North Slope."

It's easier to care about strangers than digits.

Last night, awake for hours with a sudden and severe stomachache. Painful. Remembering the radioed instructions for emergency surgery, fantasy runs wild. My imagination begins to play the worrisome game of "What if—? What if—?" For the first time since our arrival in the wilderness, I know a twinge of fear. Staring into the darkness, reach for the rational. I've felt this same uneasiness trying to maneuver my car into the five o'clock expressway traffic in New York City; heading down a steep San Francisco hill on a rainy, foggy night. Is this really very different? Two of our "neighbor" families in the Koyukuk own small planes. All have two-way radios and can call out for assistance. We have neither.

To choose to come to live in isolated wilderness without means for making contact with the "outside" was not a lightly made decision. Risks were measured and the advantages of isolation in terms of this year's experience far outweighed the disadvantages. But we did not ignore the risks.

Among preparations for the year were complete medical and dental checkups. Through searching and a bit of unexpected good luck, we found a doctor in San Francisco with firsthand knowledge of the Arctic—a mountain climber, physician on several expeditions. The fifteen minutes he could allot us out of his busy schedule expanded into an hour as he became caught up in our project. He supplied us with a series of prescriptions designed to cover most medical emergencies. Recommended a comprehensive medical textbook on arctic survival; briefed us on the newest data on safeguards against and treatment for frostbite and snow blindness. Clarified the physical principles behind his own personally tested preferences for particular types of arctic clothing, foot- and handwear, which led to the usual animated discussion whenever arctic enthusiasts speak of the "right" kinds of clothing.

We left his office feeling well equipped and only a trifle guilty for the time he'd given us. It was obvious that this vicarious revisit he'd just made to the Arctic was for him as tension-breaking and soul-saving as a week's vacation. The harried, pressed doctor who had greeted us an hour earlier looked, as we said good-bye, as if he'd just dropped twenty years and many pressures.

His reaction was not surprising. I think it was arctic explorer Freuchen who wrote that once a man has cast his eyes over the infinite sweep of the frozen Arctic, he has seen eternity, and will never again be free of the pull it has on him to return.

Small risk, then, this bellyache, and a twinge of fear, for a glimpse of eternity!

I got up from my warm sleeping bag, lit the kerosene lamp and pulled down our well-stocked medicine chest—a cardboard carton with a red-crayoned FIRST AID crudely lettered under the printed label, "Drano." After a mild pain-killer pill and a dose of Pepto-Bismol, I returned to my warm bunk, read a half page of an Agatha Christie yarn and fell asleep.

Freeze-up takes place before our eyes!

Several clear, cold nights and days have extended the lake ice out from the small bays and inlets—well into the lake. This morning we watch the ice forming, creeping out toward the lake center, spreading, moving as storm clouds in the wind reach out, expand. A light, steady snowfall begins, and whitens the ice. All day this white sheet has moved farther and farther out. Now the entire lake is covered, looking like a great white valley merging into white slopes of mountains.

We had heard that freeze-up seemed to happen overnight. It does, suddenly, even though the process leading to it has been under way for many weeks, and is not yet ended.

The bell-like sounds of thin ice breaking and moving are gone now. In their place, silence emanates from the white plain now covering the blue waters. All motion is stilled—all ripples, waves, eddies locked tight under a cover of ice.

Winter has now covered all the land.

WINTER

THE BIRDS

When we step outside each morning, our constant companions, four chickadees and seven arctic gray jays, all fly round, perching on the nearby spruce or the cabin roof, chattering raucously, even lighting on our heads or hands if we carry food for them. If we are late coming out, they stand on the snow just outside the windows and peck at the glass, chirping softly. All it really means is that our cabin is now their restaurant and the service this morning is too slow.

These wild birds have apparently never seen man before, and they are both curious and unafraid. Often the jays will fly along partway with us when we are out on the trails, but never too far from home territory, which seems to be centered in a square-mile area around the cabin. On our return, they rejoin us at the same place, with a greeting very different from their usual chatter —this call is a prolonged, several-noted, beautifully melodic song. When we return their greeting with an awkward whistled imitation, they repeat their melody once more, then fly on ahead of us to the cabin.

In contrast, the little chickadees seem seldom to leave the camp. But, equally gregarious, they will carry on a conversation for several minutes if they like the sound of your returned call, "Chick-a-dee-dee-dee. . . ."

But this morning not a bird is in camp, even though fresh moose scraps and crumbs have been placed on either side of the cabin. Not until dusk do two jays suddenly reappear to peck at the meat scraps. Then off they fly, to the west. This must mean that there has been a "kill" in that direction. As scavengers, jays are particularly partial to suet and fresh meat. Since the wolves are the only predators here in great number, the kill must be theirs—perhaps the moose Sam met yesterday on its way up the trail toward the cabin, or one of a band of passing caribou.

Sam goes to investigate, finding no signs of the kill or the birds. But in breaking trail to the northwest, up on the mountain behind camp he found a plentiful new supply of dead trees for firewood.

FULL MOON

The moon takes on new meaning here.

As we sit down to a moose-roast dinner, through the east window we catch a glimpse of the newly risen moon—full and golden, balanced on a craggy peak like a huge gold bauble atop a Christmas tree. In a twilight sky of deep, rich blue, the moon looks immense and very close. Below, a wide golden swath of moonlight cuts through the reflected blue of sky on snow.

As did our ancestors—and the Eskimos—we now measure our months by moons.

If our speculations are accurate, in two days we may have a mail drop.

Whether Daryl will fly on here from Wiseman, or if the weather will let him through, we don't know. We'll know if and when he comes. I'm anxious to film a "drop," if possible. I've heard that the bush mail pilots use various marking devices for air drops—in winter, a long bright-red streamer tied to the materials dropped; in summer, a long streamer of toilet paper. In any event, an air drop must be a riskier task than casual talk of it indicates. Unless the plane flies low, close to the ground, drift may take the package a long, hard hike from its target. And flying low to the ground in these mountain crosscurrents carries its own built-in hazards. But bush pilots in the Arctic are accustomed to risk.

Blizzards, sudden storms, whiteouts, landing on gravel bars, frozen creeks; flying over vast wilderness hundreds of miles from airports and mechanics, with ground temperatures that reach as low as seventy degrees below zero, in small Super Cubs or Cessna 180s—why do they take the risk? It's not even a question to be asked here in the arctic wilderness, where everyone has chosen to live with risk.

Yes, there's a certain excitement in anticipation of a drop. Mail will be welcome, of course, but I'm even more curious to see just how the drop will be made—if Daryl comes.

Fourteen degrees above zero tonight, and the sky is dancing pale green light!

Today we take the big sled up the mountain to the new place Sam found yesterday, snowshoeing and packing the trail as we go. This bigger sled is not only much heavier than the other, but is an unwieldy eight feet long, with an added eight feet of gee pole in front. Pushing it up the mountain, empty, is not an easy task! Sam snowshoes in front of the sled, I behind, to pack the snow for the return trip down.

Here at the crest of a slope, the forest is more dense, with many fine virgin spruce, some thirty feet tall, their trunks a foot in diameter, some of them between two hundred and three hundred years old. So far we have found few remnants of virgin forest around Koviashuvik. The axes of the departed prospectors were ruthless.

The day is bright and sparkling, deep-shadowed in the thickest woods, sun-slanted where the trees stand apart. As in all forests in all seasons, there is an ancient hush here, too, a great stillness deepened more by the snow cover blanketing the forest tundra, subduing the voice while exciting the imagination. These moments of connectedness with what we know as the primeval are so very rare today as to be unknown to many.

We "walk" down the snow around several dead trees, then remove the snowshoes. Each sharp bite into wood of the double-bit ax comes back sevenfold, as the echo bounces between the mountain faces. Dry branches snap like small firecrackers as they are knocked off with the back of the hatchet blade. Though the temperature is less than twenty degrees, we remove our parkys, for the work is hot. The day is so pleasant and the harvesting goes so well that after filling the sled we go on to ax more logs for a tepee stand next to the trail, to bring down at some future date.

There is no such thing as level ground here—everything is up or down. Trudging up the slope in heavy insulated boots, I find the snow a hindrance—but a boon in dragging the logs down, much easier than dragging logs over tussocks of summer tundra. Sam is very good about not criticizing my ways of dealing with some of the chores. Since women never handle weights as do men, I devise my own carrying style, clutching one or two logs, trunk end, under each arm but letting the weight rest on my hipbones as in carrying a child, and dragging the lighter tip end of the logs through the snow. (Carrying the logs reverse-ended adds ten pounds in resistance.)

Finally we are ready to go down. The problem now is just the reverse of pushing a loaded sled *up* a mountain. The question is how we are going to slow this down once those iced runners get speeding down the mountainside with six or seven hundred pounds of logs. This time Sam does not get into the rope harness —he may have to jump clear if the sled starts moving faster than he can run. But the sled must be steered by the gee pole on the right side at the front to keep on the narrow "trail" we've snowshoed, so he takes up the rope in his left hand. I will be the "brake" at the back of the sled.

We start off gingerly to get the feel of things. All seems to go well. We pick up speed—then more speed. At some of the steepest stretches I find myself churning up clouds of snow as I dig in with both heels, pulling back on the sled handles with all my weight. At one of these sharp declines, my feet fly out and I find myself being dragged along at fifteen miles an hour, which, I note, might be an interesting new sport were I not so concerned about Sam being overtaken and flattened out like a piece of cardboard. We are about halfway down the mountain and gathering even more momentum. The sled is no longer just a sled. It has a life of its own and *it* is in charge. I dig in my heels even harder and feel as if I'm at the final moment of the losing end of a tug of war. Sam runs even faster. He is now being chased by this thing, no question about it. I'm reminded of Buster Keaton with a locomotive at his heels and I wish I could stop braking to watch Sam run. But we are reaching the gentler slope now, and the speed finally begins to slacken, almost imperceptibly, but enough for me to jump on the back runners and ride into camp, stopping just short of the sawbuck.

We have had a great day in the forest. We've run a good race. And the woodpile is replenished!

ARCTIC JOE

When we were out in the boat early this fall, we scanned the landscape carefully for game. In the process, we familiarized ourselves with landmarks—certain trees, outcroppings of rock, willow brush, the few groves of birch growing on the slopes. After the snows covered the land, we saw something new. Two or three miles to the north, halfway up a gently sloping mountainside, was a cabin. Only when the snow had outlined its roof, presenting a striking new horizontal line across the landscape, did it become visible.

Today we snowshoe over to this cabin, taking the narrow game trail along the rim of the lake until we are directly below the site. Turning inland and moving up the gradual rise through the silent forest, we follow a trail crudely marked by old blazes hatcheted into the spruce. The smell of burning spruce logs will carry on the wind for miles, seeming to linger among thickets of trees long after a stove has grown cold. But there is no scent of burning wood here in this stillness.

Well before we have traveled the mile or more to the cabin, we know it has been uninhabited for a long time. Only game has passed over this trail in recent years. It must be a favorite route for moose and wolves; their tracks and droppings are fresh and numerous.

We come upon the cabin suddenly. The forest stops abruptly at a clearing dotted with spruce stumps which show where the logs for the cabin have come from. Twenty-five feet to the left, a thick tangle of willow screens a creek now silenced by thickening ice.

The cabin is a ruin. Buckled walls, windows gone and frames askew, part of the sod roof collapsed inward. Yet inside, though chill and dank, and though the spruce-pole bunk and whipsawed shelves and table have been gnawed by porcupines, there is a feeling of livability about this one-room shelter. The rough-hewn furnishings are placed for most efficiency, with an aesthetic rightness in their proportions and balance.

While the cabin appears to have been built long ago by a miner, it has since belonged to and been used by an Eskimo family, if the clues are accurate. Materials are used economically. The spruce-pole bunk is simply constructed, with no waste effort or space. Nothing is overdesigned or overbuilt. There is a tentative quality about many of the arctic native's dwellings which probably stems from his history as a nomad. Non-natives, with equally few consumers' goods, seem to have a need to build a sense of permanent indestructibility into their wilderness homes, with bunks attached solidly to walls, everything nailed down as if it is to be there forever, as if in such "permanence" immortality may be guaranteed. Native homes even in permanent villages often have a more casual, even transient, quality, as if at any moment whatever can be transported might be piled onto the sleds or snowmobiles and moved on to the summer fish camp or the caribou-hunting grounds.

Other clues are here in the things we find. Although all residents in isolated areas become fairly proficient in making multiple use of hard-come-by materials, the native far northerners more often rely on indigenous materials. Here the door hinges are fashioned of skillfully worked moosehide. Hanging in a corner is a string of short lengths of caribou leg bones, weights for a gill net. Scraps of caribou, moose and wolf skins in the corner show a fineness in scraping and tanning that indicates an expert's hand.

The outhouse has none of the usual arctic jerry-built construction of spruce-pole frame held together by canvas, boards from wooden supply boxes, old Blazo tins. This is a simple two-sided tepee of spruce logs, just high enough to enter and with a board seat at one end. An original "A-frame."

In the dogtrot, a cluster of tattered mailing tags used for shipping furs are labeled "Arctic Joe"—a name we know. This must be the trappers' cabin Arctic Joe and his wife used when they came over to Koviashuvik by dog sled from their permanent camp in Wiseman, to hunt and trap and ice-fish.

Arctic Joe's name is well known to those interested in arctic mountain lore. He is, at the same time, a mystery. Piecing together the scraps of local hearsay: Arctic Joe is considered a "famous Eskimo in these parts" because "long ago, when he very young," he suddenly appeared on the scene "from out of the North." Still another tale has it that his pregnant mother walked all the way from the arctic coast into the range across the wild frozen tundra, so that her son could be born and raised free from the danger of conscription into the "white man's army."

Whatever the truth, a mystique surrounds Arctic Joe, even among the natives. We first met him in a village where he and his third wife ("other two lost on trail when they hunting with him") seem to live, by comparison, a solitary existence in the middle of village sociability. He is called "The best hunter man in the Arctic," and in the Arctic the skilled hunter has always been held in the highest esteem. Because of this, his more gregarious fellow villagers seem to respect his solitary wanderings in the mountains, where he may disappear for days before returning, as silent and noncommunicative as he departed.

The men of the village hunt caribou, still the primary diet staple of the inland Eskimos as it has been for thousands of years. The caribou hunts are no longer communal as they once were. A few hunters hunt alone; more often they join with a brother, brother-in-law or friend. A few trap wolverine and wolf as well as fox and ermine. These pelts add a little to the family income if they are not used for the family's own needs. But the traditional, centuries-old hunting and trapping economy of the Nunamiut continues to disintegrate swiftly under the exponential acceleration of change. Arctic Joe represents the artistry and skills of the "old ways," even to his fellow hunters.

The village Eskimo men with little or no elementary school education who have had the opportunity for training in mechanical skills have proved adept, quick to learn, able to work with sophisticated tools and machines. If there is a "work" problem, it is in part the hardship in adapting to the day-to-day routinization of the white society's work ethic. Being forced to live and work away from their families and village while on such jobs is equally difficult. Being uprooted from their homeland—the lands of the Nunamiut ancient hunting grounds—is a problem unrecognizable to restless, mobile white workers who shift from city to city, state to state, as easily and as indifferently as they change shirts.

One of the Anaktuvuk men said of a proposal to move the entire village from its present location to the flats nearer the oil fields north of the range, "Who can live on those flats where there is nothing to see all round? I am mountain man." Then, stopping to study us as if he were not sure any outsider could really grasp the meaning of what he was saying, he explained, "My home here!" with a sharp nod down at the tundra. "Not worth nothing to go live on flats! I die away from mountains!"

Still, most of the men continue to make the effort to adapt to the urban work world. Money, always in short supply, must at present come from outside the village. They continue to take the occasional jobs offered them by oil and mining companies, public agencies and a few local firms in Fairbanks and Anchorage. But most soon return home, frustrated and disenchanted by the strangeness and dulling tedium of regimented dailiness in the outside world.

"Not worth it," one said to us with a laugh and a disbelieving shake of his head as he recalled his job "outside."

"It's crazy place out there," added another, studying us intently as if wondering how *we* could find it tolerable.

But behind the shrugs and laughter, there seems to be unspoken uneasiness over the contradictions between the two worlds. Whether from some anxiety that their inability to solve their financial stress in this fashion might, in the non-native's eyes, represent personal failure, or from fear that we might interpret their comments as criticism of us and "our" world, I do not know.

In any case, I share their wonder at how we can live lives of day-to-day routinization, circumscribed by time clocks and machines. Sun, wind, cold, seasons, moon are routinizers that enhance life, but not if one's quest is for ever more efficiency, productivity and dollars.

The old hunting economy of the Nunamiut has already been replaced with new, and in many ways more uncertain, ones: welfare assistance, the making of masks for tourist gift shops "outside," and the short-lived odd jobs. Among the latter, one seasonal occupation drawing on most of the manpower of the village seems to contain within it some rewards similar to those in the old communal hunting culture.

We were in Anaktuvuk Pass during the peak of the annual summer rampage of forest and tundra fires in the state. Some government sage of recent history had the imagination and foresight to see the native villages as a logical, and excellent, source of manpower to fight the yearly sieges of fires. The men of Anaktuvuk and other villages have been trained by the Fairbanks Bureau of Land Management firefighting division as professional firefighters.

For this work, which may last anywhere from a few days to several weeks, an hourly rate of portal-to-portal pay, plus food, first aid and medical care, if needed, are provided. Hard and dangerous work, calling for strength and endurance, courage and skill, it is, nevertheless, looked forward to with anticipation.

As radio reports announced the outbreak of each new fire, and the spread or containment of each of those already raging throughout the northern part of the state, the men of Anaktuvuk followed the news like generals plotting the course of a battle, predicting where and when the next forces would be most urgently needed. For days, all in the village were restless, waiting —women and children included. Then the announcement came over the radiophone: the Anaktuvuk firefighters were to be ready to go in two hours' time. The big transport plane was on its way.

The village buzzed into action. Men and women erupted from tents, moving pruposefully from one household to another and back again. Children ran excitedly up and down the village path. Older men and women began to drift down toward the airstrip, where they stood expectantly in little waiting clusters. A sudden run on the Paneaks' "store," a sod hut next to the family's tent, emptied the supply cartons of canned soft drinks and packs of cigarettes, most of the "sales" listed on the credit ledger against the pay the firefighters would bring back.

As the big plane was heard in the distance, villagers spilled once more out of their tents and moved in waves toward the gravel airstrip, the children shrieking, *"Air-plan! Air-plan!"* As always when planes set down at the village, many of the women were dressed in their most colorful summer parky covers, made of bright cotton prints cut to mid-calf length and full enough to accommodate babies on their backs.

But the men, some of whom also wear their handsomer parkys for meeting planes, were today in their sturdiest work clothes and jackets, like men everywhere setting off of a morning for the job at the plant or construction site, except that each freshly slicked-down and carefully combed head was topped by the protective white plastic helmet of the firefighter brigade.

As the plane landed in a cloud of gritty dust and taxied to a standstill, the men surged forward, led by their "fire chief," Jack Aghook. They quickly climbed aboard, laughing and calling out jokingly to each other and to their waving families and friends. Jack stood at the plane door, counting the entering men, clapping some on the shoulder and wisecracking with others, wearing a beaming smile. This was not the quiet, soft-spoken man we had seen in other situations. This was the chief, the man in charge, apparently relishing every minute of it!

The Anaktuvuk firefighters speak with unself-conscious pride of their reputation as the best pumping crew among the BLM firefighter crews. As members of this village "team," working as part of a unit composed of men who are brothers, cousins, life-long familial associates, they communicate an unabashed sense of self-esteem and pride that one does not often hear expressed in the talk of other areas of their lives except in discussion of successful hunts.

These are the strong, younger men of the village—the youngest nineteen or twenty, the oldest forty-five to fifty. The women and children and the elders watch them depart, with smiles and waves.

Arctic Joe is not at the edge of the airstrip to see the big plane airborne. He may be off in the mountains alone. It is said by some that he and his wife would not be living in the village if circumstance had not required it. They would still be living the seminomadic, solitary life of hunting and trapping the wilds, of ice-fishing at Koviashuvik, returning now and then to their one-room log cabin, their permanent camp at Wiseman. The old "hunter man" cannot escape the paradoxical price extracted for contemporary "well-being" and "security." A lingering illness requires periodic medical attention, costly beyond all the income now to be garnered from a good year of fur harvesting.

We were told by Arctic Joe's old Wiseman friend and hunting companion that to qualify for the public health service provided the native population, Arctic Joe had to become a resident of an officially recognized native village.

"Otherwise," the old sourdough commented with a snort, "old Arctic Joey might have fouled up the whole public health department trying to figure out what to do about him!"

Spend the early part of the day tanning the caribou skin. Rub sourdough sponge into the hide, then put the skin under the bunk to "set" overnight. Tomorrow another application, working the sponge into the fibers with the motion used in doing laundry by hand—rubbing one part against the other between the knuckles.

BLACK WOLF

Late afternoon, Sam hikes down to the lake to check for tracks and to see what is happening with the lake ice. When I see him return, pushing the sled up the slope with a large, dark-furred animal on it, I race out to meet him.

On the sled is a black wolf. Its thick, soft undercoat is a deep smoky gray, blending to black, tipped with silver guard hairs. Even the inside of the mouth is blackish. A beautiful creature, looking at first glance like a very large, long-haired dog, but something about it has a look of wildness, even in death.

At the shore, finding fresh wolf tracks all around the old cabin, Sam rounded the far corner and found this young female caught in the trap at the foot of the "ramp" log up into the meat cache. An older, wiser wolf would have avoided the trap or, if caught, pulled himself free of it. This one, caught solidly by a toe, curled up in the snow and went to sleep. No way to get close enough to free it, so the .22 was used.

Dusk and turning colder. The wolf must be skinned tonight before the carcass freezes solid. We hang it, head down, from a spruce-pole frame near the cabin. An hour later, after a rushed dinner and chores, we're ready. Sam brings in the carcass, which weighs sixty to sixty-five pounds, and places it on the table. A strong musty odor edged with a slight acridity fills the cabin— the smell of a wild thing. Sam sets to work with his skinning knife. First a slit along each hind leg opens the pelt, which gradually separates from the carcass as the skinning blade moves along gently, severing the connecting fibers. I'm surprised at the thinness of the skin in which the fur is embedded, much more delicate than that of a caribou. The carcass without its thick fur is gaunt, the lean muscles stringy, streamlined—a miracle of construction, designed for speed and endurance. The knife eases the pelt free; it peels off the way a woman peels off a girdle. Working around the head and ears is more difficult, but at last the job is done.

With a flashlight, Sam scrounges around the storage shed for a board which once was a part of the miner's sluice boxes. Smoothing down the edges and surfaces, he makes a stretchboard and eases the pelt over it, skinned side out. As the pelt dries it can be scraped right on the board. We will use the wolf pelt to make ruffs for our parkys as the Eskimos have done for centuries. Wolf and wolverine fur, framing the face, are the best protectors against wind, snow and frostbite.

Sam takes the carcass outside and leaves it at the side of the cabin until tomorrow. The stretchboard stands in the cabin corner. We tidy up and have some hot chocolate as we talk over the day's events. Tonight I feel as I did the day of the caribou hunt, the day of the moose—a sense of reward and accomplishment; at the same time, a vague sense of loss.

Before turning in, we step outside for a quick look at the night sky, but we rush back for our parkys and mitts. The northern lights are out in full panoply and have taken over the heavens. A sky full of dancing motion as the lights race across the blackness, erupting in sudden streaks from behind the mountains, creating a spectrum of ephemeral jewel colors—intense emerald greens, deep reds, golds. Shimmering, incessantly moving, changing, vanishing, reappearing, they congregate finally in an iridescent canopy just over our heads.

Our initial cries of "Look *there!*" . . . Did you *see?*" . . . *Look!*" soon subside, and we stand silent, enveloped in a wild and magical event of light and color. It is the Night of the Wolf—a fitting acknowledgment. . . .

FIRST MAIL DROP

A loss of six to eight minutes of daylight each day now. An hour a week? Four hours a month? What will the "long night" be like? But the sunrise, coming now between eight and nine o'clock, is still with us, appearing suddenly this morning out of the dawn in bands of crimson, gold and deep gray streaked across the southern skies.

A sharply crisp morning at zero degrees. The lake is growling again today—the sounds of freezing as the ice contracts are like moans and cries of some huge beast. A crack begins near the shore, zigzags like a rifle shot gone berserk across the entire lake, then ricochets and echoes back. Quiet—waiting—until the next explosion of sound. . . .

Sam scrapes the wolf pelt on the board with a gentle touch, for the thin drying skin tears easily. Midmorning, he sets off for the shore while I tidy up the cabin and begin the dishes. Five minutes later, at the tail end of an echoed wail from the ice, a hum of another sound approaches from Jim Pup Pass in the west. A small plane, coming in so fast and low that it has almost passed over before I get out the door.

It is Daryl's plane. He's over and headed for the lake. Will he try to land on the ice? Not safe yet. For a moment I lose sight of the plane as it disappears against the dark spruce on the sides of the mountains, then pick it up again as it circles, recrosses the whiteness of the lake ice and heads this way. As he passes overhead, I can see Daryl very clearly. I wonder if he can see *me* —he won't make a drop unless he knows someone is here (we might never find the mailbag). Remembering how animals can be sighted against the vast tundra only when in motion, I begin to move, jumping up and down, with both arms whirling like windmills. Then he's gone past, almost as far as the pass to the west before he circles and returns, this time very low and close to the ground, aiming, it seems, right at the cabin.

There is a flash of bright green at the plane window. It rests there until the plane is no more than a hundred feet from the cabin, then suddenly plummets like a falling bird to hit the snow with a solid thump—right in the middle of the trail to the outhouse and only fifteen feet from the cabin. The fall has driven the green bag down into the snow, out of sight. As I race down to get the sack, I have a sense that the plane has barely skimmed the cabin roof as it soars on and over the lake again.

Once more Daryl circles back over the camp. This time I swing the retrieved big green U.S. Mail bag in circles over my head, and again wave and jump like a maniac to show him that the drop was right on target. He waggles the wings in acknowledgment and turns east, looking against the immense setting like a sparrow sailing over the mountain summit.

In front of the cabin the sun is warm, the wind still. We bring out fresh mugs of coffee and settle ourselves comfortably on two upended spruce log stumps in the sun. There is a touch of the ceremonial in our preparation. It does seem a rather special occasion. The metal seal on the bag is broken, the mail brought out. Letters from family, friends; business mail, bills, magazines, books—even the junk mail seems interesting for a change, worthy of careful inspection before wadding it up for the fire-making trash box beside the stove. An hour passes while we are caught up in the news of the world "out there." Finally the last of the letters is read.

In the last few minutes, the sun has slipped behind clouds that have moved in over the southern mountains, and the chill wind resumed from the west. For a brief moment, as I look across the endless snowfields to the western peaks now wreathed in misty clouds, I feel caught in limbo, between two worlds—here and "outside." It's wonderful to get the mail, but ambivalence runs beneath that pleasure. Viewed from this world where we perch on our spruce stumps, these letters and commentaries speak of a world that takes on some of the aura of a strange, remote planet. Where does a "night of the wolf" fit in?

The wind blows colder. We go inside, hang the empty green mail bag on a nail. The fire is warming.

Awakened this morning to the smell of perking coffee mixed with something else—a strange musky, meaty aroma coming from a bubbling pot on the stove.

Sam, who has been up for a while, explains that he's cooking the wolf skull. Wonder in my half sleep if he plans to introduce me to a new form of survival food for breakfast. But it is only the skull he's interested in, and this is a faster method than waiting for the birds and shrews to clean it.

Last night it was minus four degrees, with a bright gold half moon. This morning the moon is still visible. It does not "set," but remains clearly visible all day, moving around the sky above the peaks in a circle. Appearing to "rise" late in the day, it actually turns from white to a golden "night" moon, as the sky deepens in color.

My tobacco supply runs low. Have had to salvage what tobacco is left in the butts; open the newspaper "papers" and pour the remaining shreds of tobacco back into the can. Soon even that will be gone and I will join the ranks of the nonsmokers!

PARKAS: PORTABLE IGLOOS

The wolf pelt has been dried, scraped, tanned with sourdough.

A skin sewer with the skill of the Eskimo women can get several ruffs out of a single wolf pelt. But the prime fur is that of the wolf's own thick natural "ruff," below the neck and across the back and shoulders. Working with the sharpened ulu, we cut the pelt into wide strips. Two joined end to end fit around the parky hood. Ideal would be an entire prime "ruff," but we'll make good use of these narrower ones.

Sam zips himself into his parky so that I can position the fur correctly before sewing. With the hood up, the ruff frames the face so closely that only the eyes are left uncovered.

We have no skin-sewing needles, but a large-eyed sturdy needle from my sewing kit can be ground down flat on three sides of the point. This punctures the hide more easily and neatly than a smooth-pointed needle. Nor have we enough sinew to sew on the ruffs. Many of the Eskimo women now use dental floss as a substitute for sinew. This we have.

With the sewing finished, we try on the parkys. Only wolverine fur would better protect our faces from frostbite. Our parkas, chosen carefully after examining those of various Fairbanks friends, seem to be adequate so far. With more "layers" added under them, they should do as well when the temperatures drop to minus fifty and sixty degrees.

As with all else here, details make the difference. These parkys are much longer than the more common just-below-the-waist style but are lighter-weight than many shorter jackets. They are down-filled, the inner lining stitched with enough seams to hold the down in place, evenly distributed; sturdy nylon makes the outer shell. Sleeves that hold snug at the wrists keep out wind and snow. Four huge pockets hold an assortment of "emergency" necessities always with us—waterproof vial of matches, bar of baking chocolate (denser and smaller than a chocolate candy bar), neat wad of toilet tissue, binoculars, cartridges, face mask, extra wool gloves, miniature trail first-aid kit and, until the long night, sunglasses. Heavy-duty zippers, openable top or bottom, most important for moving freely and for stopping on the trail; a button closing as well. Hoods are warmly lined with fake mouton.

The only fault in this otherwise excellent design for arctic wear is that the zipper ends at the neck. When the hood is pulled tight around the head by means of a drawstring, there is a small but vital gap between parky neck and hood which exposes the throat to cold and wind. A wool scarf helps to some extent, but not in arctic midwinter cold. We've filled in this gap at the neck by sewing on a patch left over from an old fleece-lined leather slipper found among some caribou-skin scraps in the storage shed. This now buttons across the neck.

Snowshoeing down the mountain trail today, we find the tracks of three Dall sheep that have crossed the trail, headed toward the shore from the peaks to the northwest. The deepening snows must be bringing them down for better forage. As we near the old shore cabin, a covey of ptarmigan rise up in a sudden stir of deep-throated cluckings and a great whoosh of wings as they scatter into the air and wheel toward the trees in the north. They have been feeding on seeds in willow thickets beside the cabin. These arctic grouse are now in full white plumage, with only a touch of black on their tails. Once they set down on the snow, white on white, they are impossible to see. The thickly feathered feet make distinctive tracks on the snow. They must have found good feed in these willows, for hundreds of ptarmigan tracks crisscross the snow here. Every willow branch has been stripped of its dried seeds and leaves.

On the shore twenty feet in front of the old cabin are fresh tracks of grizzly bear. (Only luck that he chose to by-pass our cached meat!) The pawprints are immense—three times the length of a moose's hoofprint and twice as wide. The tracks continue on along the shore for a hundred or more feet, then veer up into the tundra of the mountainside. I wonder if he is headed toward our camp.

There is something undeniably awesome—and worrisome—about these fresh tracks. Their very size gives an image of a build and power that triggers an undercurrent of alarm at the possibility of a close encounter with such a creature. The Anaktuvuk women express fear of only one animal—the grizzly. I understand. At the same time, based on my knowledge, the fear seems irrational.

I know that despite the surfeit of hair-raising bear stories one hears in the far north, the facts are that most bears in their wild native setting will avoid any close encounter with man. The danger is in the unexpected close and confined confrontation, in which the bear, feeling cornered, may charge. A sow with cubs, especially, is always to be kept at a good safe distance, for she is quick to attack if her cubs appear to be even remotely threatened.

I know, too, that bears have an exceptionally acute sense of smell and hearing, but extremely poor eyesight. Being curious, particularly these in the wilds seldom invaded by men, they will move close to get a better look at anything strange on the land-scape. And if the object of their curiosity suddenly breaks into a run, the bear is likely to give chase; they move with amazing speed. Outrunning a grizzly may be difficult! Best then to stand absolutely motionless, since the bear will be intrigued more with a moving than a stationary object, which may well be only another tree or rock on his poorly sighted horizon.

If, though, he continues to advance, the unexpected noise of loud shouting or, better yet, clanging metal will often frighten him off. On one of Sam's backpacking trips through the range, he spooked an approaching curious grizzly off at a fast gallop by rapping a Sierra cup on the metal frame of his backpack. A last resort (south of timber line) may be a tree. Unlike the smaller bears, grizzlies do not climb trees. While one of our spruce with their brittle slender branches may not be the easiest to climb in a hurry, it can be done if a seven- to eight-hundred-pound creature is right behind you!

Still, several Alaskans each year are killed or badly maimed by bears. Approximately five thousand grizzlies roam the wild mountains of the Brooks Range. The grizzly in particular is known to be unpredictable; foot travelers in bear country should carry firearms. But knowledge of, and respect for, the wild inhabitants of a territory are even better protection.

We wonder if this is the bear who has torn apart a miner's boarded-up cabin, eight miles to the northeast, for two years in a row. Once a bear has taken over a camp as part of his partic-ular territory, it becomes very difficult to persuade him other-wise. I cross my fingers that this huge fellow is not headed for *ours*.

The lake ice is covered over with a thin layer of rippled, wind-swept snow. As we walk out onto it, I move cautiously, testing for thin ice. But even the cracks have refrozen solidly. We walk through a great field of "flowers." Thousands of deli-cate little blossom-shaped formations of fine-petaled snow and ice crystals glitter and shimmer in the sun's shifting light.

Sam scrapes away the crystals and, with the ice chipper, begins to chop a hole through the ice. Each blow of the sharp metal sets off a round robin of echoes as the sound, airborne, reverberates back from around the mountain faces ringing the lake. At the same time a different sound flashes out, racing through the ice itself. This hits the shoreline and ricochets back, returning through the ice by different routes, at different pitches. And still another note, deeper than all the rest, seems to begin right at our feet and to move out under the ice. This hollow rumble is short-lived and does not come back but is quickly swallowed up somewhere beneath us. The bowl of the lake is a great, silent amphitheater in which each chop of the ice chipper sets in motion a new variation on a recurring theme until we are ringed by unbroken sound.

Water begins to seep, then floods through the hole, and again all is silent. When all the ice chips are cleared out of the hole, and we get down on our hands and knees, faces close to the water, we can just barely see out through the darkness. Lake-bottom grasses and mosses sway gently from the disturbance we've made. It seems a world untouched by the winter that surrounds us above.

The ice is now about five inches thick—strong enough to take a light plane. We will have to begin work on the "runway." We have a "snow shovel" made of a short, worn board wired onto a spruce pole. Sam pushes this along in front of him, pacing off a thousand feet from the shore out onto the lake ice, in a straight line. This marks off one edge of our "airstrip." Wandering along the shore waiting for him to return, I begin to feel the cold even though it is only ten degrees above zero and the wind is slight. The toes of my left foot are feeling numb. One can't stand around inactive for very long in the cold.

Scouting the shoreline while waiting for Sam, I see that the Dall sheep have come down onto the ice here, and headed out across the lake. Wolf tracks are everywhere along the shore— a family of at least five or six has been all over this area earlier today. A little distance on, the huge grizzly pawprints reappear. They come down out of the tundra brush onto the lake ice and continue on along the shoreline. He is headed south at an easy steady lope. We wonder that he has not hibernated yet.

Delicate, evenly spaced parallel streaks on the snow turn out to be the wing-tip landing marks of a covey of ptarmigan. Their prints mark a trail from their landing strip along the shore and up into the willows. Here, too, they have fed well.

The light is beginning to go, the wind rise, the cold increase.

We have a long hike to home. In all the silent white miles that stretch around and beyond us as we trudge along across the flat of the frozen lake, we seem to be the only two creatures in the world. But all around us are the signs, proof that we are only a very small part of a busy, many-creatured land. Life is here with us in great abundance. Room for all.

After our dinner of moose roast stuffed with cornmeal dressing, of stewed dehydrated carrots and chocolate brownies, Sam pulls out the oil paints. The wolf skull, now clean and dry, is brought to the table. Its lines are as stark and simple as if a sculptor had shaped them. Mixing the paints to earth and sky colors, Sam carefully, sparingly extends the eye hollows with ocher— shadows the cheekbone hollows with clay red—enhances the long, sloping nose cavity with lines of deep turquoise. A raven feather found beside Raven Lake at Anaktuvuk Pass, and carried on my backpack all summer, is added to the narrow cranium.

Sam hangs the wolf skull over the heavy frame inside the cabin door. It is a beautiful artifact, one a shaman would appreciate. We have our totem.

CHILL FACTOR

The cold does not move in gradually, a drop of a few degrees each day, as I had expected, but moves from plateau to plateau. For a week and a half now, morning and night temperatures have ranged from minus four to ten degrees. Midday temperatures vacillate from ten to twenty degrees above zero. But this means very little, really; like playing the numbers game. The figures on the thermometer have almost nothing to tell of the cold, in the way that a wristwatch tells little about Koviashuvik time.

A snowstorm and whiteout produce a milder temperature than a sunny day, for example, for the cold of outer space is closed off by the thick overcast. Now the sun's warmth is deceptive, more imagined than felt. No longer high in the sky, the sun moves along just above the rim of the circling peaks to "set" by 4 P.M. behind a western mountaintop.

The real key to the cold is wind. Cold in combination with wind produces the "chill factor," which, more crucial than either temperature or wind velocity, can also be measured.

Here in the mountains wind can come up so unexpectedly that within minutes the stillest day can turn bleak and frigid, with a harsh arctic wind that drops the temperature equivalents of ten to thirty degrees.

Dressing for hikes which take us a good distance from camp is a tricky problem in this time of early winter. Best to dress for the worst, and in layers of clothing. Mitts and parkys and sweaters can always be removed if we have them with us. If not, and the weather worsens, the next best thing is to keep moving!

Today we breakfast on T-bone moose steaks and sourdough hotcakes. With plans to spend the day working on the cabin remains down at the shore, we fuel up for the weather, whatever it may bring.

Our main chore at this point is to clear out the fallen roof turfing from the interior of the cabin shell. Sam has patched and rebuilt the cabin's rusted old Yukon stove and now it is installed. And it works, helping to thaw the top surface of the solidly frozen sod that is a foot thick over most of the floor, several feet deep in some spots. We set to with the ice chipper, sharpened spruce poles and a shovel. The loosened earth is carried outside and packed around the base logs of the shelter as wind-and-varmint-proofing. To our surprise and pleasure, we discover a floor of sorts under the dirt. The well-weathered planks are crude adzed

WIND-CHILL FACTOR

COOLING POWER OF WIND EXPRESSED AS EQUIVALENT CHILL TEMPERATURE

WIND SPEED–MPH	TEMPERATURE																				
	40	35	30	25	20	15	10	5	0	-5	-10	-15	-20	-25	-30	-35	-40	-45	-50	-55	-60
0	40	35	30	25	20	15	10	5	0	-5	-10	-15	-20	-25	-30	-35	-40	-45	-50	-55	-60
5	35	30	25	20	15	10	5	0	-5	-10	-15	-20	-25	-30	-35	-40	-45	-50	-55	-65	-70
10	30	20	15	10	5	0	-10	-15	-20	-25	-35	-40	-45	-50	-60	-65	-70	-75	-80	-90	-95
15	25	15	10	5	-5	-10	-20	-25	-30	-40	-45	-50	-60	-65	-70	-80	-85	-90	-100	-105	-110
20	20	10	5	0	-10	-15	-25	-30	-35	-45	-50	-60	-65	-75	-80	-85	-95	-100	-110	-115	-120
25	15	10	0	-5	-15	-20	-30	-35	-45	-50	-60	-65	-75	-80	-90	-95	-105	-110	-120	-125	-135
30	10	5	0	-10	-20	-25	-30	-40	-50	-55	-65	-70	-80	-85	-95	-100	-110	-115	-125	-130	-140
35	10	5	-5	-10	-20	-30	-35	-40	-50	-60	-65	-75	-80	-90	-100	-105	-115	-120	-130	-135	-145
40*	10	0	-5	-15	-20	-30	-35	-45	-55	-60	-70	-75	-85	-95	-100	-110	-115	-125	-130	-140	-150

DANGER OF FREEZING EXPOSED FLESH FOR PROPERLY CLOTHED PERSONS

LITTLE DANGER	INCREASING DANGER (Flesh may freeze within 1 minute)	GREAT DANGER (Flesh may freeze within 30 seconds)

*Winds above 40 mph have little additional effect

Adapted from Arctic Aeromedical Lab Technical Report 64-28

and ripsawn spruce boards; the heavy layer of earth over them has kept warping and buckling to a minimum. Discovering the wood floor is akin to finding a shining nugget at the bottom of the rocky muck in the gold pan! Gravel or earthen floors were commonplace in these old wilderness cabins, board floors a luxury.

By early afternoon our floor, if not spotless, has only an inch or two of iced-over sod left on it. We're satisfied to leave it at that. The ice will melt with time and a fired-up Yukon stove. With only one small window, the cabin interior is fairly dark. From open gaps all around the roof edges and between the logs, daylight streams in. Our box of stuffing materials holds scraps of cardboard, egg cartons, canvas and rags. We use them all to plug the gaps. But still it has the look and feel of a large sieve.

Our next job today is to finish the runway. Now that the ice is thick enough to allow a plane to land, markers will indicate a safe landing place for any passing plane and be ready if and when Daryl comes with the mail. Sam has already marked off the two thousand-foot boundaries, a hundred feet apart, with the snow shovel, using some rusty old tins as a sighting aid in keeping his lines straight.

Around the immediate location of the camp here at the shore, the surrounding timber has long ago been cleared for firewood or mining. We need two live tall trees for airstrip markers. Sam axes them from a dense cluster of spruce further along the shore. This thick little grove will benefit from careful harvesting; the larger trees are already choking out the smaller ones. The branches of the two we take make two- to four-foot-long fronds.

Piling the sled high with our "markers," we head out along one of the boundary lines. Every hundred or so feet on the line, Sam chips a small hole in the ice and sets a frond down into the water. Within minutes the hole freezes over again, holding the marker firmly upright. We move along, planting the fronds to the end of the line, then move back along the other. It begins to look as if a carefully spaced nursery of fledgling Christmas trees has sprouted up through the ice.

By the time we're finished, the sun has dropped behind the western mountains and the wind turned strong. At such times of fatigue and chill, a parky with its fur-lined, wolf-ruffed hood seems more than ever like a warm snug house to burrow into. We head up the trail.

A good day. From halfway up the trail we can look down on our "airport" and get a sense of what it must look like from the air. Unmistakably, the two very straight thin dark lines of spruce stand out against the immense unbroken sweep of whiteness that is the frozen lake as something manmade. To arctic pilots it can only mean a safe landing strip, and that, in all these endless miles of isolated wilds, someone lives here at Koviashuvik.

Finishing up our journal notes tonight, we fight falling asleep at the table. The cabin warmth, the soft hiss of lantern, the long hours outside today in brisk, cold air—and the soft, warm bunk looks very inviting. Sleep in this setting has the quality of childhood. Total. No sense of wasted hours, but as enjoyed as waking hours.

The wolves are singing at the shore. There will be wolf tracks on the airstrip tomorrow where they will have investigated the human goings on in the territory.

Before giving up and crawling into the warm sleeping bags, we have to find an answer for Sam's taste for something ice cold. Strange to find the arctic cold so consistently dehydrating. I understand why the men at the South Pole stations drink great quantities of iced tea throughout the winter. We can make some snow-cold iced tea. But discussing what we will have, we begin to fantasy tall ice cream sodas, floats, sundaes, remembering evenings in the city when we walked down to the corner ice cream parlor to satisfy a craving for "something ice cold."

Ice cream is a favorite dish among the Eskimos. I didn't understand why Dishu made a point of including her recipe for Arctic Ice Cream among those she gave us. Now it makes sense. *Akutak*, Eskimo ice cream, is made with great quantities of caribou back fat and ground caribou meat. On the coast, seal oil is used.

Cranberries or blueberries can also be added to the mixture. Tonight I think we'll skip the caribou fat and meat, and try straight Arctic Ice Cream.

DISHU'S ARCTIC ICE CREAM

1 cup milk (evaporated preferred, but instant milk will do)
⅓ cup water
½ cup sugar
⅛ teaspoon salt
1 teaspoon vanilla

Mix well. Set outside until mixture starts to freeze. Then beat until it looks like whipped cream. Set out to freeze again, then beat again; repeat until ice cream is good thick consistency. Serve straight, or with chocolate sauce, cranberry or jam topping.

Until I have time to teach myself how to make some fur boots, our army surplus "mukluks" will have to do. From the early-winter heavy rubber insulated boots, we change now to our warmest winter footwear. These arctic boots are even heavier weight, thicker-soled, than the others, but they're an excellent and inexpensive answer. Water-repellent, heavy-duty canvas uppers zip almost to the knee, where they tie snug around the leg with a drawstring. Across the instep, laces hold the boot snug, too, or the weight of the thick rubber insulated soles would pull the boot off. Two felt insoles in each add further insulation. Inside the mukluks go three pairs of wool socks, plus thick felt booties, ankle high. None of these layers can be too tight or binding if frostbite is to be avoided. The boots are big enough to accommodate all these layers around the feet and still have room to spare for a pocket of air space for insulation.

A good design, but only substitutes for the natural inland arctic boot of caribou-skin uppers, moosehide sole, innersole pads of tundra grasses or bear or caribou fur, with inner socks or booties of caribou calf or fox. So far few synthetic materials can match these caribou fur boots for warmth, and none for beauty.

But unless one can get *oogruk* (seal) skins from the coastal Eskimos to make more waterproof soles, the fur boots become a problem in the wet snows of spring thaw. The moose-skin soles get wet, and in drying, shrink.

Our army surplus boots seem warm enough. But they take some practice. On the trail I find that my feet swim around inside the boots—like walking down a slide with a cardboard carton on each foot!

CHRISTMAS TREE

We leave soon after breakfast to plant a Christmas tree on the lake ice.

On our way down the mountain we select a tall, interestingly shaped spruce from an overpopulated cluster of trees and sled it on down to the lake. We may be jumping the calendar holiday season, but who knows what the weather will be for putting up a Christmas tree in December?

I also want to film this event. The increasing cold creates more and more photographic problems. Now I carry the movie camera in a scarf sling inside my warm parky. Otherwise the mechanism will be too cold to run by the time we get out to the center of the lake.

At the old cabin shelter, a fire is already laid. Firewood is frozen, and the paper and spruce shavings ice cold, but careful tending soon gets a blaze under way. A pot of moose stew now kept at the shore camp for emergency meals is a frozen mass. But it will be thawed and warmed by the time we return.

We've gathered together scraps of Blazo and other tin cans, which will be our Christmas tree "ornaments." So that they will hang free for the wind to catch, we tie them to the branches with two-foot lengths of string.

We must break trail to get out to the middle of the lake. I snowshoe ahead of Sam, who, also on snowshoes, pulls the sled. This double packing firms the snow enough for the tree-laden sled to ride reasonably smoothly in our path; otherwise the runners would sink down into the soft snow. Breaking trail has a quality about it that is more than satisfying. A first step onto a strange planet: the great flat snowfield of the lake has the look of a pristine clean new world. Making one's way across it has adventure and mystery built into the experience. We want to be sure of placing the tree where it can be seen from the upper camp, and keep moving farther out on the lake until we have a clear view of the upper cabin.

Here is the place. Ringed by enormous space. The center.

Sam scrapes away the snow and begins the chipping of a hole through the ice. With it begins the ice-chipping "music."

The camera is warm, but in between filming sequences I quickly place it back inside my parky. Even so, I have only a minute or two each time to work before I hear the mechanism begin to slow down as the lubricants and metal get colder and colder. My fingers just about equal the camera's tolerance for cold. The big, warm arctic mitts come off while filming and the wool gloves underneath are not much protection. By the time the camera freezes, fingertips are also numb. To warm my hands between rounds, I put them inside my parky as well, thrusting them up into the armpits, where body heat is always high.

I photograph Sam finishing up the chipping, struggling to pull the eighteen-foot-tall spruce upright from the sled, bracing himself when the tree turns into a sail in the blustery gusts of wind, sliding the tree into the hole in the ice, hauling to keep it from slipping on down through the hole while he kicks ice chips and snow up around its base to hasten the refreezing.

Against the immensity of the lake's white wilderness, the lone man and the solitary spruce appear to be engaged in some ancient, ritualized and joyful competition.

Within minutes the hole is frozen over enough to hold the tree in position. Sam steps back for a longer perspective on his work. The tree leans ten degrees to the west, which is easily remedied. Now the spruce stands tall and erect, and Sam moves slowly all around it, nodding his unqualified approval. A gust of wind sets the ornaments in motion. They catch the sunlight to sparkle and flash. And there is a sudden clear sound of bells as some of the wind-jangled ornaments strike each other.

This lone flashing tree in the middle of a frozen lake may seem a very strange object to a passing pilot.

"This is more than a Christmas tree," Sam remarks. "It's our airplane trap as well!" A curious plane coming down low enough to investigate will see our runway—and land for a visit. On our way back, Sam snowshoes in the snow a greeting. In ten-foot-tall letters he walks out: "W E L C O M E!"

I have used up all my film. Although we've been physically active, we feel chilled. Striking out for the shore camp, I hitch a ride on the sled for a short way. A great way to travel! Sometimes I think a dog team would warrant the care and feeding. But how many *more* caribou to hunt, dress, haul . . .

At the shore cabin, we warm ourselves and fill up on hot moose stew before heading up the mountain. All along the trail we can look down and see our Christmas tree flashing and sparkling in the low afternoon sun. From our cabin we can just barely see a small dark speck down in the middle of the lake. Then a glint of light flashes! and another!

"W E L C O M E! Anybody!"

Yesterday Sam hiked over to Jim Pup creek to check for tracks. En route he left the big sled near a stand of cut logs, then continued on. Much wolf activity along the way—and wolverine tracks. For ruffs, wolverine fur is even more resistant than wolf to collecting and holding ice crystals formed by frozen breath vapor, and the guard hairs are less likely to break off when stiffened by ice. We can use a wolverine pelt.

Sam has set a snare to the west about a half mile beyond the last tepee of logs. Today we hike over to the sled to bring back a load of wood. The trail as far as the tepees is well packed. At the sled we decide to continue on, and check out the snare. On with snowshoes, for the snow beyond the end of our trail is deep and soft. The terrain under the snow here is a stretch of large tussocks. We go over three- and four-foot-high hummocks covered with willow and alder scrub, slipping, sliding, stepping firmly down only to discover that what looks flat on the surface is the sloping side of a high tussock; like running a field of invisible hurdles.

I'm relieved when we finally reach ground where the tussocks diminish and the contours indicate a natural "trail" across the snowy tundra, marked by the tracks of a moose, a wolf family, a single snowshoe hare and the wolverine. A little farther on, we reach the snare, set across the "trail" and anchored by a heavy wire to the thick base of some nearby willows. There are no trees near enough to anchor the snare, which is undisturbed. But the tracks around it tell us many things.

The wolverine, *gulu gulu*—"the glutton"—has come close, investigated the snare and then turned away from the path and gone its way up the mountainside. In the animal folklore of the Arctic, the mystique of the wolverine almost surpasses that of the wolf. His ferocity is legendary. Observers have seen wolves and bears give way at carrion feeds to wolverines. He is about half the size of a full-grown wolf; his powerful jaws are only one of the wolverine's superb survival tools.

Wolverines are still trapped or snared on occasion by native and bush trappers. But the animal's wildness force is so dominant that he will chew off his own foot or leg to escape the trap. Only in the past few years has the bounty been removed from wolverine. When trapping was a primary means of livelihood among far northerners, the wolverine was a menace to trap lines, raiding traps and ruining pelts. Fast and ferocious when cornered, driven by insatiable hunger—and, like the wolf, superior in intelligence—the wolverine has as his primary adversary today the hunter with a powerful rifle. In the arctic mountains fewer wolverines are now taken for profit. Like most one-man gold-mining operations, the one-man trap line demands too much time and hardship for the financial returns possible.

The snare has also been investigated by a family of four or five wolves. Their tracks, headed toward Koviashuvik, show that they have come single file along the trail to within five or six feet of the snare. Here they pause, those behind the leader breaking out of line to mill about, but none preceding his large prints on the trail. Then all move off the trail and away from the snare, the large wolf still in the lead, followed by a smaller adult and at least two even smaller pups. A pause to the side of the snare, where they leave their signs (which seem cogent commentary on the snare)—bright splashes of yellow urine and two mounds of scat. The tracks circle back onto the trail and continue on, again in single file, the large tracks still in the lead. So much for our outsmarting the wolves.

We head back. Reaching the edge of the tussock field, I have the feeling I'd rather just sit this one out. I'm tired, sweaty under my parky, while at the same time my nose is running from the cold and my toes are beginning to feel numb. I reach down with a sigh to tighten up the stretched snowshoe harnesses for this last scramble. Raise up to meet Sam's eye as he waits for me to catch up. There is something about that eye that makes me take a deep breath, set my jaw and charge ahead.

But the charge doesn't go anywhere. One snowshoe takes a mighty swing forward, the other is glued fast where it is. Somehow, in a kaleidoscopic whir of events, I am standing on myself, watching the world spin by upside down through the sinew mesh of a snowshoe which seems to be up in front of my face, burying my head like an ostrich in icy darkness, feeling my legs being jerked into a pretzel knot.

I remain where I am, exactly as I am, buried head down in the deep snow. All I can think of is that with no mail plane until next month, it would not be wise to break an ankle today. Until I can decipher where my feet are in this tangle, I had better stay where I am. But my face is stinging with icy needlelike jabs, and I can't open my eyes.

There are sounds of muffled laughter in the distance. I cannot stand up or back out of this entanglement, but by moving very slowly and tentatively, I can roll over on my back and undo the tangle of legs, feet and snowshoes. Fortunately, Sam can't be seen very clearly through eyelashes thick with white crystals, for which my snow-covered mitts are no help. But as I lie there squinting at the world from this new ground-level perspective and summoning every remnant of dignity for a last grand effort to get upright once more, I can see that Sam is staring fixedly at the northern peak we have named Truth. His shoulders are twitching.

Somehow, like Queen Victoria, I am not amused. When I'm at last back on my feet and have freed my snowshoe from where it has been hooked on a willow root, brushed myself relatively clean of snow, emptied out my mitts, squirmed the snow down inside my long johns into less troublesome spots, he turns, and with a carefully bland face and voice says, "Ready?"

We move on. In a heavily dignified silence, we reach the sled, load it and start back to camp.

Wrestling the heavy sled the half-mile haul back does for wounded vanity what nothing else can! Pushing and braking, huffing and cussing, jumping onto the runners for the last fifty feet's victorious ride up to the sawbuck, injured pride seems as inconsequential as a Cadillac in Anaktuvuk Pass! We unload the sled and stack the trees into a tepee beside the sawbuck.

As we amble toward the cabin, a distant mountain seems to catch fire. The moon, golden and almost full, rises from behind it as we watch. The crimson fades slowly away and the stars appear. It is three o'clock and dusk turns the vast snowscape deep twilight blue. Outside the cabin door we look across the lake and can just see old Rooney's cross, etched white by the new moonlight.

Sam throws back his head and shouts, "Rooney—are you there?"

The answer comes back echoed sevenfold: "THERE . . . THERE . . . *there* . . . there . . ." Sam throws back his head again and calls to the wolves. "Ow-w-w-w-oo-ooo-ooo. . . ." The answer comes back echoed sevenfold, but ends in a fresh round of song that is no echo. The wolves reply from down on the shore. And then from the mountaintop behind the camp, a new

Billie Wright

Sam Wright

The Brooks Range in summer

Koviashuvik, looking south

Koviashuvik, the cabin in the foreground

Scraping caribou skin in mid-September

Planting the Christmas tree on the lake ice. The camp is on the mountain behind the tree.

Back from the trapline

Hauling the sled up the mountain for wood

Snow block for winter water supply

Clearing pitch to prevent chimney fire

The day the sun returned

The mailplane arrives

Icing the runners on the sled

Early winter view of the shore cabin, now ready to be lived in

At breakup, Sam using the boat as a sled on the floe ice

voice is added. Sam howls again—and echoes and wolf songs make a great chorus circling round and round in this world within the ring of jutting peaks.

Overhead a streak of green light shoots across the sky. Another from over the eastern peaks ripples like a moving curtain of gold and red. The sky dances. And the creatures sing.

It is All Hallows Eve. . . .

GOOD-BYE TO THE SUN

Two days ago, the morning sun emerged from behind the mountains shortly after noon, rode low along the southern crest for a brief half hour, then "set" behind the peaks to the south.

Yesterday, the full day's passage of the sun above the horizon lasted only ten minutes.

Today the sun has vanished.

At midday, its light from behind the far mountains is only a bright distant glow backlighting the horizon. Within our mountain-ringed world, the sky is clear but the light is gray, sunless. By two in the afternoon, the highest mountaintops to the north are crowned by sunset pinks—but there is no glimpse of a setting sun.

The "long night" has begun. Not until winter solstice, December 21, will the process reverse. If the return of the light approximates in time the fading of the light, the sun should reappear sometime in early February. That is a long time away. A long time not to see the sun.

Two days ago the temperature was seven degrees above zero; yesterday, zero. Today the thermometer reads twelve below zero. At "nightfall"—at three in the afternoon—twenty below zero.

All my knowledge, my data, my life experience with sun and warmth, with its absence and cold, has not equipped me to grasp this stark connectedness of earth and sun, as has this day while I watched for the sun to reappear and it did not.

The long night begins.

THE COLD IS A TEACHER

The thermometer slides gradually downward—minus sixteen, minus twenty, twenty-two degrees below zero. At twenty-four below today, we go out for a load of logs. Sun touches only the very tips of the highest of the surrounding peaks. All below is in shadow. The shadow blues the snowscape a different hue from that earlier time when it reflected back a brilliant turquoise sky. This blue *looks* cold. With the sun gone and the sky devoid of overcast, the cold is at once of a different quality—more penetrating. Under my warm parky, I add a wool sweater over flannel shirt and long johns, for I expect the trip to the forest to be a chilly one.

This time we go north of camp, rimming along the slope of the mountain to where we have tepees of cut logs. There is only a moderate wind, and the day is crisp and invigorating. Coming back, the heavily loaded sled responds to the downward pitch of the "trail," leaning hard to the downhill side. From his harness rope at the front, Sam has no control over the tilt of the sled. At the back, I try to hold it on the trail but it leans sharply over on its side. Jumping down into the deeper snow alongside, I throw my full weight against the load. It does not right itself, but now rides along at its not quite forty-five-degree angle.

This is hot, hot work. I slip my sweaty hands out of my outer heavy mitts and throw my parky wide open to cool off as we move on. But within a few minutes, my perspiring hands inside the inner wool gloves begin to sting with coldness. This sensation of being overheated everywhere except for cold face and hands is not a good or comfortable feeling.

At one point, downhill gravity and slippery hummocks prove a combination beyond my strength. The sled suddenly hurls itself over on its side. Heavy logs scatter like spilled matches out into the deep snow. We reload, weighting the sled on its uphill side, and are on our way again. But it is a struggle all the way back.

At camp, we unload the logs into a stand beside the sawbuck and come inside. Not to warm up this time, but to cool off. I tear off my parky and sweater, and sit down to rest. I cool off quickly, so quickly that within a very few minutes I begin to feel a shaking chill. My clothes are still slightly damp with perspiration and snow. Though the cabin itself seems warm, I stoke up the fire even hotter and put on my sweater again. But my own chill is very severe now, an inner cold that is not affected by outer warmth.

I feel a little sick, with a reaction like that of the delayed shock that follows a physical emergency. Dull, light-headed, taken over completely by the sensation of internal coldness.

I remember that our Mount McKinley–climbing doctor had warned us about becoming overheated in the cold. The cooling-down process happens too rapidly, the change is too radical— and at extreme subzero temperatures can be fatal. This recall snaps me out of my lethargy. Immediately changing all my clothes to dry ones, I sit huddled as close as I can get to the roaring fire, drinking scalding-hot coffee until the chill at last begins to dissipate.

This is contrary to my expectations of the cold. While one could tolerate and deal with an excess of body heat at zero degrees and above, at subzero temperatures the stress is much greater, the adjustment back to normal body temperature more severe. I think the added layers of clothing may actually be harmful if hard physical labor is to be done. It seems I have much more to learn about this arctic environment. What I *have* learned from this small misadventure—and how fortunate to have learned it early in the winter's cold—is that cold is never just cold.

A sudden loud thumping and bumping in the dogtrot. Sam rushes out, is stopped short in his tracks by a barrage of small but furious barks coming from almost beneath his feet. In the middle of the dogtrot is an ermine, pure white but for a tip of black on its tail and bright black eyes. The handsome little creature rears up to stand erect, but his tiny forepaws stay firmly fixed around a frozen moose roast. It is four or five times his own size, ten times his own weight at least.

Since the meat carton is up on a high, narrow shelf, the small thief must have used some tactical logic to maneuver the heavy chunk of moose up from the depths of the box and over its side to fall to the ground. Now he launches a battery of scolding, chattering barks, stretching up on his hind feet to glare fiercely at Sam. Then, startled by Sam's chuckle, off he rushes, abandoning the meat, dashing out the dogtrot door. Around the cabin corner, he stops on the snowbank outside the window and rears up to look about. The window is just above the end of the bunk where I am sitting, face pressed to the glass, peering out. Suddenly he sees me, and there we are, three inches apart, eye to eye.

We stare, then, like jack-in-the-boxes suddenly sprung, spook each other. He jumps straight up into the air, I almost off the bunk. And off he goes again, around toward the back of the cabin.

He will be back, unfortunately. This is too good a find to be frightened off!

In five minutes he returns to get his—our—roast. But this time a trap is below the carton.

Now we have another ermine pelt, one we didn't wish to have. But then, it's nip and tuck for all us predators. . . .

At twenty-five below zero, a head-on thirty-knot wind makes breathing difficult as the icy blasts reach my lungs. I wait at the shore shelter while Sam hikes north to check his traps.

Inside the old cabin, the punishing gale is cut off, but neither cabin nor stove is very warm. The frozen spruce firewood is not burning well; the chimney fights a losing battle with erratic wind-swirled drafts. Taking off my mukluks, I put my wool-stockinged feet up on the edge of the stove surface. The toes are numb. The heat doesn't warm them at all, but this is all I can think to do.

Sitting alone in the dark cabin, listening to the whistle and howl around the door and roof, huddled deep down into my warm parky, the soft wolf fur almost completely covering my face, I slip into a half-waking, half-sleeping world where time does not exist, mail never comes, life simply *is*. Hibernation.

THANKSGIVING AT KOVIASHUVIK

For a memorable holiday to my specifications, three things are required: a great feast, congenial people, and celebration, preferably with singing.

Even though some of the forms take on an unexpected aspect, Thanksgiving Day at Koviashuvik meets all the requirements.

Puzzling over the menu for our feast, I feel like one of Somerset Maugham's British travelers, who tries to carry a little piece of dear old England within his pocket to the far exotic corners of the earth.

However, for the "traditional" Thanksgiving dinner of our past, we have no turkey, no dressing, no fresh potatoes, no green beans, peas or any other fresh vegetable, no white tiny onions, mushrooms, fresh fruits, relishes, no salad greens, nuts, crisp red apples, no pumpkin. Well, I will make us a Thanksgiving dinner with arctic bounty and trail foods; many good things to eat, and more dishes than we could dream of for a "regular" meal, which, even as I think the word, applies to no meal we've ever had at Koviashuvik.

With the arrival of the light, Sam sets out in search of our Thanksgiving bird—ptarmigan. He carries the .22 rifle and a long spruce pole. I watch him snowshoe briskly down beyond the cache and disappear into the willow thickets along the creek bed; listen for the familiar throaty squawks—or the high ping of the .22. Hearing neither, on my way back through the dogtrot I select a fine fat moose roast and place it next to the sourdough pot up on the shelf behind the warm stove to hasten thawing.

Sitting down at the table, I make out our menu and begin work.

Every dish is an experiment, an improvisation for which no

recipe exists. Soon the cabin begins to fill with savory smells from pots and pans crowded together on the stove; every surface fills with utensils, mixing containers, spices.

Sam returns, birdless but in good spirits. A covey led him a merry chase all the way down the frozen creek bed to the lake ice before he decided against a Thanksgiving bird. While the last dishes are cooking, we have an apéritif of sherry, with hors d'oeuvres of pie-crust leftovers spread with caribou fat, crushed dill seed, salt and freshly ground black pepper, and oven-toasted. (Sam has lined the blackened, rusted little camp oven with reflective Blazo-can tin, and now it can produce miracles.)

As the cold winds outside whip around the corners of the cabin, flinging hard snow crystals like small pebbles against the windowpanes, inside we are warm and comfortable. Full of anticipation for the coming feast, our holiday mood starts Sam to singing. With full-voice renditions, we sing all the old songs we can remember, eventually getting to the old-time hymns and gospel songs learned in childhood and still delighted in, leaning over the table to catch the full round resonance under the big kettles hanging from the ceiling beam. Then, having perfected our two-part harmony, we remember "Wonderful Words," and begin:

> Sing them over again to me,
> Wonderful Words of Life;
> Let me more of their beauty see,
> Wonderful Words of Life . . .

We have not sung this old hymn since our last visit to Anaktuvuk Pass. The words trigger an immediate association of a summer Sunday morning in the village. The spruce-log chapel set high on a rise along with the schoolhouse, above the village sod huts and tents which dot the rich green tundra of the high valley. The thirty-foot-long logs for this small church in the treeless mountain pass north of timber line were hauled by the village men from the nearest forest many miles to the south. Just inside the chapel door is a big oil-drum stove, cold and silent on this particular morning when the steady drone of mosquitoes marks the time of the year.

Nearly everyone in the village has come to church, parents, children, infants, teen-agers. Every bench and folding chair is filled, with children held on laps. Some of the men have been tutored as lay preachers. They take turns conducting the services. This morning Jack Aghook stands grave-faced and solemn before the attentive men and women. The children, like children everywhere in church, squirm, cry, fidget, sigh, look over their shoulders to stare and smile at anyone who will smile back.

The service begins with a brief scripture reading, delivered by Jack in such a soft, quiet voice that it is difficult to hear him halfway back in the room. And then, before the sermon, the singing begins.

As Jack calls out a page number in the Eskimo-language hymnal, there is a stir, an expectant murmuring rustle. Jack begins the song, and on the second note, half the congregation joins in; by the third, all are singing lustily. Here and there one hears harmony, but most of the voices sing in unison—the men in deep tones like reverberations of skin drums, the women in soaring, nasal, singsong tones, a keening but at the same time joyous voice. Practiced in these simple songs only through the singing of them in the church services, the voices lift in unabashed, uninhibited pleasure; the collective pitch unerringly true, the musicianship untutored but natural and marked. These are singers that *hear*. There is surely not a formally trained "musical ear" among them. But these men and women live where life depends on the highest development of *all* the senses. Like a well-trained and experienced choir, they are obviously listening to themselves as parts of the whole, as well as to the other voices filling the chapel. It is undeniably a joyful, happy sound.

The Nunamiut have been called "the happy people," but the concept of happiness in the western sense does not accurately reflect what is intended. *Koviashuktok*, which is a state of general well-being, joyfulness, of being fully and pleasantly in the present moment, without anxiety or worry but rather with laughter, better describes the general mien of these mountain people. While their life in the Arctic has always been demanding and severe, the Nunamiut are often described as people with a great zest for living, a keenly developed appreciation of both joy and sorrow, an awareness that *koviashuktok* is the best, most desirable state to live in.

Whatever else is to come this Sunday morning in this log chapel, for me the singing is the most rewarding. Hymn after hymn is sung, first in English, for there are guests. We, and a passing planeload of four touring University of Alaska summer students, have been invited to join in the service. Earlier I filmed the children and their parents as they played and chatted outside the chapel. But I have left the camera outside.

Next to my feet on the floor, a tape recorder unobtrusively records these songs of worship. Sam sings so lustily next to me that I worry that his will be the only voice on the tape. I nudge him and whisper, pointing to the small microphone I hold, "Sshhh . . . you're drowning out all the others!"

Still singing, he looks at me, puzzled, then whispers back as if explaining the obvious to an imbecile, "But I *have* to sing!" I understand. It *is* contagious! I forget the taping and join in, too.

Another hymn, and another, now sung in Eskimo—"in our *own* words," as one old woman requested. More members of the congregation call out. Jack softly repeats the number; the initiator starts the song off. All are recognizable by the old familiar melodies, even though the words are strange to us, and we hum along with each.

One robustly rendered tune we recognize as

> There is power, power, wonder-working power;
> In the blood, in the blood.

Maybe it's only our imagination that this song is sung with special insight and gusto—for these are, after all, the Caribou Hunters. . . .

Suddenly the music seems to be over. Jack, speaking almost in a whisper, greets the guests and bids them welcome. As quietly, he invites Sam to "lead us in prayer." I can tell that Sam is startled, caught momentarily off guard in his relaxed role as a full participant among the congregation. He rises, pauses for a second, and responds to the words of welcome Jack has just given, speaking briefly of the warmth and friendship and grace with which we have been made welcome by the people of this beautiful mountain valley, and of our feeling of oneness with them—then he begins in slow and measured words the prayer most likely to speak to people to whom ritual and form as much represent meaning as content: "Our Father, who art in heaven: Hallowed be Thy name. . . ."

He deliberately chooses the particular phraseology used in the formal liturgy in which the mountain people have been instructed by their missionaries. When Sam sits down, for a long, long moment the room is hushed except for the sighing babies and buzzing mosquitoes. One of the older women sitting near the front, her face hidden by the fur ruff of her colorful summer parky cover, leans forward and murmurs something to Jack. He nods, and her clear, high-pitched singsong voice begins, and is immediately joined by all the others, in:

> Sing them over again to me,
> Wonderful Words of Life;
> Let me more of their beauty see,
> Wonderful Words of Life:
> Words of life and beauty
> Teach me faith and duty:
> Beautiful words, wonderful words,
> Wonderful Words of Life;
> Beautiful words, wonderful words,
> Wonderful Words of Life.

Jack's sermon is a very long reading from the Bible, given first in English, then repeated in Eskimo. I cannot hear a single word from where I sit, only a soft monotone hum almost indistinguishable from the steady drone of the cloud of mosquitoes hovering in the open door.

The room is warm, close, but not unpleasantly so, scented with insect repellent worn in liberal amounts by everyone present. I watch the children's faces turned toward us, beautiful round little faces with their black-eyed direct way of looking, their quick smiles darting in and out of sober stares.

I watch the adult faces of those I can see near me. All seem completely engrossed in the ritual of the Sunday sermon. Perhaps their keen ears, more accustomed than mine to hearing the subtle sounds within the stillness of wild places, can hear these hushed words as I cannot. Some are following their own copies of the scriptures, with pointing finger, word by word.

Few in this room have had more than three to four years of elementary school education, and these among the younger adults. Several adults as well as children hold certificates from Head Start programs. One woman villager is said to have gone through the second year of high school. With the teen-agers sent "outside" to high school and the younger children taught in English in the village school, almost everyone now reads English to some extent.

As with all other peoples with one foot in the ancient traditional world, the other in the contemporary western world, education is the dream. "Education" will resolve all dilemmas, fulfill all promises, make all things possible. The *children* will be educated, and thereby made free to move more easily and more wisely than can the "noneducated" elders in that other world "out there." Education as a solver of all human difficulties is the "white man's" dream the Nunamiut have now assumed for their own, even as they look askance at its consequences in the world "outside." If the old hunters have other thoughts, they are too courteous to express them except through gently poking fun at some of the oddities prevalent in the white world.

It is also the "white man's" religion that has been assumed. But while church attendance is high, and while the few lay leaders seem to be deeply and sincerely committed to this religion, one is nevertheless left with the strong impression that the chapel is filled because it is a place where all the people can come together at once for a sociable gathering, and the villagers are gregarious, sociable people.

Much of the afternoon we spend with one of the "patriarchs" of the village, a philosopher and wise man, one who has lived many years outside the village, held responsible jobs there before returning to the mountains—a shaman, were there still shamans today. He calls himself "the unbeliever" in the village, accepting fully neither the formal dogma of western man's Christianity nor the Eskimo legends of creation—but he is neither atheist nor cynic. He is a poet, artist, historian of these ancient peoples of the arctic far north, a gentle, fragile, silver-voiced old man who breaks his own backward-looking reveries with a sudden wry comment:

"Simon . . ." he begins. (Simon is the other major figure among the elders of the village, philosopher, historian, sage and interpreter.) "People come to Simon, who calls himself a believer, and say, 'Simon, tell us the old Eskimo stories of how the world began.' And they come to me, 'the unbeliever,' and say, 'Jimmy, tell us the old Eskimo stories of how the world began. . . .' Finally I go to Simon to talk about this problem. We say to each other, 'What we going tell these curious people who want everything explained? who want to know this, that? who want to hear stories? Do we tell 'em *my* stories? or *your* stories?' We think awhile and decide. We say, 'I tell 'em my stories. You tell 'em yours. They be pretty mixed up then! Must make up their own minds!'"

Unasked, he shares some of his stories with us; plays the tapes he's made of Eskimo dance drums and chants on his new portable tape recorder. With great scientific interest, he shows us an arrowhead he has found nearby which is fashioned as the earliest known men on the North American continent worked their arrowheads. This is proof, he feels, that his ancestors did not cross over to the American continent from Siberia, but originated here in the Arctic, and spread southward. Here, Jimmy believes, man began. And that first man was Eskimo.

From Jimmy's hut, we go back to the chapel, for at two o'clock it is time for Sunday school and we have been invited—rather, made to promise by a number of the children that we will be there. They are already gathered in full force. Each has been given an outlined drawing of a biblical scene to color at home. The pictures seem irrelevant to anything they know, but the children delight in them as gifts.

The youngsters are really here to sing, and impatient to begin. Their two young teachers are teen-age girls, initiated thoroughly by someone into the formal "language of the faith," competent with the small ones, but also a trifle shy in the presence of visitors though we try to be unobtrusive, sitting quietly in a back row. But the children are obviously glad for our presence. They have an audience—know, without any question, that they are good singers. They turn around again and again to study our reactions, which are openly appreciative, for the same keen sense of musicianship of the morning is here in even greater measure.

Listening intently to the lovely child voices, I wonder at the state health statistics, which report a high incidence of hearing loss from disease among Alaskan native children. One of the harsher consequences that came with the end of the nomadic life, with the closeness of community living and regular contact with the white world, was the inevitable sharp upswing in disease among the native peoples. Respiratory maladies—influenza, pneumonia, tuberculosis—though more and more controlled by public health programs, still take their toll, often leading to chronic infection of the middle ear among children. Untreated, the problem can lead to significant hearing loss. Where Anaktuvuk Pass stands in relation to health standards of other native communities I do not know. But in terms of the general mood toward the physical well-being of its people, it is spoken of as superior to that of those coastal and southern interior native villages that have had more prolonged and involved contact with white populations.

But it is impossible to think of *these* children in terms of statistics and programs of any kind! Their exuberance shakes the log walls! The old Sunday school songs they are roaring full voice make as good sense in Eskimo as in English (both are sung). These boys and girls see nothing real or alarming in ideas such as "crucifixion, sin, redemption," for such concepts are outside their frame of reference.

The concepts are relatively modern attachments to the Eskimo language, assimilated first from coastal Eskimos who were in earliest contact with the missionaries, then from the missionaries themselves, who came only on occasion to visit the isolated mountain village. The forms were obligingly accepted along with some of the other curious ideas brought by the white world, for the Nunamiut are hospitable and obliging people.

The children are here because it is a gay Sunday-afternoon party. Gregarious and boundlessly energetic, they are here to sing—and it is even better to have someone new to sing *for*. Their young teachers must share this feeling, for they speak to their charges in English.

When the singers are dismissed, they shoot out of the door like small firecrackers going off, and down the hill path at breakneck speed, hooting and shouting and still singing at top volume.

Whatever blend of folk religion, western Christianity and amused gentle disbelief the villagers live with individually, their missionaries, white and native, might best be content with the collective joy and meaningfulness of that gathering on the hill. I could not help contrasting the mood of these celebrants with some spirit-constipated Sunday-morning throngs I have encountered in other places, other times.

> Beautiful words, wonderful words,
> Wonderful Words of Li-i-ife;
> Beautiful words, wonderful words,
> Wonderful Words of Life. . . .

On impulse, remembering that particular and special summer day of song and celebration in the high green valley at the remote heart of the range, we reach for our own Eskimo hymnal on the shelf here in our solitary cabin, and thumb quickly through it.

On this Thanksgiving Day, we send a greeting of sorts to our neighbors, the people of the mountain pass, now locked in frozen winter as is Koviashuvik. For our celebration here, we return their welcome and acknowledge our feeling of oneness with the same song that they shared with us. . . .

Awkwardly, slowly, for we must sound out the long Eskimo words and try to fit each syllable to the right note, we sing:

> *Unipkautigiksuamik atutkigsaktugut*
> *Sivinigiksilaananik ilitchisaktugut*

CHORUS

> *Jesus unipkautainnik kilanmukutainnik*
> *Ukaluinik nakuuruanik kamasuksaktugut*
> *Ukaluinik nakuuruanik kamasuksaktugut.* . . .

THANKSGIVING DINNER AT KOVIASHUVIK

Fried Arctic Ptarmigan in Country Gravy (canceled)
or
Prime Rump Roast of Moose
and
Sourdough Bread and Dehydrated Onion "Stuffing"
Instant Rice Steamed in Instant Tomato Soup
Dehydrated Carrots in Caribou Fat
Cold Wild Cranberry and Raisin Relish
Lime Jell-O with Wild Cranberries
Hot Sourdough Muffins with Honey
Instant Yam and Cinnamon and Honey Open-Face Pie
Dehydrated Apple and Wild Cranberry Pie
Thanksgiving Special Oatmeal Cookies
made with Chocolate, Raisins and Honey
Dishu's Arctic Ice Cream with Wild Cranberry Sauce
Instant Milk   •   Coffee

Sherry over Arctic Snow

DECEMBER 1

Thirty below zero today. We are now well into the "long night."

Out for buckets of snow "midday," and in a piercing deep-blue arctic sky, the waxing moon "rises"? "sets"? Despite the absence of sun, the day has a muted but sparkling quality about it. Every spruce and willow looks as if it had been inked in a fine black pen line onto a huge white canvas. The neatly stacked woodpile a beige and black sculpture, topped by a white snow dust cover. Night arrives at 2 P.M.

Except, sometimes, in the middle of the night, the cabin is always warm enough, snug and windproof. But the stove works hard—not from "morning" until "night," but from getting-up to going-to-bed time.

Window frost thickens on the inside of the glass. Corner ice patches grow larger. Nailheads are now small white gleaming points of ice in the bright, far-reaching light of the lantern hanging just over the table center from a wire attached to a ceiling beam.

But for one to two hours midday, a light is needed in the cabin. During that brief time without a lantern, we must sit close to the window for reading or handwork. When the day is overcast, the gasoline lantern is on all day. For a change now, we use the kerosene lamp, with its old hand-blown chimney, for first light and fading light; save the gasoline lantern for the rest of the many hours of darkness. The lamp's soft yellow glow gives off a beautiful warm light, but the brightness of the other is easier to work by.

The "long night." Not quite what I expected. At first the darkening daylight seemed to alter the snowscape. Distances looked different, proportions became distorted—but no longer. One soon learns to adapt in a grayed-down world to a new way of "seeing."

Few of the old arctic journals and diaries say much of the perils of being enclosed for long periods of time in a very small and solitary cabin with one other human being. Yet without fail, our few friends who have weathered an arctic bush winter (if not the aforementioned situation) had comments they seemed determined to make to us when they learned of our plans for this year.

Dishu, with a merry, knowing giggle, said, "You like each other? You better like each other pretty good you spend long arctic night in little cabin together! No place to go be mad!"

Our old prospector friend Jacob, and his wife, Dorothy, were matter-of-fact about the hazards. She told me, "Oh, it all works out somehow. If you decide to go home to Mother, by the time the mail plane comes in to get you out you'll have already forgotten what it was that made you want to go in the first place!"

Her husband had his own firsthand insights on the problem, which he saw as hers. "Well—it's harder on a woman, you know," he said. "They get cabin fever, don't get out as much as the man—not as much chance to work off steam. You have to make allowances for *that*, you know."

Dorothy turned to me, intense in her remembering. "Well, you miss someone to talk to, you know. *That's* what's hard. Why, one winter up on the creek it got so bad," she said, "that I went with Jacob twenty miles from our mine over to Wiseman, and twenty miles back, snowshoeing all the way at fifty below zero, just to get to talk to somebody besides Jacob!"

Men living in far northern towns or cities or on military bases often talk wistfully of how they would "give anything" to live the solitary life of the wilderness "if only the wife would agree to it." I've heard some of the wives discuss the idea. Their husbands are quite right not to press the point.

If an informal poll were taken of the men who *have* taken their wives into the wilds to live, even briefly, the results would surely show three-quarters of them divorced by the following year. One doesn't hear many of the details of what went wrong. From the women, the complaints seem to have little to do with the living conditions. It is usually said that "he" was impossible to live with. From the men, perhaps a less personalized reaction.

"She didn't take to the life"; "She didn't much care for the isolation"; or "The life is too hard on a woman."

All that the wilderness experience seems to contribute to the cause of these rumored statistics is a speed-up in the process of marital disillusionment if the seeds are already sown, albeit in a hidden garden plot. By stripping away all the diversions and crutches, the rationales and scapegoats of "civilization," and by moving straight into the essence, into the very heart of relationship, the wilderness life forces relationship to survive—or not— and in either case, dramatically!

In the early gold-mining days, few prospectors could conceive of taking a "refined, gentle female" into the crude hard life of working a claim or surviving a bitter, lonely arctic winter. But on occasion two men partners would go into a venture together, contribute equally to a grubstake, work the claim and share the confined space of the one-room log cabin year after year. An often-quoted and reportedly true story in the Arctic tells of two such old-timers of long partnership who, bound close to the small cabin by the long, cold night, had a midwinter quarrel over something. Something trivial, of course, as trivial as one hanging his wet socks to drip on the other's bunk, or forever shirking the scrubbing of the skillet, or spilling bacon fat on the other's precious book. With nowhere to go, as Dishu warned, and not being as quick on the trigger as some other settlers of frontier quarrels, these two settled theirs by agreeing to draw a line down the center of the cabin floor. From then on, half the cabin would belong to one, the other half to the second. That line was not to be crossed. Nor was one word to be spoken between them ever again. And so the winter passed—without argument, and in silence. And the following year as well. And the next.

The arrangement lasted for twenty years, until one of the partners finally succumbed of old age. Was he missed by the other? The story doesn't say. If one had been a woman, would the story exist?

Communication, as the wave of interest in nonverbal communication rediscovers, often has little to do with words. But what the nonverbal-communication enthusiasts overlook is how much the human ecology has to do with what happens in communication. In this the Eskimos are innately wise. The land has been their teacher. Whatever small interpersonal stresses are under way in the little winter-bound sod hut, let a band of caribou pass, a wolf howl over the rise, a stove flicker out, the sun return—and life makes an abrupt shift back to what's *really* important!

And so it is at Koviashuvik.

Dorothy had said, "After a while the two of you have said all there is to be said, and you start saying the same things over and over until you get so tired of hearing each other, you stop talking. *That's* when it's bad!"

The reverse may be the case here. The happy accident that brings two people together who share a great and varied spectrum of common interests, and enjoy verbalizing all of them, is merely a matter of good fortune and intelligent choice. But while words are a rich and powerful tool in communication, being a human tool words often carry a potential for sudden and near-inexplicable misunderstanding, for seemingly irresolvable friction, especially if used carelessly when one is tired, in a wistful mood, has a bellyache, frostbitten toes, or even a perverse need to provoke a little excitement just to counterbalance the sweet blandness of tranquillity!

Therefore, after an unusually quiet supper, Sam took a long hike in the moonlight last night. The cabin atmosphere was less one of strain than of awkward confusion. From it, Sam's departure was abrupt; my mental message to Mother to prepare for my arrival via the very next mail plane not entirely as amusing as Dorothy's suggestion had seemed. I read, and wondered if Sam could see the trail in the darkness. The moon was misted over, night visibility limited. I wondered, too, if he had taken the rifle—then realized that he couldn't see to use it anyway. I hoped he would not encounter any nonhibernating grizzlies or night-roaming bull moose.

Then I heard the snowshoes on the trail, moving rapidly

toward the cabin. The door burst open and Sam came in on a blast of frigid air, beard, brows, eyelashes and parky ruff thick with ice crystals.

"I was snowshoeing along the trail to Jim Pup, not paying much attention to anything," he said, getting out of his parky, "when out of the corner of my eye I saw something move. . . ."

Life in the cabin makes an abrupt shift.

"What was it? What happened?" I pour fresh coffee, sit down, and listen eagerly as Sam describes how he was moving briskly along the trail toward the snare, enjoying the bracing cold beauty of the night, when he caught sight of a slight blur of motion just beside the trail directly in front of him. . . .

All senses are jarred awake. Freezing in his tracks, he peers through the filtered light. A few yards away, by the willows where the snare is set, there is a dark silhouette, now still and motionless. Moonlight strikes yellow eyes. Wolf eyes.

As the two face each other, the hairs at the nape of the neck slowly rise—wolf *and* man. Is the wolf caught in the snare? if caught, securely so? or was he just investigating it, interrupted by the sudden arrival of still another night roamer?

They face each other, still unmoving, the immense silence seeming to shrink down to enclose them, lessening the short distance between them even more. A low, soft murmur of sound, barely audible, comes from the wolf's throat—a faint low half growl, half hiss. There is a clink of metal. The wolf *is* snared, but may be only lightly caught. If he pulls free, his survival is uncertain, dependent on the injury done to the leg caught in the steel wire. If he is caught securely, he'll settle down in a hollow burrowed in the snow, curl up and sleep until morning if intruders are not near to threaten.

Sam begins backing on the trail, moving slowly, easily, avoiding any sudden or extreme motion, then turns himself and snowshoes about and starts back home, his back to the wolf, listening between the crunching slurs of the lift, fall, slide of snowshoes on frozen snow for any added sound. There is none; only the silence, now vast and absolute once again.

There is nothing to be done tonight. Too dark to return with the rifle. If the wolf is still there with the morning light, we will have to end what has begun.

This morning, we take off toward Jim Pup at first light. Sam has the .22 rifle, checked out and ready. The movie camera is inside my parky. The day is clear; cold. At minus thirty-seven, facing into the slight wind, my eyeglasses, even with the automobile-glass antifreeze rubbed on the lenses, frost over at once with a thick film of ice. My mitt comes off just long enough to take off the glasses and put them into my parky pocket, and I wonder if the camera lens will frost up as quickly.

We move along at a good pace. I press to keep up with Sam, for I want to be ready for whatever happens when we reach the snare. In this past week, he's packed a good trail through the white tussock field. The cold has firmed it to a hard, solid surface.

"Almost there," he says suddenly, in a low voice. "Camera ready?" We stop for a second while I remove my mitts, take the camera out from its sling inside my parky, set the lens wide open (I'm not certain I can get anything in this gray winter light), focus at infinity (I don't plan to get in too close). We move on, very slowly, quietly. The snare is just beyond a white hummock rise immediately ahead.

Sam stops, says, as if disappointed, "Yes, he's still there."

He raises the rifle. I raise the camera and before I can focus with my own, the camera's eye has framed the gray image against the white. Fifty feet in front of us, the wolf stands motionless, head turned toward us, wary, poised. In the half light his eyes are startlingly yellow, fixed out of the long slanting face directly on us. Through the zoom lens pushed to its full magnification, I can see the black lips pull back hard over sharp pointed teeth. This is what Sam came suddenly upon in the moonlight last night. A blur of motion fills the camera frame as the wolf hurls himself against the wire of the snare caught tight around one foot, lunging first away from us, then toward us. Involuntarily I draw back. The camera viewfinder goes black under a cloud of breath condensed into ice, but I keep filming, pointing the camera blindly in the direction of the wolf. The crack of the .22 rifle in the stillness is like the thin sound of a child's popgun. I keep the camera running until Sam says, "That's it," then follow him over to the hummock. The head shot was clean; immediate. A young but large and full-grown female; the pelt prime, thick and deep, of gray-white color tipped with black. The willows ringing the snare have been pawed and chewed down to the snow in the wolf's attempts to free itself. Only the thickness of the roots to which the snare was anchored held it.

Deciding to take the carcass back to camp for skinning, Sam hoists the heavy weight—this wolf weighs eighty to eighty-five pounds—onto his back, and we start for home. Aircraft wolf hunters say it is nearly impossible to snare a wolf—they are too wise. The expert on hunting wolves from the air may not have the same experience as the earthbound hunter.

As we head home, the trail parallels the low-hanging half moon, which seems almost to keep pace with us as it rolls along in the gray midday sky.

We had hoped to snare the wolverine—and snared the wolf instead. This fine pelt will not be wasted. But something is required by way of acknowledgment. Glancing again at the pale noonday moon, I hope that tonight the northern lights may help to close the circle.

Meanwhile, I think I understand a little better the truth that underlies the Nunamiut's ability to set aside the interpersonal conflicts of dailiness, not allowing them to totally dominate existence as they seem to in the world "outside." To live close with the daily realities of life and death demands a perspective that relegates human irritabilities to their proper place.

LADY MOOSE

In the forest today the wind shifts and suddenly carries on it the strong smell of animal. Caribou? Wolf? Not wolf; this is different. We stop work, sniff the air, listen; hear twigs break in the forest. Wait, unmoving. Over a rise a barren cow moose soon appears among the trees. Though we're downwind of her, she senses something, stops abruptly, head lifted, big, awkward, the long exaggerated face and pendulous nose almost a caricature. She sees us, remains motionless staring curiously for several minutes, then turns and moves slowly back into the forest, the massive, powerful shoulder and haunch muscles rippling in slow motion as she breaks trail, thigh deep in the crusted snow, strangely graceful and elegant.

I succumb to the lure of the new Sears, Roebuck catalogue only for "necessities." Equipment for making a hand-hooked wool throw rug arrived in the last mail.

The wool yarns a spectrum of color—like dipping into a jewel case of bright precious stones. The burlap backing has been treated with something that gives it a sweet, exotic fragrance; a fantasied Persian bazaar. The simple wooden-handled hooking tool a classic design of functionalism.

Pleasure in the ancient craft plied by my grandmothers, and satisfaction in the reds and golds, purples, blues, pinks, avocado greens, forest greens, yellow-greens, blue-greens, and in the feel of soft but sturdy skeins. The rug grows, beginning to look, by contrast to our blue-white frozen world, like a child's bright bold painting or a wild-flower tundra garden in sunset light of late summer. . . .

A VISIT

A leisurely, lazy morning, dawdling over breakfast, talking of many things as morning slowly lights the world beyond our two small windows. Then we hear an engine, low and close, and rush outside to see a small green skiplane circle overhead. It passes on toward the lake and circles back again, barely skimming the mountain slopes to the southwest. A strange plane. It buzzes the camp. We can see its two occupants only as faceless silhouettes. We wave as it passes on over to circle the lake and descend toward the far end of the runway.

Our lazy morning has left us unprepared for the unexpected. Sam rushes into mukluks and outdoor clothes, and takes off down the trail to greet our visitors, whoever they may be. Like every hostess in the world, suburban split-level or one-room log cabin, I am immediately concerned with proper hospitality for our guests. Stoke up the fire, refill the coffeepot, warm up the caribou roast. No sourdough chocolate cake due to Sam's gluttony at supper last night, but frozen oatmeal cookies from the dogtrot go onto the stove to thaw.

For all this readying, they may not even come up the trail. It depends on time, and on where they have come from. Surely not Fairbanks, for there's not enough daylight for a small plane to make the round trip in one day at this time of year.

I watch the trail, and soon three tiny figures crest the plateau into sight. One, appreciably smaller than the others, races on ahead. He must be a youngster to move with such agility. My curiosity is great as I step outside to make my greetings. As the small round figure bounds up to the cabin, I'm surprised to discover that it belongs to a little middle-aged Eskimo woman. Coming toward me with outstretched hand, she says, "I'm Minnie."

My own greeting is as uncomplicated. "I'm Billie. Welcome!"

These are our "neighbors" who live some thirty miles away, across several mountain passes. Minnie is the wife of the bounty hunter. We go inside. A tall man, bending very low to get through our low-slung door, soon enters, followed by Sam.

This is Ralph; we shake hands. He removes his metal-rimmed eyeglasses, which have immediately fogged over with a curtain of steam from the cabin's warmth. His eyes are a bright direct blue. I'm struck by the pallor of his coloring until I realize that all of us but Minnie have the arctic winter look of washed-out paleness which seems even more pallid in contrast to the deep bronze summer color given white skins exposed to blazing arctic sun.

They make themselves comfortable, Minnie across the table

from me, Ralph on the bunk, Sam on our spruce stool between bunk and stove. An intimate circle, for the cabin, after all, is only twelve feet square.

We get acquainted in the arctic bush fashion, asking the latest whereabouts of the caribou, news of other game sighted. Though it is early for lunch, they are pleased to join us. As we gather round the table, our talk continues, soon moving inevitably onto the wolves and then to the caribou once more, completing the cycle.

Ralph and Minnie are licensed by the state to hunt wolves from an aircraft. There is a set limit on the number of wolves that can be taken in this fashion. But the law becomes a matter of conscience because of the obvious difficulties game authorities face in enforcement of these air-hunt controls.

Ralph is a soft-spoken, slow-moving man—not at all my stereotype of a bounty hunter. He has lived, mined and hunted wolves in the isolated arctic wilds for many years. But he has strong opinions on the present ways of the world "outside," which he states unhesitatingly and as forcefully as a soft, quiet voice can communicate. He seems to be the prototype of the nineteenth-century frontiersman—the "rugged individualist," self-made, courteous, appearing much concerned with religion as he describes a vague attachment to an obscure "nonsectarian" sect of "Brothers" and "Sisters" who devote themselves only to "serving others" through manual work and prayer.

This part of the world is Minnie's home territory. Her nomadic family, she tells us, camped all over "this place," hunting and trapping. Growing up in Wiseman, sporadically attending the one-room log cabin grade school there, Minnie refused, unlike many of the others, to go "out" to high school. Ralph smiles at her and says that for this stubbornness he blesses her, for it gave him his "helper."

Of Eskimos today and their changing ways of life, both express sharp disapproval. They feel very negative about what they interpret as the natives' seemingly willing shift from a self-sufficient hunting life to one of welfare, "dependent on the dole." Hard work, self-reliance and godliness are the primary virtues in Ralph's world. Thrift, too, for as he says, "The one-man gold-mining operation no longer provides a decent living. Even with income from the wolves added, you can't make much money in this wilderness. But the trick is not to get into debt. Pay cash or do without." I'm reminded of my friends in the "lower forty-eight" who own nothing outright, but have everything they've ever dreamed of by the simple expedient of living in chronic debt.

Ralph grins, and adds as illustration, "When that tractor of mine goes, I can't replace it. That'll be that." A plane and a tractor. Must cost many wolves, I think.

Minnie remarks that they waited two years for a sale on the right wallpaper for their cabin. A wallpapered log cabin? I ask her to describe their "house." It is about six times as big as this one, she says. And the wallpaper covers over the dark cardboard insulation. "Looks pretty! Gives light!" she explains.

Ralph has heard that we backpacked into the central range north of timber line last summer to plant trees. In their hunting forays they've become familiar with much of the mountain territory from the air. Men who know it from the air find the idea of foot travel across this wild terrain unthinkable except in dire emergency. Sam tells them about his interest in Robert Marshall's tree-planting theories concerning spruce tree growth north of timber line—and Ralph is reminded of his surprise in sighting from the air some patches of young cottonwoods growing inexplicably on the barren treeless tundra of the arctic north slope.

Talk of trees soon leads to porcupines, who probably destroy more spruce than cold, storm, browsing moose, summer lightening and fire, all put together. Minnie says, "Porcupine all over spruce round hereabout. Porcupine in all the trees. Taste like spruce."

The light is getting dim. Dusk is not far off. Without any spoken agreement, both our guests begin to put on their outdoor things. I comment on their handsome caribou-skin mukluks, and Minnie explains that she made Ralph's knee-high fur boots from the leg skins of two caribou. Her own shorter-length muk-luks, cuffed in beaver fur, took only half as many caribou skins. Her warm inner "socks," she shows us, are made of fox fur.

I wish I might spend a couple of weeks with Minnie, become more expert in sewing skin clothing. At present I manage at least a few quick questions as she gets into her parky. "Yes," she answers, "I use sourdough sometimes to tan skins—some-time brown soap good. Got to rub *hard!*" She illustrates a vigorous clothes-scrubbing motion. "Later, flour rubbed in skin helps dry it, whiten. Get soft pretty skin for parky that way."

She looks over my kitchen corner. I have a feeling that she has unobtrusively noted every detail in the cabin as quickly and as thoroughly as she must scan a snowscape for a moving wolf. "You got ulu!" she exclaims. "That's good! Ulu good skin scraper too!"

Ralph wants to know if we have any objection to their hunt-ing in our territory. No, we say, not explaining that we do object to all aircraft hunting, as well as to the state's bountying of wolves, but that is a philosophical and ecological discussion which will take us nowhere in this brief time, and will only alienate and estrange our neighbors.

Like the other professional wolf hunters we've talked with, nothing can be said, we've found, that will change attitudes that see the wolf as "killer," the caribou as "victim." Minnie obviously wants to say something on the subject. She begins in a rush, "They say wolves good because they take 'diseased' caribou. No such thing, 'disease' in caribou. Only weak from starving. We *know!* We see wolves got caribou in ring; all round, wolves. Caribou can't get out to graze new feed. Starve. Them caribou glad to see little green plane come. They don' even run when we go over. Just wait for us to get them wolves. When we clear out wolves in a place, caribou better off. They don' starve. Find food. Can move round to new food."

Her serious look gives way to a quick smile, as if she has good news for us. "You get good caribou right *here!* Usually come right through *here*"—stretching her arms wide—"all over!

You don' need snowshoe trail! Caribou do it for you. Caribou turn right around soon. Come back. Then *everywhere!* All over here. With wolves!"

Sam asks if they have enough caribou for winter meat. When Ralph answers that they're late with their winter meat this year and have taken no caribou yet, we offer them a leg of moose, for we still have plenty of moose in the cache. They're grateful, but will not take it today. Later, they say, if they really need it. Of course, with their own plane they're obviously not dependent as we are on food from the land. They can ferry in their own supplies from Fairbanks when Ralph takes the wolf pelts in to be bountied.

Ralph asks if he can take our mail into Fairbanks with him, for he must soon take his plane in for an overhaul. We're grateful for the offer, but have nothing ready to go out.

As we go outside to say our good-byes, I ask Minnie the best way she knows to take ptarmigan, provided one can see them well enough to find them.

"Can make picture-wire snares for ptarmigan . . ." Her hands complete the sentence with gestures to describe the procedure. "Put extra willow round willow brush, make a tunnel." The hands describe it. "Put snares *inside*. They come in." A quick gesture of a snare in action. "Ptarmigan for supper!"

We know about the snares. But what I want to know is how to *see* the bird. Minnie looks puzzled, as if trying to make some translation in her own mind, then nods. She's found it.

"Snow," she says. "You have to know *snow—colors* of snow. *Then* you see ptarmigan. Pink." She nods again, satisfied that she has now fully answered the question. Nods again. "Yes, he *pink!*"

We all shake hands and exchange thanks—for the lunch and for the much-enjoyed visit. The sky is in its last faint twilight before darkness, and they must rush back across the mountains to their camp. They hurry down the trail on their snowshoes, waving, Minnie bounding along in front of Ralph, like a curious cub, sniffing out all the landscape as she goes.

Minnie is a force. Her lively merry way and straightforward style do not cover over the keen sharpness of a woman who can not only scrape skins, make fur clothing, cook, care for her man, but hunt as well. In this partnership, it is Ralph who flies the small aircraft down into the tricky cross-drafts of river canyons, skims along just above the steep slopes of the mountains in search of wolves. But it is Minnie who sights and reads the tracks that lead to the wolves, leans forward into the icy wind blasting in through an opening in the side of the plane and brings down the racing creatures with a shotgun.

The airborne bounty hunter works hard and takes many risks for his livelihood. After a wolf has been shot, the small skiplane must land as close as possible on some stretch of flat snow-covered tundra, river gravel bar or frozen creek, with innumerable potential hazards buried under the snow. Snowshoeing to where the wolf has fallen, the bounty hunter skins it on the spot. A "good" hunt on the short winter days can mean camping overnight in a crude, cold siwash camp in order to get all the carcasses skinned.

But between airplane hunter and quarry it is never an equal match of skill or wits, prowess or endurance. The wolf hasn't a chance, caught in the open. He can't outrun the plane bearing down on him.

There is no place to hide.

I've enjoyed this visit with our nearest neighbors. And have a sense of "community," though it is unlike any other I've ever been a part of before. But as the dishes are being done, and Sam is outside at the chores, my spirits are not as usual. I am troubled —troubled by a nagging undercurrent of sadness, rather of despair, at the complexity of what lies beyond the symbols of wolf and caribou we have talked of today.

To make a "devil" out of a Ralph avoids the problem. Whatever label extremists may choose to apply, in the context of the Arctic, of American frontier history, Ralph is no more a "killer" of the wolf than is the wolf a "killer" of the caribou. Nor can "blame" be shifted only to the overworked, understaffed, often bureaucratically restricted game management and conservation authorities, state or national. If there is "blame," I see no *single* handy target to focus it on.

The creation of "programs, agencies, budget allotments, etc." may act as temporary staying actions. But they are no more panaceas for what is required than are "law and order" programs that do not even begin to touch the question of why we are an increasingly violent nation.

Understanding the delicately balanced relationship between caribou and wolf, between the land and all its inhabitants, between "wild" animal and "tamed" man, requires more than we seem able to give as yet. Whether we're to live on an abused, exploited planet or a protected, cherished one will be determined—and sooner than we like to think—by how rapidly the perspective that guides *all* our decisions from here on out can change. Usury? or Nurturing? Which is it to be? Earlier man learned a guiding perspective from the source. Disconnected from that source, and with our remarkable record of contempt for it, where are we to learn?

My concerns came full circle. We make our choices by what matters most to us; individually, collectively. We are, all of us, "for change," all eager to solve the problems that have us in a state of siege with our environment, ourselves and each other. But who is willing to change by disenfranchising himself? What "tamed" man is willing?

Ralph's livelihood depends on wolf bounty.* His city counterpart adds one more automobile to the superhighway to get to his job each day. The air gets fouler, the garbage piles higher, the waters thicken with sewage and oil slicks. And, say the "tamed" men, the last of the wild, the last of the uncontaminated places, must be "opened up!" "Developed!" "All that 'unused' land must be exploited." Oil, timber, minerals, furs, dollars!

The dishes are finished; Sam returns. We stoke up the fire; its warmth soon dissipates the slight night chill in the cabin. My

* Since Ralph's visit, wolf bounty has been removed, and aerial hunting is not allowed at present in our area in northern Alaska.

own inner chill takes a little longer. Man, after all, is the cleverest predator of all, and "taming" is not "civilizing."

Minnie was right.

On the way down the mountain, several bassy squawks off to the side of the trail are heard. Stopping to stare in the direction of the sounds, I examine every inch of snow, every hummock, tussock, every willow root, every hollow. A snow-covered tussock moves, then another. They cross the trail a hundred feet below me, moving across the snow like chickens in a white barnyard—with a waddle, a little run, a pause, a stop to peck up a fallen willow seed. These don't seem to be particularly alarmed at my presence; they do not take flight. A dozen or more birds in this covey. They all look glossy—and fat—and just faintly pink.

Camera or .22? Fried fowl for supper wins.

Plucking and eviscerating our bird, I find the craw full of willow leaves, stems, buds, smelling sweet and springlike. The gizzard, as with other fowl, contains tiny polished jewellike pebbles. Underneath the sleek outer feathers (which inside the cabin and away from the contrast of snow look *pure* white) are grayer, softer feathers. Down surrounds the fat gland at the root of the black-tipped tail feathers.

The breast is the meatiest part, dark-fleshed and firm throughout. A good hearty bird for supper.

RECIPE FOR PTARMIGAN

Clean and prepare, as chicken.

Brown in ½ inch caribou fat in hot frying pan. Cover and simmer on medium-hot Yukon stove 45 minutes to 1 hour.

Make thick rich country gravy from pan drippings.

Serve bird and gravy with slices of sourdough bread for "soppings," and wild cranberries on the side.

WINTER SOLSTICE

December 21, the shortest day of the year. The arctic winter, reaching its zenith in the longest night of the year, reverses the process as the earth swings back toward the sun. Yesterday's loss of sunlight, only one minute. Today, no loss, no gain. Tomorrow, one minute of light will be added. We are still a month and a half away from the return of the sun to Koviashuvik, but today marks the beginning of our journey back toward it.

Christmas Eve day arrives with a break in the cold: low minus twenties and snow. By the time the light arrives, we have finished by lantern light the last touches on the packages to go out in the mail plane, if it comes today. It may not—if the snowfall thickens to whiteout, if the winds turn tricky, if the temperature at Bettles is much lower than ours, for planes usually remain grounded in the north at minus forty degrees.

Among the Christmas presents from Koviashuvik are Sam's drawings on pieces of sealskin of wolf, owl and ptarmigan; handsome fur hats made of leftover strips of caribou with bright orange linings sewn from a summer shirt seldom worn; rawhide thong "necklaces" strung with wolf teeth; small gold nuggets from Koviashuvik Creek; small packets of iridescent-colored grouse feathers gathered from across the tundra in late autumn; for gourmet cooks, a collection of sourdough recipes for orange cake, chocolate cake, muffins, hotcakes deluxe; collages made from magazine clippings, paints, caribou hair and bird feathers; an ermine pelt and a wolf tailtip; sachets of sweet-smelling spruce shavings; and large greeting "cards"—the card a folded-in-half sheet of paper with a grouse-quill-pen and ink drawing of our speck of a cabin ringed by the spruce-dotted white wild mountains, and the wish for

Shulimauragatatpianigiluragatatpialaurat

or, roughly translated, "May the entire universe be yours."

These are our gifts.

Soon after daylight, Sam is on his way down the mountain-side with the mailbag on the small sled, to wait for Daryl. I stay at the cabin to tidy up the clutter from our several days of preparations. Chores finished, time must then be taken to watch the fall of snowflakes on dark trees, the solitary jay feeding on moose scraps, to trace the rhythm of curves and slopes of white mountain ridges. I drink my coffee, look, stare as if I will never get enough of this wild beauty; but the question nags for an answer: What about Christmas here? A tree for our festivities? Everywhere I look there are forests of Christmas trees. En-circled by spruce, do we bring one inside? Somehow I feel I must decide something about the holiday at Koviashuvik before Sam comes back up the mountain. He must have a Christmas greeting when he arrives.

Another cup of coffee, a willow-leaf cigarette, decisions made. I put on my parky and arctic mitts, take my biggest butcher knife and go outside. At the largest, thickest-branched spruce tree near the cabin, I maneuver the knife in close to the lower trunk, firmly grasp a branch, bend it away from the others to cut it from the trunk, and it snaps off like an icicle in my hand. Of course, the trees are frozen solid; the large fronds break away as easily as a matchstick snaps.

Back in the cabin, from a high shelf I rout out a small "cache" of junk saved for some unknown reason—coffee and tobacco can tin lids, scraps of glossy, expensively printed advertising brochures that have come in the mail, a red cardboard box in which someone mailed us a book. And I have my carton of jeweled-colored yarns. I go to work; hear Daryl's plane arrive and take off again. Work faster. Stop to put on my parky and go down to the cache. Plans for our Christmas feast are also being made.

The first star is out in the deepening twilight-blue dome that covers the earth. It must be midafternoon, almost three o'clock, and Sam should be back up the mountain in about thirty minutes more, or by the time all the stars are out.

Now work begins in the "kitchen" while keeping a watch on the trail for Sam. When he crests the plateau far off down the trail, I can see from the bulky shape of the sled that it carries a very full load. Perhaps more supplies have come in. The bright lantern is now darkened, replaced with light from the kerosene lamp, which spreads a softer, warmer glow across the room.

When the crunch of snowshoes and sled reaches the woodpile, I throw on my outdoor things and step outside. Sam has stopped to stare in at the cabin window, where a tall candle flickers and burns. Suspended by bright yarn threads from the ceiling beam directly above, six shiny tin-can lids, decorated with scraps of colored yarn and paper, spin and turn in the window, flashing white-gold in the candlelight.

Sam comes around the cabin corner, still looking a little puzzled, and stops again to stare—this time at a great bouquet of spruce fronds hung at the dogtrot entrance, the green garlands festive with strands of bright red yarn, strings of crimson wild cranberries and four large letters cut from the red cardboard box: "N-O-E-L."

Seeing the big boxes on the sled, I am surprised, for they're not supply cartons at all, but packages with postal markings. We pick them up; I hang back to make sure Sam goes through the cabin door first. He kicks the door open with his mukluk and stops, standing at the threshold.

Bent over behind him, stuck in the lower door, I know he has seen it just as I wished him to. On the table is our Christmas "tree"—lovely fragrant spruce fronds standing tall and graceful in a pepper-red tobacco can which glows even redder against the vivid green cloth it rests on, a washcloth. The fronds are garlanded with green and red yarn and hung with "ornaments" of bright, glossy advertising brochure papers of all colors, cut into ovals, diamonds, circles, iridescent and glowing in the soft light. Above the tree and over the table, more clusters of shiny can lids hang from the ceiling beam like bright moons and suns, swirling in the breeze from the open door, sparkling as they spin.

The look of this simple arctic Christmas in our small warm cabin is strangely beautiful. . . .

The stove is hot, tea ready, Sam out of his cold, wet boots. While we have our tea, we open our packages. They've come from family and friends in California, New York, Seattle, Fairbanks. Books, store-bought cigarettes, clothes, warm slippers— but mostly food! Everyone has sent us food! Have our letters communicated deprivation? do caribou and cranberries, moose and sourdough bread sound as if we are undernourished? Perhaps what seems bountiful here, "outside" seems like deprivation. And what foods! Not only are there fruit cakes, Christmas cookies, homemade candies, but there are enough exotic delicacies to fill a gourmet's shop! Tins of smoked oysters, Alaskan salmon, turkey pâté, the finest sardines, deviled crab, ham, minced clams; cheeses, salamis, smoked salmon strips; nuts, chocolates, dried figs, apricots, peaches, pears; brandied fruits; fancy crackers, oyster soup; a comb of fireweed honey from our bee-raising prospector friend. . . .

The array is overwhelming. I've forgotten what it is like to crave food, not out of genuine hunger but out of some other, mysteriously triggered response—it must be gluttony! Whatever it is, we indulge it. Sample a little of everything! The taste of cheese is brand new. A smoked oyster, a thing of mystery. The tastes are exotic, delicious, foreign to the palate. We eat too much; feel sated but not satisfied. We need caribou and fat. I put the foods away, on shelves and in the dogtrot "freezer." These lovely treats will last the year.

We give ourselves an hour of radio. Christmas being celebrated all over the world. Christmas carols sung in Japanese, in an African dialect, Eskimo, Swedish, Italian, German—by hundred-voice cathedral choirs, missionary schools, pop singers, children's choruses, country music quartets, opera stars. We sing along with all of them. From somewhere in the world, a nonstop program of Herb Alpert's albums is played as a "Christmas treat." The music seems just right for dancing in our two-foot-wide floor space. The dancing settles our exotic fare and brings back an appetite.

The Christmas Eve dinner I've planned is a delicacy. A big pot of caribou marrow bones has been cooking all afternoon on the Yukon stove. We clear the table of gift wrappings, crumbs and mail, and Sam gets out the hammer. No other utensils are needed. Each leg bone is over a foot long. The ends are grabbed firmly in the hands, and the teeth do all the work, first tearing off the choice bits of juicy meat that cling to the bone. Since there is no neat way to eat bones, the niceties must be set aside—one just goes at it. Before long, fat and juice are running off the chin, down the wrists. Polite murmured sounds of appreciation and enjoyment begin to sound suspiciously like quiet, low growls in the back of the throat. Body hunching over the bone, teeth tearing away chunks of sweet fat meat, gnawing at the knuckle end to get into the little crevices containing succulent bits, hands gripping the bone ends, only the eyes are uninvolved, free to communicate. I see myself mirrored back in the serious concentrated look of Sam gnawing at the big dripping marrow bone— and feel the very thin edge that separates me at this moment from my hairy, low-browed antecedents hunched guardedly over the mastodon bone in the cave. I feel the guardedness, too. If Sam at this moment made a gesture toward my marrow bone, I'd instinctively crack him over the skull with it, I think. The image is jolting. I put the bone down, having gnawed it well. Take a great swath of toilet paper down from the four rolls hanging on a spruce dowel in the "kitchen." In the bush, this serves for napkins and paper towels. Wipe the fat and meat juices off mouth, cheeks, chin, hands, wrists, arms, clothes. Sam takes up the hammer, places the bones across a spruce log stump and with several sharp, hard blows cracks them open. Bone slivers and segments break away, exposing the long thin strip of light-brown gelatinous marrow inside. This is what we are after; the meat is only an hors d'oeuvre.

Even when the cache was full of fine caribou, a hunter of older times might go out and take a fresh bull just for the marrow bones. The ancient hunting camps can still be located by the cracked marrow bones strewn about the tundra.

There is no description that can be made of the taste of caribou marrow. It is atavistic; prehistory. Essence . . .

After supper, we wash up; browse through some of our new Christmas books. Our friends keep us well informed of the newest commentary on the scene "outside." Many of the books are on the problems besieging us—the war, racial injustice, environmental destruction, the human climate of malaise, of despair. Scanning the pages, the problems look overwhelming—so many, so complex, so very urgently in need of solution.

A wolf cry begins down on the frozen lake—a soaring note, thin and lonely, drifting faintly up the mountain and into the cabin's warmth. From the peak behind the cabin, an answering call begins, and then another, joined finally by a lone hunter on the lake ice below. The mingled cries become a song, no longer lonely but a howling glorious cacophonic song of sheer joy.

I close the books, set them aside. I have my own stubborn faith, and my experience, that dreams are better than blueprints, people worthier than machines, joyful songs preferable to battle hymns. And my irrefutable conviction, reinforced by this frozen, vast and exquisitely beautiful land, that it is a great and marvelous miracle to be alive, a gift which we must not allow to be sullied or uglified, treated with indifference or contempt—not any life, anywhere. . . .

Bedtime—but, with the wolves, the northern lights are calling.

We step outside into the great vibrating hum, and watch the swirling curtains of greens, golds and reds sweep across the sky. There is something miraculous about the way they all soon come together out of the eastern sky, from over the mountains to the west. Within minutes, the heavenful of jewel-faceted light has converged into one single pulsating dancing cloud above the cabin. It hovers, glows, and wings of light shoot suddenly out from the center, shimmering, dispersing, fading, at last vanishing over the white peaks until the sapphire night sky seems a void as empty as a dark, cavernous theater after the play is over. But into the darkness comes the glow of stars. The North Star, directly overhead, glitters and sparkles blue, green, gold. The red planet seems close enough to reach up and touch. Sirius flashes iridescent blue, then emerald green—a signal.

Yes, greetings, world—and a Merry Christmas to us all!

Christmas Day. Dawn lighting the horizon moves the circle of our mountains closer; wind stilled; snow falling lazily, white on white; carols played on our harmonicas, chairs tipped back, feet up, in two-part harmony; Sam flushing a ptarmigan for the Christmas feast; a raven circling the camp and breaking the big silence with whooshing wings and calls of "Tuk-tu! tuk-tu!"; reading aloud one of the Christmas books, Tom Neale's enchanting *An Island to Myself*, and learning of his life alone on his Pacific island, knowing an immediate sense of at-homeness there; running outside to wave at a strange small plane that buzzes the cabin and flies on northward—a fitting holiday greeting between otherwise strangers in the Arctic; watching the sky turn crimson in a fiery red sunset from a sun we have not seen for a month and a half; gaining one more minute of light today as the sun moves on its inexorable path back into our lives . . . Christmas in the Arctic, a reminder, a connecting thread to tomorrow and beyond . . .

SOUND OF WINTER

Today Sam sets off across the creek for one of the highest peaks on the south ridge, a good vantage point from which he intends to map the contours of the lakeshore. As I bring in firewood, I can hear every crunch of his snowshoes as he rims up the slope, breaking trail, but I can't see him anywhere. When finally I catch sight of him halfway up the mountain across from me, where the spruce look as if they were only a foot tall, he is a speck against the white. The distance between us is approximately a half mile. Yet when I halloo across to him and he answers, I discover that we can talk in conversational tones and hear each other as distinctly and easily as if we were twenty feet apart.

The Eskimo hunters say that in winter, caribou can hear a man moving across the snow a mile away. All the extraneous sounds of summer that distract and confuse—wind in trees, in willow and grasses, the humming of insects, whirring of wings and the singing of birds, trickling melt and running streams—all are stilled by winter. When the thick blanket of snow and ice muffles the land, any sound breaking the silence is magnified a thousandfold.

I can hear the wings of a raven flying a mile away; its call two miles away. The song of the wolves from across the lake travels two to three miles to reach us. In winter, everything listens.

We scan the airwaves for evening news. Fairbanks disappears into wild shriekings of static, Anchorage is only a wail, the lower forty-eight a void. But a Canadian Northwest Territory station is bringing in the New Year with great enthusiasm— with shouts, applause, whistles, bells, bursting balloons, popping corks, "Auld Lang Syne" at its usual funereal beat. Provoked in thought, a kaleidoscope of past celebrations of this night, memory-hazed places, people—impressions of smoky living rooms or drafty ballrooms, of dull-eyed, thick-tongued greetings exchanged, of resolutions confessed with embarrassed laughs and crossed fingers, of individuals blurred into amorphous crowds, of worked-at gaiety with a sense of expectation betrayed somehow, of celebration gone awry, of synthetic experience.

This night, a great near-full white moon lights up the land for miles around, sprinkling many-colored brilliants across the snow. We howl to the wolves, but no answer comes back. The hard winter hunt takes them far from home territory these lean days. Long before the magic midnight number brings in a "new" year, we're in bed. Every day here new, no breaks in the continuity, no resolutions required. Awake sometime in the night from dazzling moonlight streaming in the window into our eyes. We think at first it is midday, for the moon is bright as an arctic winter day. Judging from the amount of chill in the cabin, the hour must be close to 4 A.M.

We get up for fresh-brewed coffee and supper's leftover Jell-o. Sit at the table in the light of the moon, watching the red glow from the open draft in the door of the roaring Yukon stove, talking of beginnings. The new year has arrived.

STORM

At minus forty-five, the cabin floor is frigid. We wear our warmest mukluks, indoors and out, now. The eggs under the bunk freeze.

Three days and nights of constant gale winds have changed the face of the land. All trails and paths are gone, no trace of them evident anywhere. Waist-high drifts fill the footpaths around the cabin. We dig our way out each morning. The force of the wind is so great that we can lean into it and be held. But at the same time, breath is sucked out of us.

Everything around camp is stowed safely away or tied down, but still the furious blasts rattle the glass in the window frames, shake the cabin door, tear away sections of canvas, rip loose boards and Blazo tins, sending them careening through the air. No snow falls, but the air is thick with ground snow swept up into driving sheets of stinging whiteness that race across the frozen tundra. Trees bend under the weight of the wind, leaning over several feet at each roaring blast. In summer these winds would tear the shallow-rooted spruce out of the tundra. Only the deep hard cover of snow keeps them from being uprooted now.

Wild voices seem to fill the air with shrieking, wailing cries. They will not be ignored. We are always listening—for what I don't really know. Perhaps for the momentary lull when the sound shrinks down to a muted babble. But at these moments, we listen even harder, waiting for the fury to resume, and when it does, are awed by the power the voices symbolize.

Like the Eskimos and all the wild creatures of the Arctic, we burrow into our shelter to sit out the storm. Only dire necessity could drive us outside for more than the most urgent chores. Frostbite and exhaustion are the great dangers if caught on the trail away from home in these windstorms at subzero temperatures. The recommended procedure in such an emergency is to follow the example of an old Eskimo woman heading home on foot from a visit to the next village and caught midway on the trail by one of these midwinter storms. Digging a hole in the snow, she burrowed deep enough to be protected from the wind, and went to sleep. When the storm had passed three days later, she continued on her way home.

The wind reaches us, even inside the cabin, seeping in around the chinking, up through the floorboards, along the doorjamb and window frames. All the things hanging from the ceiling beams are in motion. Icy drafts swirl about the room. The stove, stoked high, labors hard but the heat is dissipated only a few feet from it.

Over our double long johns we wear flannel shirts, wool pants, thick sweaters, scarves, but still it is necessary to warm up every few minutes by hovering directly over the stove. Feet and hands feel the chill most of all.

We wait out the storm—trying to keep warm, going to the warmth of the bed early, rising late, reading, talking, but mostly waiting.

On the fourth day, a quiet lull lengthens, silence deepens, the cabin warms, frigid drafts subside. We hurry out to do the chores before the wind returns, but when it does a few minutes later, it has lost its furious punishing power. This now is the familiar, easy wind we live with all the time at Koviashuvik.

The storm has passed.

Four and a half minutes of light added today. At midday, a bright full golden moon in the northwest sky hangs above pink-tipped peaks. The rays of the hidden sun, still low behind our horizon, reach the pinnacles for the first time in many weeks. The light slowly returns. . . .

The cold increases; the thermometer continues its downward slide below zero—minus thirty-five, minus forty, fifty, fifty-five. All the land a frozen stillness. This small cabin an insignificant speck in infinite space, too small to be glimpsed from a mile away high on the mountainside. The cabin becomes the focus of our existence, the hub from which all our forays into the bitter cold radiate out and return. An average of twenty to twenty-two hours of each twenty-four spent in this one small room. All the myriad business of dailiness taking place in twelve by twelve feet of space—working, sleeping, eating, bathing, dreaming, reading, skin scraping, snowshoe repairing, thinking, fretting, talking, relating, cooking. . . .

A friend's letter asks, "But how can two people function in that limited space? Don't you suffer from claustrophobia—from lack of privacy?" I find that I don't know how to answer the letter. It asks the wrong questions, "wrong" in that they're based on a set of assumptions that have little meaning here. The assumptions belong to life in an eight-room suburban house, not to life in a wilderness cabin.

The cabin is "shelter," in the word's most basic, most universal sense. Here, warmth, food, rest, comfort are to be found. At the same time, a paradox exists. The cabin is not a refuge from the world around it as shelter *from* something implies, but is a natural extension of the world outside it. A connection exists between inner and outer space that seldom occurs between house and surroundings in more "civilized" parts of the world, where one's shelter helps to shut out the outside, becomes a retreat from life outside, from masses of people, noise, action, mile upon mile of other such shelters—from all the surfeits of public life which invade the private life.

Just the reverse is true of our wilderness here. With a universe in which to move freely about and with a feeling of at-homeness and oneness with the world, "home" fulfills the basic needs of a place to sleep, a place to get warm, eat, move about in, a little. Not much space is required for that.

The casual visitor to the Arctic often fails to understand this spatial relationship, and the attitudes it inculcates. His interpretation of the size of the shelters, based on the status given "outside" to spacious dwellings, is that the smallness is a sign of poverty.

One of the younger, more outspoken Eskimo men at Anaktuvuk Pass told us, "We didn't realize that we were a 'poverty-stricken' village until the white men told us so." He then added with a shrewd little laugh, "Now that we know how poor we are, we want to be rich like everybody else!"

The outsider also judges the apparent lack of privacy in the arctic one-room home by his own standards and needs. He comes from a culture in which a value premium is placed on a separate room for each member of the family, in as spacious a "private world" as he can afford to rent or buy. He then sees the Nunamiut family living together quite cheerfully in their one-room house or canvas tent—parents, several children, perhaps a grandfather, aunt, niece or nephew, plus a constant stream of visitors—and, applying his own values as a yardstick, he measures incorrectly.

Missing the point that wilderness is an intensely nonpublic world, and that all of it is "home" to the wilderness dweller, the outsider is almost certain to feel that in this enjoyment of the crowded gregarious intimacy of family life, there must be less sensitivity to others, less awareness of the individual's needs and "rights," than he himself possesses.

Yet one of the most striking features of the Nunamiut is his acute awareness of the other, expressed in all his personal relationships. Although always intensely interested in other individuals, and curious about them, the mountain people do not pry. Though jokes are made about each other, a good joke on oneself is equally appreciated. To be *koviashuktok*, even though the concept is seldom heard verbalized, is the state most desired. If one suffers the loss of *koviashuktok* and falls into a prolonged period of irritability or brooding, all those around him experience the loss as well.

Untouched so far by the influences of the psychotherapeutic view of personhood, the Nunamiut family seems burdened neither with self-consciousness nor with the emotional problems common-place among the families in the lower forty-eight.

The usual petty grievances and irritations found in all human communities are of course present: envy, competitiveness, cliqu-ish-ness. Some larger guiding perspective in the Nunamiut life view keeps these in enough balance so that differences and quarrels are resolved, often spoken of with humor and a shrug, lived with, contained within the community. Tensions within the individual do not seem to get translated into the usual marital or parent-child conflicts.

While the concern exists that children be educated, it seems more a tribal concern for the future than the individual family's drive to see its own children learn to achieve, to compete, to be "successful" by the standards of the white world. If any "sacrifice" is made for children, it is only incidental in that the presence of the school does in part define village life. Children are otherwise treated affectionately but matter-of-factly—scolded, hugged, ignored or enjoyed, seldom indulged or "spoiled," and never excluded from the total life and activities of the entire community of families. Inquisitive and gregarious, undemanding but assertive, all the children are treated with an offhandedly casual, accepting and often amused affection by all the village adults.

Marital relationships and sexual love seem equally taken for granted. These subjects often enter peripherally into conversations. What is communicated by both men and women is that these are, of course, "good"—good in the same way as the first bright days of spring, the spring and fall migrations of the caribou, the first snowfall of late summer. Mention of any of these enjoyable matters brings quick smiles of acknowledgment and pleasure.

Despite the restricted choice of partners available in the small community, marriage nevertheless seems based on strong mutual affection, physical attraction and a conviction that marriage is a highly desirable and essential institution for both sexes. While husbands' and wives' roles and duties are in general separate and distinct, the marriage relationship provides full equality to both members, cemented by a strong bond of partnership and cooperation.

Family emotional relationships among the mountain Eskimos are so far still firmly based in a history of a very real physical dependency in which the well-being and survival of each member is necessarily rooted and nurtured.

In such an atmosphere, crowd terms like "aloneness," "alienation," "respect for the individual," "privacy" have little significance. Individuals, having no fear of losing their selfhood either to the group or to solitude, are at home and at ease with both.

One can learn from these arctic peoples, but it is the land one must look to for understanding, for it is the land that defines the size, shape and materials of the home as well as the life view of those who dwell within it.

From these assumptions, I can write about our living space; of cabins, of our cabin.

Shelters in the Arctic are traditionally an extension of the land itself.

In Anaktuvuk Pass, where no timber grows, sod huts replaced the caribou-skin tents of the nomadic life. To make the houses of sod, large slabs of moss-covered earth were stacked like adobe or concrete blocks into sloping walls, braced inside by thick willow supports and rounded over across the top to resemble a Quonset hut covered over with green turf, willow shoots, berry plants and sod. Built on the site of the removed turf, the earthen single-room house nestled low in the tundra, protected from the full force of arctic winds.

Windows, once made of bear intestines, were replaced by plastic or glass. With a stove inside, the frozen sod structures were relatively warm and dry until spring thaws brought a chill dampness inside. Then the family shifted into the white canvas tent which lets in sun and light.

A few plywood dwellings were under construction to begin replacing the sod houses on my first visit to Anaktuvuk. There was much debate among the villagers on whether the poorly insulated wooden "boxes" would keep a family warm in midwinter when winds reaching velocities of eighty to one hundred miles per hour sweep through the pass from the Arctic Ocean. With an air-freight cost of over twenty cents a pound added onto the high cost of building supplies, few families could afford an alternative to the sod igloo. Only with the assistance of public agencies can the new structures be made available to all.

In our own part of the Koyukuk, the log cabins are seldom larger than twelve by twelve to twelve by fourteen feet, slightly smaller in size than the sod huts north of timber line. The average length of suitable logs to be taken from our local spruce is about twelve feet, but the diameter of the slow-growing spruce is such that twice the number of trees are required in cabin building than farther south. To the south, timber is more plentiful, trees grow thicker and taller, trucks and tractors are available to haul and hoist; cabins are therefore larger.

One of the smallest cabins in the Koyukuk belonged to an old prospector whose gold-mining claims were located in the arid gulches of a ridge of dry timberless mountains, twenty miles south of Koviashuvik. To cut corners on the number of logs he had to drag or haul on his shoulders from the nearest stand of trees many miles away, he built a three-sided cabin backed into a hole in the rocky mountainside. Some of the local old-timers with claims on more wooded lands chuckled over this shack. "Not any bigger than a clothes closet," they said. It was not tall enough inside for its big, burly owner to stand erect. It had the essentials, however: bunk, table, Yukon stove—and a snug-fitting door to keep out cold and varmints.

Along with these essentials, an amazing amount of equipment, supplies and furniture can be crowded into a twelve-by-twelve-foot area. My first impression of our cabin was not of how little space there was in it, but of how efficiently every inch of it had been utilized—ceiling, walls, floor.

Every piece of "furniture" is multipurpose. Stretched out across the foot of the big fur-covered bunk, with the window behind my left shoulder, the stove only a warm two feet away, I have the most comfortable reading couch ever designed.

The middle of the bunk is perfect for sitting cross-legged and rugging, mending, writing letters, thinking. The oilcloth-covered table is big enough for a wolf to be skinned, an afternoon's baking to be mixed, a caribou skin scraped, moose ham butchered, card games played. Two can write letters, spread papers about.

What is harder to describe is what is below and above the furniture. The wall behind the narrower bunk is covered with nails for hanging up parkys, mitts, jeans, shirts. The walls everywhere else hold shelves—shelves made of old wooden crates, roughly adzed spruce planks, water-worn sluice-box boards. On the shelves, books, magazines, film supplies, mail-order catalogues, radio, kerosene lamps, first-aid carton, rifle-cleaning kit, paints, varnish, repair kits, writing supplies, small boxes of odds and ends: replacement parts for gasoline lanterns, boot oils, sewing materials, leather thongs, playing cards, binoculars, ammunition. The wall next to the stove is decorative with hanging skillets, lids, pots, spatulas. In the "kitchen" corner, shelves under the work surface hold the large varmintproof cans of supplies. Shelves above hold dishes, cups, smaller supplies, spices. What can't fit on a shelf hangs from the ceiling. With its many hanging items, the entire ceiling looks like an old general store in a farm community on the midwest plains. Lines strung between the big spruce beams hold sweaters, eight pair of wool mittens and gloves, six pair of leather and canvas work gloves (all clothes pinned to the lines), wool socks, extra blankets, towels, flour-sack dishcloths, wool scarves, ermine and squirrel pelts. From nails driven into the beams every two feet hang lanterns, cameras, two big kettles, tools, plastic bags of sourdough bread, of instant soups, bags of yarn, bags of rags and scraps of fur, coils of rope, wire, boots and mukluks.

Over the two-foot-wide "aisle" in the center of the cabin hang the wet things: dripping mukluks and mitts, laundered clothes, defrosting moose or caribou. There is also room in the aisle for dancing.

Under the bunks, a warehouse of things: a carton for our clothing—our "chest of drawers"; cartons of stored summer clothes and boots; two of my rugs-in-progress in heavy plastic bags to protect the wools from nest builders; a wooden toolbox (working with metal tools that have been left out in subzero cold can tear flesh from the hands); cartons of papers; work files. Under one end of the table, a twenty-five pound tin of flour, another of sugar, a fifty-gallon box of instant milk. Everything else that is not regularly needed and that will not suffer from freezing goes into the dogtrot or the cache.

In the cabin is all that we need—roughly in order. Still, to a visitor fresh from "outside," it would look cluttered beyond belief, as the homes of the villagers looked to me the first time I visited and wondered how they would ever be able to locate anything in the casual jumble of clothes, toys, furs, supplies, cookware, dishes and food. In one way, the confusion of things in the sod huts and tents was less noticeable than that in some equally small log cabins because there was less clutter of furniture. Some of the dwellings had a folding chair or two. But most sitting was done on fresh willow boughs spread on the tundra floor, or on the family bed, a pile of caribou skins and blankets raised off the ground by a pad of cut willow boughs, and filling the entire space across the back wall.

With no timber for furniture building, and furnishings flown in from outside exorbitantly costly, one very sensibly improvises better answers: wooden boxes and crates become supply cabinets; a piece of plywood or lumber boards nailed together, set on wooden boxes, makes a low table. The sheet-metal stove, also set low, rests on four tin-can "legs."

Out front, a new snowmobile may be parked beside the villager's house. Inside, however, only surface variations mark a change from the old nomadic way. The atmosphere of the villagers' homes always seems snug, homelike, comfortable, busy, welcoming. But in the absence of many material goods, of chrome and plastic, of foam-stuffed upholstery, nylon carpets and power appliances, the casual visitor may miss the richness of what the people create and communicate of "home," and see only poverty.

With wood available to the log cabin builder in the timbered areas of the range, furniture is more readily constructed. Much of it is crude, jerry-built; some, made by sourdoughs with carpentry skills and hours of leisure in the long night, lovingly crafted.

Most of the old cabins in the Koyukuk were built by lone men for their own occupancy. Women were not in the picture. Many of the old prospectors were spartan in their needs and tastes. They were here to get the gold out of the ground. Everything else was a waste of time and energy. Others of the old sourdoughs imported curious mementos from "home" into the arctic frontier. In one of the rotting old cabins which belonged to a lone prospector at Jim Pup, there is an enormous, elaborately wrought, brass-plated double bed. The springs are rusted through; the mattress shredded, carried off by birds, voles and squirrels for nests. But the big golden bed still stands among the collapsing log walls and sinking floorboards. A long and expensive journey by sea freighter, river boat and dog team brought that monument of "civilization" into the Koyukuk wilds.

The early gold seekers prospecting the wild creeks of the Arctic were in the tradition of all frontiersmen. Some came for adventure, and quickly satisfying the craving in the dramatic climate, among their burly cohorts, grew restless and moved on to new horizons. Some came to escape unpaid debts, a nagging wife, dull job, law-enforcement agencies. Most came to get rich quick in order to go back to wherever they had come from with the gold fruits. Most returned home instead on borrowed fare. Few came in search of a "home." But those few who remained did so because they were caught, not by the dream of the "yellow stuff," but by limitless sky, the thin lonely night cry of the wolf, endless ridges of horizonless mountains, the mysterious arctic winter twilight.

I think of my friend Jan in her eight-room suburban house . . . and I see her "confined" within walls, ringed by a narrow moat of carefully cultivated green and a six-foot-high fence. I try to imagine her in a one-room cabin or sod hut, ringed by infinite universe. The universe can be frightening if one is closed off from it too long. Many have lost connection with it.

Were I to return to the city now, I suppose that my perspective would be forced to reverse itself. Remembering the jangled sounds, the crowds, the cement canyons, the cold steel, glass, neon, the grime and thick air, the hurry, the search for green or a glimpse of sky—where can the need for space be satisfied? Or the need to move about easily, take one's time, enjoy the walk, smell the fresh natural smells of clean earth and grass, move about the places of people without tensions and fears? No; like Jan, I would be forced to disconnect myself from the world, to find a shelter closed off like a fortress from what lies beyond the walls —a place that offers nurturing of the inner life, provides some respite from the din and freneticism of crowds.

I do not know what the answers are. The alternative to city-suburb is not the wilderness for more than a very few people. Not only is there not enough wilderness left to absorb more than a very few, but once the wilderness is invaded by the many, it will no longer be the wild.

The great ecologist Aldo Leopold and many others have stressed the need for wilderness as a laboratory, a living example of the land in a natural ecological balance. The concern has been repeatedly expressed that soon there will be no land left that has not been manipulated, cultivated, exploited, changed by man's hand. Perhaps the wilderness needs also to be protected as a laboratory in human values, a place where the land, not man, is allowed to determine in large measure the human relationships to nature's ecological balance—a place where man discovers firsthand the kinships, harmonious interdependencies, the essential connections of all life systems.

While broad institutional answers which may yet prevent us from destroying the planet or our own humanness on it are being sought—or ignored—or rejected—we individuals might begin by making our own individual choices, taking our own individual actions toward these answers.

A letter to Jan ends:

The value study has led us to a choice. When the "year" is up, we will remain here in the wilderness. Build our own small cabin on one of two silvery, rushing creeks that tumble down from the white peaks into the deep waters of this mountain lake. When the sun returns in the spring, we'll begin to explore the territory along the two creeks and decide whether to build on "Holy Moses" or on "Last Chance" Creek, both obviously, perhaps prophetically, named by two old prospectors.

But we're after a different gold. It can't be found by "going back" to old frontiers, although this is what some of our friends "outside" will believe our decision represents. But no one moves back in time or space to what is past.

The present frontier, for all of us, is the crucial one. It has to do with the life quality that the Nunamiuts are in the process of losing as that dinosaur of old and outlived frontiers, "progress," continues to gobble up and to devastate the planet, along with the uniqueness and diversity of all its human inhabitants.

That amorphous quality is still here in the smiles and nods of these inland people, in their recognition and acknowledgment of the "good" in merely being alive. The frontier we are all on at present is where commitment to that "good" is to be discovered.

Here, the value of one's own life is a prerequisite for hope in the future. Here there is a conviction that life is better than anti-life and that a concern for others is expressed in the acceptance of one's own responsibility for answers. . . .

. . . at Koviashuvik, which might be—anywhere. . . .

Learning to recognize the limits of subzero cold is like exploring an alien environment. The fine line of safety can be crossed over without warning. In the minus forties, I go to the cache and without stopping to think take off the arctic mitts to work only in my wool gloves. All the body heat is sapped swiftly from my hands by the frozen supplies handled. Within two minutes, I can no longer hold onto anything and my fingers feel burned.

Rushing back to the cabin, I immediately immerse my hands

in hot water. The pain is excruciating but reassuring as normal sensation slowly returns.

END OF JANUARY

We have not seen the sun for more than two and a half months. Today Sam calls me outside at about noon, and bets fifty cents that the sun will reach the cabin in less than an hour. Each day the line of light has crept across the land, coming closer and closer to the cabin. We see it moving. The golden color, like a white-frothed tide, slides down the slopes, over the northern end of the plain of the frozen lake, reaches the tip of the small island, creeps up the mountainside to touch treetops behind the camp. But in the south, toward Jim Pup, where the sun itself will have to clear the mountain peaks before it can strike our camp, there is no sun. Not today. Our camp remains in deep blue shadow, encircled by distant golden light. In two days . . .

MINUS SIXTY

The hint of promised sun holds no warmth. These days are bitter cold. The thermometer slides steadily downward, reaching minus forty-five, then minus fifty, fifty-five, and holds at minus sixty degrees Fahrenheit. With the wind stilled, there seems at first to be little difference between the more familiar minus forty and forty-five and this new low. But after only a couple of minutes outside, beneath a cold white aurora, I sense the difference. Exposed face skin instantly grows taut, numb. Hands and feet begin to sting and grow numb, even in heavy mitts and arctic footwear. The frigid air hits the lungs with a jolting, savage bite. To remain inactive for very long at these temperatures could result in freezing to death. Men can and do survive in this severe cold, but survival is borderline. No room for mis-calculation or error. But one never really gets "cold" in this extreme, subzero cold. One stays warm or dies.

Today the cabin looks cluttered. It is too small, too confined. The blue-shadowed world that we have lived in for months now seems permanent. The cold, wearing, wearying, eternal.

Just once I'd like to race out the door fast and far over the tundra without first having to put on six layers of footwear and strap myself to clodhoppers called snowshoes! I feel snappish, claustrophobic, irritable, trapped, which means a full-fledged first attack of Cabin Fever!

And for Cabin Fever there's no remedy but bootstrapping.

After sawing two big logs with the Swedish bucksaw, and stacking them onto the woodpile, and panting furiously from the exertion at minus forty-eight degrees, it's very nice to come back into a spacious, well-ordered, cheerful little cabin. The fever has passed.

VISITOR

Stepping out of the cabin to do our chores this morning, we come face to face with a great white wolf. He stands fifty yards away, silently watching. His yellow slanted eyes glitter; he does not move. We do not move. We three seem frozen together in a fragment of time, like a stopped frame of movie film, action jammed midaction. On a faint stir of wind, I can just smell his wild smell. His yellow eyes do not waver. He still does not move. We wait. His stance does not change, but a sudden tension enters it. Still watching, his yellow eyes fixed steadily on us, he takes a few steps; the hairs on the back of his neck are up, the tail up, ears alert. His body begins to draw itself together, shoulders hunching, the fine deep ruff of thick white fur across his back rising as he walks slowly, watchfully away, and disappears down into the creek bed. . . .

RETURN

By late morning, light has almost covered the land.

By noon, the moving edge of gold has reached three-quarters up the plateau, sweeping steadily on toward our camp. I will make no bets against the sun's arrival today! Mukluks go on to be ready to dash outside, if, today . . .

At twelve-thirty, the tops of the spruce just below the cache catch golden fire. The blue-black winter look of spruce turns warm green in an instant. I thought the trees were black because they were frozen. It was the absence of sunlight.

We hurry outside, and the whole world lights up.

The great bright glow moves surely, steadily, across the limitless snowfields. Reaches the woodpile behind the cabin and turns the stacked split logs a warm tawny yellow. Touches the back corner of the cabin roof and turns a long blue icicle into a glittering diamond dagger. The paths around the cabin fill up with brightness. The cabin is bathed in light.

Sun pours over our camp as, above the mountain peaks toward Jim Pup, the fiery globe itself appears in a blaze of hot gold. Sunlight now embraces all the frozen land. Sun warmth strikes our faces in a sudden gentle blow. We lift them to the light, dazzled, blinded. Shout greetings to the sun as if welcoming an old friend who has been missing too long. Raise our arms and reach toward the source of warmth, toward the light which wraps around us, and everywhere, blue snow now gold-warm and splashed with a skyful of dancing brilliants.

A strange and joyful madness erupts in our camp. And we dance a lunatic, gleeful jig round and round the cabin with our boots making the music as they clump over frozen snow with drumming, bassy, crunching sounds. We come around the cabin corner and meet our shadows, seen for the first time in seventy-seven days. Elongated and distorted by the low-in-the-sky midday sun, our shadows start a contest in mugging and jumping and dancing, and I wonder why elsewhere shadows have come to belong only to children!

Dashing into the cabin for a camera, I'm stopped at the threshold by the newness of an interior aglow with yellow brightness which streams in through the frosted windowpanes, spilling over onto the oilcloth on the table, reaching out in golden fingers to probe the farthest, darkest, coldest corners behind the bunks.

The sun crawls along the white mountain crests for two, four, five minutes—which stretch to a precious ten. We are content to stand in its warmth, quietly watching the landscape of our journey through the universe as our planet, on which we have passage, tilts its range of mountains up into the sky and slowly covers the great glowing circle.

The sun is gone. It does not reappear today, though we see its bright rays above the ring of mountains as they glide on past it. Tomorrow its passing will take longer, and still longer the following day, until long sunlit days of spring will become the arctic day of summer and the world will be light, both day and night.

The blue shadows of sunlessness resettle over the land. There is a different quality in the vast white sweep of frozen mountains and valleys—or is it in the way that we now look at them? The long arctic night of winter is past. The sun has returned, a miracle. At Anaktuvuk Pass, as at Koviashuvik, and in all places where the sun's absence has been most deeply felt, its return today was greeted as it has been for centuries, with smiles and joyful greetings and uplifted faces. Our sun has at last returned.

A GIANT REFLECTOR

The sun has been back only a few days. Although it is still low in the sky and its warmth feeble, we're already troubled with sun glare. A letter from Dishu warns to be careful of snowblindness as the sun returns.

She writes, "You better watch out eyes getting burned, sun coming back. Potato poultice good. Cover eyes with potato if you get snowblind." I hope instant potatoes will substitute.

Apparently the unfiltered sun's reflection off the snowscape burns right through the eyelids. Caught out without sunglasses, rubbing soot on eyelids and around the eyes is helpful—or a pair of crude goggles with narrow eye slits cut into them can be carved out of wood. Meanwhile, sunglasses go back into parky pockets as part of our trail emergency equipment.

Weather, raw and uncertain. Erratic winds and skittish temperatures, as if the return of the sun had triggered quiescent forces into uneasy, conflicting motion.

Mail day today, and here at the cabin it is minus forty-five at noon. The winds blow hard, first from the west, then the north, then from the camp itself, in swirling clouds of ground snow as if wind were being created right here on the premises.

Right after breakfast, Sam heads down to the shore to wait for Daryl, who finally arrives at about three o'clock, with light to spare. He is airborne again almost immediately. His rushed departure must be due to the extreme cold of today—and the cold is always most severe down in the bowl of the frozen lake where the coldest air sinks and winds from the Arctic Ocean sweep through the pass from the north and over the open plain of lake ice.

When Sam returns with the mail sack tied to his packboard, his red wool face mask is white, coated over completely with a thick layer of ice crystals. Hanging up the frozen mask to defrost over the slop pail, he rubs his face briskly. A bitter day at the shore: minus fifty-six degrees at the shelter when he left. Daryl stopped only long enough to pass the mailbag out the plane door, grab the outgoing one and take off.

Coming up the trail, the wind was head on, sharp as a knife, Sam adds. Halfway up, he realized he'd better put on the face mask. Now, as he turns toward the lantern, I see a small patch of yellowish white on the soft flesh just above his cheek. The rubbing has reddened the skin around it, but the mark remains white, a sign of frostbitten flesh.

The danger of frozen skin is one of the primary reasons why

the "buddy" system is recommended for arctic travelers. In sub-zero temperatures, especially with winds, exposed skin freezes without warning, without even the knowledge of its owner. Once the skin is frozen there is little to be done out on the trail. The danger in stopping to build a fire in order to thaw out is that thawed skin is highly susceptible to refreezing. This more drastically damages already damaged tissue. Whether surface tissue has suffered frostbite, or fingers, toes, hands or feet have deep-frozen, it is wiser to leave them frozen and to continue on to camp to avoid the danger of thawing-refreezing. Rubbing the frozen limb or skin with snow was commonplace treatment until fairly recently. Its effect was just the reverse of what was intended. Toes and fingers were unnecessarily lost in the "treatment." The current recommended procedure on reaching a warm shelter is to immediately immerse the frozen area or member in hot water. As the frozen part warms and thaws, there is also a general loss of body heat from cooled blood circulating through the body. Alcoholic drinks, which give an illusion of warmth, actually lower body temperature, and should be avoided at this time.

Sam is fortunate to have escaped with such minor frostbite but another problem has also been created by the bitter cold of today. His body temperature returns to normal, but his feet remain numb. Stripping off the layers of mukluks, felt boots, wool socks, we discover that his feet also show signs of frostbite. The lines of white around the heels and across the toes match almost exactly the outlines of his snowshoe straps. Snow must have accumulated and packed down under the straps, then frozen to an icy ridge. During his long hours out in the intense cold, the ice penetrated all the protective layers of footwear to freeze the skin beneath.

I brush aside an uneasy recall of tales told of isolated arctic wilderness dwellers who have been forced to amputate their own fingers or toes, and in some desperate cases, a hand or foot, to stop the spread of gangrene, which can be the aftermath of deep freezing of the flesh.

In seconds, the metal washbasin is filled with boiling water from the teakettle, cooled down with snow water to a temperature Sam can bear to hold his feet in. Every few minutes, more hot water is added. Thawing frozen skin is intensely painful. But the treatment begins to work. Feeling and color slowly come back into all the toes but one. That and the heel skin remain discolored and numb.

Considering today's temperature of minus fifty-six degrees, and a wind of at least ten mph, maybe more, the chill factor reached down to at least a Fahrenheit temperature equivalent of eighty-five to ninety degrees below zero. Luck has been ours this day, really!

We have done all we can. Sam dries his feet and gets into warm wool insulated socks, settles down with another cup of steaming coffee, and then we remember the unopened mailbag. Today the news from "outside" seems irrelevant. . . .

The bitter cold of the day holds into the night.

By evening, all wind motion has ceased, leaving a vacuum which seems gradually to fill with a new, strange and massive kind of silence. The night has never been this still.

Despite the roaring fire, tonight the cabin is cold: continual, unrelenting cold. All the window glass has disappeared under dense coats of ice. We hang blankets over the windows, but chill cuts through the heavy wool. The cardboard insulation covering the log walls is heavily stippled with ice crystals. Small icicles form long fringes along the corner shelves in the "kitchen." Our washtub snow-water storage tank across from the Yukon stove is frozen solid, radiating a wide circle of frigid air out into the room. We use the ulu to chip out chunks of ice to fill the teakettle. The filled teakettle seems to cool the stove, to radiate its own cold waves.

We turn in two hours earlier than usual to try to escape the inescapable icy pall that has permeated the cabin, crawl into bunks not half warm enough tonight, with their sleeping bags designed for subzero weather and their piles of furs and blankets.

We take turns reading aloud to distract ourselves, holding the book in mittened hands, but fingers stiffen quickly and the unrelenting presence of the arctic cold overshadows any meaning of the pages' words of elsewhere. We blow out the lantern and burrow deep into the bunk, fighting to relax against the tension prolonged chill brings. Time suspended. . . . Our own interior heaters, well stoked with caribou fat, begin in the snug enclosures to warm us at last, the warmth held inside the den of the sleeping bags.

The tension of cold dissolving under the comforting, reassuring waves of warmth, from deep down in our secure burrow we listen to the mammoth stillness that is the crash of silence, the sound that is frozen sound at minus sixty-five degrees Fahrenheit.

Two hours of direct sun today. Only a little more than a week since it returned. It rides higher in the sky each day—rather, earth tips on its axis a little more each day. Morning light now arrives close to 6 A.M., usually in a "painted desert" sky of fluorescent reds and yellows! Twilight falls between 4 and 5 P.M.; our "day" seems long.

Winds and temperatures continue to vacillate from day to day. There seems to be no stable plateau in the weather. A week ago, minus sixty-five degrees; three days ago, minus thirty. Yesterday, up to minus five—and today, sliding back down to minus twenty. And still the erratic winds, suddenly shifting direction, unpredictable.

A parky squirrel poked its head up through the snow this morning. He sat there in the mouth of his tunnel, just dug out from his burrow, unmoving, fixed, as if he'd fallen sound asleep in the sunshine. A blast of icy wind suddenly swept across the snowfield, leaving a wake of snowclouds. The moving mists engulfed the squirrel. In a flurry of swirling crystals, he dropped instantly from sight.

Sun or no sun—he must be as confused as I!

Thirty feet behind the cabin, the tracks of a lone caribou where it paused to paw down through the snow to reach the lichens, followed by the tracks of one large lone wolf. In the wolf tracks, a large snowshoe hare's bounding prints, which look like those made by a three-legged creature, and following the hare, one very small ermine trail.

What words are right for snow?

A fresh snowfall. Sun bright and hot by early afternoon, when it reaches its highest point just before slipping again behind the peaks. The snow cover changes under the sun's few hours of heat. The top layer has begun to thaw, and the smooth iced surface we are accustomed to turns to a consistency resembling melted marshmallow. The snowshoes sink down almost a foot deep with each step. Without snowshoes, boots break through even the crusted layers below, and a leg can unexpectedly get jammed down in a hip-deep hole in the snow. Getting out of the trap without injury is as tricky as summer tussock-hopping across an arctic bog.

Wrestling the sled, even unloaded, through the soft stuff calls for all one's endurance and patience. Now the sun replaces the light of the long arctic night to determine when we do our chores. Travel and sledding are best done early in the morning before the sun has had a chance to soften the surface snow, or a few hours after the sun has disappeared, when cold and wind have had time to refreeze the surface.

As I come to know the myriad kinds and conditions of snow, English words for them become inadequate. To be able to use the Eskimo terms would be helpful. The many dialects of the Eskimo language seem to be deeply rooted in the special ecology of the Arctic. Unwritten and unrecorded until recent years, Eskimo is spoken language with the emphasis on action words, rich in descriptiveness and immediacy, or present tense.

There is no single Eskimo word to represent "snow," for in the Arctic there is no such thing as just "snow." Instead there are

terms for "new snow," "old granulated snow," "very old granulated snow next to the ground," "snow to be gathered for water,"
"snow spread out," "snow that is drifting," "snow like salt," "snow
newly drifted," "snow piled up near the bottom of a hill," "snow
mixed with water," "snow on clothes," "it snows," and so on. In
all of these terms, there seems to be no root word for "snow."

A NIGHT VISITOR

Tonight on my way down the outhouse trail, I hear footsteps
in the snow. I've just left Sam inside the cabin; therefore, I freeze
in my tracks, listening. Then hear them again—a methodical
crunch, crunch, crunch of heavy steps breaking through the
crusted snow. They stop. No moon. No light anywhere but for
the dim glow of lantern light from the cabin window. I turn
and race back up the path and inside for a flashlight.

Outside, listening again in darkness, waiting to see if the sound
will resume before turning on the light, I stand absolutely still,
aware only of the sound of my own breath. I, too, am being
listened to.

Then the footsteps begin once more, from somewhere down
the slope in front of me, close to the cache.

Switching on the small flashlight, I aim it toward the cache.
In the cold, the batteries work poorly. The light is faint, but it
immediately stops the footsteps. Moving the feeble flicker of light
methodically across the white slope below, I can barely make
out the three shadowy spruce near the garbage pit, the vague
outline of a rusted hulk of mining equipment, and then a new
trail of dark patterns across the snow. The trail ends at two
slender dark posts sticking up out of the drift. Attached to them,
a very large moose. Staring curiously up into the dim light, he
stands motionless, a shadow creature who seems, in the yellow
glow, unreal, like a cardboard cutout propped against the landscape, until he drops his head with its mossy stunted new growth
of antlers, turns, and slowly ambles away into the night, the

crunch, crunch, crunch, crunch of massive hoof on icy snow taking a long, long time to fade off into silence.

HARES

More snowshoe hares are moving into the territory. More tracks seen in the fresh snow cover. But this is not a peak year for the arctic hare. And not enough have moved in to bring in the lynx and fox, their primary predators.

High population density among snowshoe hares reaches a peak cycle approximately every ten years. The once held view that food supply alone was the key to the cyclical nature of wild animal population must now include many ecological factors— food supply, climatic conditions, mating, nesting and maturation circumstances, predator relationships. All these factors, if favorably balanced, may be conducive to increases in populations. But these same favorable factors in balance will not sustain high-density population beyond the point at which stress, arising out of conditions of overpopulation, begins to decimate those numbers.

The size of the lynx population and, to a lesser extent, numbers of fox apparently have a direct relationship to the snowshoe hare cycle. The old trappers say that almost no lynx have been seen in the far north for a number of years now. But whether this is because of the nonpeak years of the snowshoe hare or because the lynx has been largely trapped out of existence, I don't know. We have seen no signs of lynx or fox here at Koviashuvik. And only a very few snowshoe hares.

RECIPE FOR SNOWSHOE HARE

Skin, stretch and scrape pelt. Good for making socks, mittens or for trimming parky.

A fat young buck, like the one Sam brings home today, is prime. Prepare as for fried chicken, dipping all pieces into seasoned flour. Brown in caribou fat, along with all the hare fat that can be salvaged. When browned, cover and simmer, allowing slightly longer time for cooking tender than chicken or ptarmigan requires.

PORCUPINE SUPPER

The porcupines eat on and on: more fine spruce are killed. Another of the oldest and handsomest groves found stripped; the culprit only a few feet away. Sam loses patience. We have porcupine for supper.

Sam's mood, when he returns to the cabin with the porky tied to his packboard, is noticeably ambivalent. There's no sense of a "fair hunt" involved in the taking of a porcupine. The slow-moving, slow-witted rodent is a "sitting duck." But the general destructiveness of these creatures on our slow-growing, sparse forests is a concern and an irritation.

When the packboard is removed, Sam's ambivalence shifts. The back of his parky and wool pants have been thoroughly doused by the relaxation of the porcupine's sphincter muscle.

In the bush, porkys are considered good eating, a fine change from other game meats. And since nothing is wasted here, we will, of course, eat the porcupine. Although we can't think of what use to make of a porcupine pelt, Sam decides to save the skin. Hoisting the carcass onto the table for skinning, I get my first really close view of a porcupine.

Its fur is surprisingly thick, long-haired—a rich deep brown, golden-tipped. Hidden down in the back and bottom hairs are the quills, seemingly thousands of them, each long and needle sharp, so dense they are like a coat of spiked armor. The belly is quill-less, soft, almost downy to the touch, a velvet brown color and obviously very vulnerable to attack. It is suddenly clear why the porky tucks itself into a ball and keeps its rear to its enemies when threatened. This is a male with a small, rough-skinned circular pouch beneath the penis, and at the bottom of the pouch, the anus. Each paw is tipped with sharp, hooked claws with which it grips the trees it climbs to feed on.

Sam lashes together spruce poles to make a stretching frame. With the skin-sewing needle, he stretches the pelt on the frame with cord. The inner side of the skin glistens with oil. The meat should be fat and tender.

With its golden-tipped guard hairs making a broad, light band down the center of the skin, the stretched pelt is a handsome fur. But reaching out to run my hand over its softness, I remember just in time to move the hand lightly *down* the pelt. The other way and my palm would be instantly studded with quills. We decide that there are probably a few people for whom we'd like to make a porcupine fur pillow, but can think of no other use for the pelt except to appreciate its beauty.

RECIPE FOR PORCUPINE

Marinate two porky legs in leftover pickle juice for a few hours (even fat porcupine tends to be a little tough). Dip legs in salt- and pepper-seasoned flour, and brown in moose fat mixed with porky fat. Cover and let simmer for an hour.

As Sam notes, porcupine is basically processed spruce, therefore the meat should be seasoned only lightly or the delicate sweet taste will be overpowered.

Porcupine quills are a good substitute for paper clips.

The wolves are back. Once again their songs roll around the mountain faces, to echo and ricochet and come back sevenfold to set them off once more, with Sam joining in the wild song.

Wolf tracks are now everywhere. If the urine signs are really a mark of territorial claim, they've taken over Koviashuvik! Down at the shore, a baited trap has been raided by a very large and very wise old hunter. The bait well gnawed, three-quarters of it gone; the rest defecated on!

February passes with few changes since the advent of the sun's return. Yet one senses change under way—or is it only my expectation of the spring to come? After the long quiescence of the arctic winter night, faint, indecipherable voices seem to come from the great plain of ice covering the lake. How can it be? The ice is now four to five feet thick. And the snow on top of the ice, dependent on drifts, adds another two to four feet of deep cover. All sound should be locked in, frozen—and yet there are faint but unmistakable sighs and whispers coming from beneath that deep crust that covers the waters.

Is it merely the effect of the return of sun—or of a hidden, ancient time clock somewhere, a companion to my own inner clockworks, unknown to my consciousness but sensed in some other realm of my awareness, that moves lake waters and me toward spring?

MARCH 31

The last day of March is our first day of spring! Only a vole could stay in his burrow on this sparkling day. Fifty degrees in the noonday sun. In the shade behind the cabin, it is less than half that reading, but in the sun, the day is exhilarating! Roof snow and icicles melt and drip and splash into their puddles in the snowbank around the cabin. Patches of crusted snow begin to slide off the roof edges. Sam climbs up on the roof and shovels it clear; protection against the turf roof absorbing the melt, and rivulets running down inside the cabin!

With this first day of "spring," we decide to start work on our summer camp. We've purchased the old shelter on the shore from Dishu. While these derelict hulks of old log cabins have little actual value once they've begun to collapse and rot, the exchange of money for property, no matter how derelict, has a symbolic value in the Arctic. It recognizes "ownership," and ownership in the remote wilds represents somewhat intangible qualities like acknowledgment of another's hard labor, a shared kinship with the land, respect for another's love of a special place.

While we still plan to build our permanent cabin beside one of the creeks up the slope of a mountain, we want a summer camp on the shore. This shift from winter to summer locales is traditional among the people of the Arctic. From winter hunting camps, families moved to the shores of deep mountain lakes or the banks of swift-flowing rivers to make their fish camps for the summer. Here, birds, berries and roots were to be found in abundance and fish enough to feed themselves and their dogs through the "long days" of summer.

Our immediate task is to start building a small but tight little log cabin on the site where the shelter now stands, fifty feet from the water's edge, facing the sunrise, with a sweeping view of the lake and of the mountains to the north, east and south.

Most of the shelter's logs will have to be replaced. Ideally, the new logs should be cut, stacked and allowed to season for a few months to prevent warping out of alignment when they are part of the walls. But if we're to get the cabin up and enclosed before mosquitoes arrive, we will have to use unseasoned logs. To get our logs cut and hauled before breakup has turned the land into a slushy quagmire, we need to go to work immediately.

Setting off down the plateau, we have to remove our parkys. The blazing unfiltered sun warms our faces and backs like a tropic sun. I feel my face breaking into a silly grin again and again, for no reason but that the day is a great day! And remember one of the women at Anaktuvuk breaking into a smile at my comment that "Spring must be wonderful when it finally comes after the long dark winter. . . ." With nods and smiles, she answered, "Everybody smile when spring come. Everybody walkin' round with smiles on them springtime days. Nice, spring!"

Nice! Across the plateau, the constant sweep of wind offsets the sun's heat, keeping the surface snow fairly well frozen. Frozen well enough for Sam to hop on the back of the sled at the beginning of the down-the-mountain slope and pump himself along to pick up speed, and then to zoom down the curving trail

at a furious pace as if he were on a toboggan in a chute, until
he hits a too-sharp unbanked curve that pitches sled and rider
headlong into a deep snowdrift.

Three-quarters of the way down the trail, we cut off to the
right into the forest nearest the shore camp. Here we struggle
through the sun-warmed, protected-from-wind deep snow, breaking through the surface crust at every step. In the golden slashes
of sun that pierce the blue shadows of the woods, the glare is
blinding. The drifts of snow under the trees are alive with
millions of dancing multicolored crystals of light.

Sam begins to ax the trees he's selected, trees of varying heights
and diameters, harvesting only where overcrowding exists. As
each spruce crashes to the ground, the ringing sound of the ax
is suddenly replaced with an equally voluble hush. I trim the
branches off the fallen trees with a hatchet. The jays who live at
the shore camp soar in and out of the trees around us, twittering
and scolding, making certain we know we are invaders of their
territory.

Harvesting the logs is hard work. Moving about in the mushy
snow, we step out of one hole back onto the uncertain surface
above, which under the weight of that next step immediately
collapses into another deep hole. We move in slow motion, like
the moose in winter.

Still, the afternoon passes too quickly. The lowering sun slowly
elongates forest shadows, and gradually lets in the glacial wind
that blows from the north.

Sam's final chore is to girdle a fine and very straight spruce,
almost thirty feet tall, the trunk more than a foot in diameter.
This monarch among the many shorter, more slender logs will
be a roof beam. The girdling blaze around the trunk will stop the
flow of sap and kill the tree. We and the porcupines have our
different needs.

Ready at last to go, we load our trees on the sled; these logs,
still weighted with sap, are far denser, heavier, than the dead
dry trees we take for firewood. The loaded sled at once mires
down, runners disappearing, the body of the sled buried several

feet deep in soft snow. There is no way to make this haul any easier unless we want to come back tonight after the snow has refrozen. We strain and struggle with the load the half mile down to the shore, park the loaded sled beside the shelter and start up the trail.

With the sun's setting, winter seems to have returned. But we are too weary—and too pleased with the day—to care!

Awakening to the Second Day of Spring, we find that a thick, hard-driving blizzard has moved in in the night. Winter resumes.

Fully awake, we find unexpected consequences from yesterday's gloriously hot, brilliantly undiluted sun. It has left us burned and snowblind. Sam's scorched red face explains why my own is flaming hot and stinging. Our eyes are also inflamed, almost swollen shut. They burn and scratch and throb as if they'd been filled with hot sand. Trying to focus on a given point triggers a full-fledged headache. Everything looks distorted, as if being viewed through a fine-mesh filter.

Closing eyes completely gives no relief. Worse, the slightest movement of eyeball behind lid feels like an emery board being dragged across it. Eyes open, even the subdued light of the overcast day seems blinding.

Obviously we underestimated the strength of yesterday's sun. In our hunger for it, we forgot the intensity of rays burning down through crystalline clear arctic air and onto the hot white snow mirror, deflecting the rays back into our eyes. For part of the day we wore sunglasses. But while working in the forest, we took them off. The slanted rays of hot sun slicing through the foliage threw back snow reflection no less intense than on the open snowfield.

There's little we can do except to weather out the immediate discomfort and our own feelings of irritability. In the future, more caution. Meanwhile, a soothing ointment removes some of the sting of the sunburn. For our snowblindness, we can do little but rest our eyes and avoid eyestrain and light. A cool cloth over the eyes should help, but its weight on the eyelids is itself painful.

Only in extreme and prolonged cases of exposure to bright sun on snow does snowblindness actually cause more than a temporary condition of "blindness." Painfully spelling out the data in our medical text, I read that snowblindness is a form of conjunctivitis, a form not caused by infection, therefore requiring no treatment except eye rest and protection from light. It is the mirrored and intensified sunlight bounced back into the eyes from the endless plain of white snow that burns the thin cover of skin over the eyeball. Some arctic old-timers insist that the damage is done by the burning, which goes right through the eyelids and fine tissue around the eyes. This conclusion may be based on the sensation in snowblindness that the insides of the eyelids are embedded with fragments of hot lead. Whatever the explanation, the traditional Eskimo design of wood or bone sun goggles which have only a very narrow slit to see through and which cover the eyes and all the skin surrounding them may be the best defense against snowblindness. But even these goggles cannot prevent serious damage to that narrow strip of exposed eye if the wearer suffers prolonged hours of sun glare off arctic snow or ice fields.

In our medical book, an anesthetic eye ointment is recommended for the pain, which can be severe even in light cases of snowblindness. We have an eye ointment in our first-aid kit, but unfortunately it contains no anesthesia. Our mountain-climbing physician's reasoning, which sounded very logical in his city office, was that an anesthetized eye can no longer function in a protective manner. If the eye cannot feel the wind or a wandering eyelash or a speck of dust, it will not blink or tear or close in protection. Good sense, of course, but that leaves us in our present painful predicament with no remedy other than Dishu's potato poultices.

I can see little advantage in spending the day balancing two cold, mealy mounds of cooked instant potatoes on gravelly sore eyelids. Instead we decide to give in gracefully, getting chores done at half speed, and in between, resting ourselves and eyes; telling stories in lieu of reading aloud as we wait for the effects of the deceptive arctic sun to heal and pass, along with what appears to be, on this blizzardy day, the return of winter.

Post-storm; post-spring. Subzero, and cold wind. But something new has been set in motion in the universe, and even this brief return of winter can't reverse the process. There's no way to explain this knowing; the experience is older than mere knowledge, older than the human frame in which it is carried.

Work on the lower cabin moves along. More logs felled and hauled to the shore. If we were to consider our time and energy only in terms of economy and efficiency, this part of the job could go a hundred times faster. We'd simply cut as many of the closest trees as necessary to get the number of logs we need. But we restrict the amount of harvesting in any one stand, and harvest selectively from all around the lake. The logs must then be sledded back across the lake ice. I wonder if an efficiency expert, evaluating the way we choose to spend our time and energy in this selecting and these long hauls, would consider as we do the worth of the simple beauty of a spruce tree and of the two hundred years it took to grow large enough to make a log for our cabin. . . .

At the shore, the biggest logs are barked, or skinned, with an adze. I can work with this tool for short periods, but it was not designed for women to use. Since coming to the wilderness, where all things have unique value, I've become curious and intrigued with our few tools, and with the automatic adaptations I must make in using them. I think the difference in ease with which Sam and I use the tools is less due to the usual explanation of cultural conditioning—less based in those assumptions of male competency that the culture inculcates—than in the fact that all such tools have been designed for male use, strength, dexterity and muscles.

I've learned to compensate for my lesser efficiency with some of our tools. But not with the adze, although it is a remarkably simple device, very effective in Sam's hands. Attached to a wooden handle the length of an ax's, the adze's sharp iron blade, which is about four inches wide, looks like a flattened, hammered-out pickax. The adze is swung forward and back along the log, rather than from side to side. One stands astraddle the log, and with each forward swing, the adze blade slices along the log, removing a strip of bark along with a thin layer of wood underneath the bark. Each log is then rolled a quarter turn for the next section to be stripped. When the trees are frozen, peeling them is a difficult task. The bark comes off more easily in spring, when the sap is running.

While it's not essential that cabin logs be stripped, peeled logs not only dry out faster but have longer life as well. Carpenter ants burrow in under bark and rot is introduced, eventually weakening the cabin walls. The flattened surface left on the rounded log by the removal of the thin layer that comes off with the strip of bark also makes the logs fit together more snugly as they are laid one on the other for the cabin walls.

By comparison, the small logs are a pleasure to peel. Since the cabin roof alone will require a hundred or more poles of the size most common among Koviashuvik trees, I take this job as my own, for I can hoist them about without any help. The skinning tools for these are also much lighter weight and easier to use than the adze. Our pole-skinning knife, or draw knife, has a very sharp blade about ten inches long and two inches deep. A wooden handle is attached to either end of the blade, and the knife is held in two hands, the blade pulled toward the user, peeling away the bark in neat strips. A hatchet also makes a good pole skinner, if it is very sharp. With a good strong chop, knots and bumps are easily removed.

From one of the larger logs, and four "legs" topped from the longer poles, Sam quickly puts together a waist-high sawhorse to hold the trees for skinning. This job of mine is a particularly satisfying one for some reason. Working in the warm sun and breathing in the sweet, pungent fragrance of spruce sap are part of the pleasure. Seeing the rough-barked spruce turn smooth and golden under the easy rhythm of the draw knife is also part of it. It's good to see my tepee of glossy peeled roof poles increase and grow. But it has most to do with building one's own house. These are the roof of my new home in the wilderness.

FOX

As I glance up from my book, something at the window catches my eye and pulls it back for a quick double take. A fox stands on the banked snow just outside, looking in at us. After a moment of looking, first at Sam and then at me, he turns and trots out of view.

We hurry outside; as soon as we see him, he sees us. After a second's pause in which he examines us with intense interest, he turns away and trots on through the camp, investigating everything. He sniffs the woodpile, the chopping stump, the cabin corner, the strip down the slope in front of the cabin where we toss our slops. Every few seconds he pauses to study us, then resumes his tour of the camp as if indifferent to our presence. We talk softly to him as he moves about. He doesn't respond to the sound except for an occasional glance over his shoulder or a long scrutinizing pause. But at the slightest move by either of us, he instantly stops, wary and alert. Then, as we remain still, he continues on his hurried trotting tour of the premises.

This red fox's thick soft coat is a rich auburn color except for the brownish socklike markings of his lower legs and the white patches on face, chest and tailtip. His face is slender and winsome, the black muzzle tapering to a pointed end. Small golden eyes set in two saucers of darker fur have a direct, level look. The full bushy tail is held high.

Ten feet away, he stops, sniffs the ground and begins to dig furiously into the snow. He digs like a young dog after a buried bone. His long, slender nose, as much a digging tool as his paws, shovels and scoops out the snow. Poking his head deep into the hole he has dug, he finally pulls out the frozen remains of a meat scrap. Picking it up and carrying it in his teeth like a bone to a spot six to eight feet away, he digs another hole and drops in his find. Again using the long nose as a shovel, as well as his paws, he covers the bone, then stands squarely over his cached prize, watching us watching him.

Something from far down the creek bed distracts him. He turns his head, ears cocked, tense and listening. Minutes pass and still he waits, poised, listening, staring fixedly at one spot almost a quarter of a mile down the creek. Suddenly, without even a backward glance, he turns and trots off toward the spot, to disappear behind the white banks of the creek bed.

This is the newcomer to the territory, the curious one whose delicate prints we have found paralleling our recent trails. Apparently he has decided to remain for a while. Does that mean that he—she—has a den nearby? What was it he heard or sensed far down the creek bed? That would be a natural site for a fox den, dug into the south-facing bank to catch the spring sun.

Eskimo hunters call the fox a stupid animal. The great curiosity of these animals must make them appear reckless, even stupid, at times. With little effort, we could have taken a fine fox pelt today. Perhaps he knew we would not. Who knows what his senses told him?

If our fox returns to a den in the creek bed where a mate awaits him, the old trappers who have observed such a meeting say she will greet him with great excitement, leaping at him playfully and frisking about as she takes whatever food he has brought back from hunting. Fox pups are born late May to early June and have the run of the elaborate tunnels and burrows that are a part of the den. If our fox is a vixen, and she is denning alone, life will be hard for all of them without the male's hunting skills. Perhaps we will find the answers with time, if our red fox returns. . . .

A CABIN RISES

More days of tree harvesting and stockpiling, and we now have a good supply of logs to work with. Were this to be a year-round cabin, we'd want to rebuild its foundation by digging out more of the tundra so that the cabin would be set deeper down into the earth. With tundra and snow banked high around its walls, warmth would be more easily contained. But for a summer camp the present base, which rests not quite a foot below ground level, is adequate. Our precious floorboards stay as they are.

The walls of the shelter are pulled down. New logs substituted for rotten ones. But every usable old log is salvaged and used again. Slowly, the cabin walls begin to rise.

Before being set into place, each wall log must be prepared to fit snugly with those joining it at the cabin corner. This joining, or mitering, is crucial to the solid construction of strong, permafrost-based walls that will stand a long time. With an ax, Sam notches out these joining sections near the ends of each log, on both top and bottom. The notches are approximately the size needed to fit exactly into the matching hollowed-out sections of the logs which will go above and below.

He seems to estimate these fittings with eye measurement and intuition. Whatever small miscalculation is in his initial assessment is corrected with saw, ax or hatchet when the log is laid in position on the wall. It's a little like playing with life-size Lincoln Logs except that here no two logs are exactly the same diameter, surface or shape. In building a log cabin, one becomes acutely aware that despite the way they look in the forest, trees are neither straight, smooth nor uniform. Ideally, the logs fit together on the walls well enough to avoid appreciable gaps or holes between them. But not our arctic trees. Even with Sam's skill in matching them up, narrow shafts of sunlight poke through spaces between our white spruce logs. How fortunate that the arctic tundra supplies the best of chinking materials!

Even so, our cabin rises!

The fox is back.

Surely he has a den in the creek bed. His small coyotelike tracks are everywhere. They parallel all our trails, and now are all around the camp, where he must have come often in the night, perhaps to hunt, or just to investigate. He seems to be here to stay.

Stepping outside today, we come face to face with him. He

has been digging among the slop scraps a few feet down the slope from the cabin. As we come out the door, he starts, stands poised as if ready to run, stares, seemingly listening to our voices as we speak softly to him. But he does not run away. After a minute, as if he has forgotten our presence, he turns back to his busy sniffing and digging.

Sam edges into the dogtrot and cuts some scraps from a chunk of caribou. He tosses one close to the fox, who jumps away as the small meat scrap hits the snow. Sniffing it out, the fox approaches the meat cautiously, then snaps it up in his teeth. He runs away a few feet as if he were making off with his find, then stops, drops the scrap and, pinning it down with his front paws, begins to eat. As he works his jaws around the hard-frozen meat, he looks as if he had a mouthful of taffy. Then the jaws stop grinding; one gulp, the meat is gone. He looks up at Sam, licks his chops, starts sniffing excitedly along the snow, edging slightly toward Sam.

Sam says, "O.K., Reynard—here, take it," and tosses another scrap, this time a little short of the fox to bring him closer to us. The fox stays where he is, staring first at Sam, then at the scrap on the snow, straining his head toward it, sniffing in its direction, but he does not come nearer. Then, edging slowly forward, still sniffing along the snow, he almost reaches the meat, then stops. He studies Sam's face, then, like a pup, stretches the front part of his lithe small body flat on the snow, and with his rear and bushy tail up in the air, extends his paws until they almost touch the meat. With head lowered onto his paws, ears and eyes alert, he remains where he is, waiting and staring up at Sam.

This fox is not after caribou meat. He's playing! Suddenly he makes a little leap up into the air, all four feet clearing the snow, and lands lightly to trot briskly away, head and bushy tail held high like a proud banner. But as suddenly he stops, leaps high again, and throws himself over onto his back, rolling back and forth and squirming and wiggling about in the snow. Jumping up onto his feet, he pokes his nose deep down into the snow, and holds it there for a second. Then, prancing up onto his hind feet, he tosses his head and flings the snow off his nose up into the air. Again and again he buries his nose in snow, leaps up, tosses the snow off, like a seal tossing a ball into the air. Abruptly the game ends. His easy playfulness switches instantly into alertness. His head is turned toward the distant creek bed, eyes fixed and probing. For a long moment he stands very still, staring, listening, ears and tail erect with tautness. Then, with a last look in our direction, and a final playful little leap, he starts off toward the creek at a brisk run.

SPRING

RAISE THE ROOF BEAMS HIGH

Like the days of autumn, these, too, go fast in work to be done.

Yet the line between "work" and "nonwork" is less clear to me here than at any other time or place! Is it "work" to spend these sparkling spring days outside, soaking in sun and beauty, and feeling the good feeling that comes from handling materials as natural and familiar as one's own hands?

As the shore cabin goes up, some of the jobs to be done look impossible at first. Hauling about the dead weight of twelve- to fourteen-foot-long wall logs calls for all one's strength, but they *can* be lifted and hoisted into position. Compared to the huge roof beams, which are longer, denser and infinitely heavier, the wall logs begin to feel like jackstraws. We have five of these giants to be hoisted up, and strategy is necessary to raise them—brawn alone will never do it!

In less isolated surroundings, these massive logs are lifted by hoists attached to tractors or pickup trucks. Here it has to be done with no power but our own. By rolling and jockeying the beam logs along the ground snow, we can get them into place parallel to the half-built side walls of the cabin. The snow that has been banked around the cabin base makes a natural ramp. We add to the banks to make them even higher. Then we can roll the beam up the ramp by inching it along, bracing it with a chock to keep it from rolling back down. At the top of the ramp, one beam end is rolled and maneuvered, raised high enough to brace it up on top of the back wall of logs. Then the other end is jockeyed and inched up onto the front wall. From there, the massive beam can be rolled on up along the slant of the two supporting walls and into position.

Once in place, these huge beams will take the full weight of not only the roof logs, but also the insulating tundra that will cover the roof logs.

At the end of the day, looking at our mighty roof beams all securely in place, I feel ready to take on any task that can or will come our way at Koviashuvik. What intrigues me about this enforced problem-solving in wilderness living is the sense of self-sufficiency it produces. I wonder about our increasingly complex world which forces us into greater and greater dependencies on specialists and institutions and machines. From where will we learn the kind of selfhood that comes of the necessary self-sufficiency—how else do we find our way through the rat mazes, survive in them, live despite their antilife qualities? As for me, I'd rather raise the roof beams of Koviashuvik!

THE BEE

Spring moves in on new sounds. To the hum of flies, shrinking snow cover and northern lights, shifting cabin and talking metal, a new song is added today. A very large bumblebee arrives. Flying in through the half-open door, she finds the window glass and hovers, buzzing, against the pane. I pick her up gently with the flour-sack dish towel and take her back outside. Her droning hum as she hovers near the sun-warmed cabin logs is a solitary one. There are no other bees to be heard.

A little while later, she finds her way into the cabin again. Back at the window, she soon tires of the glass and drops to the sill to crawl about, still buzzing. Exploring the wooden sill, she is suddenly quiet. Her needle-sharp feelers busily flail the air in front of her. Then she lifts to find the glass again, and her song begins once more.

Alone in the cabin except for the company of this newest spring arrival, I find that her presence dominates my awareness to the exclusion of everything else I should be doing and thinking about. There is some curious kinship here that cannot be explained, and I give in to the mystery, sit down close to the window and just watch her.

The fuzzy yellow of her striped body, bordering on a luminescent green, is strikingly beautiful like the bright new green of spring leaves that have fallen into a shallow stream aglow with sun gold. The rest of her is a glossy patent leather black.

Her arrival here seems premature, with deep snow still covering the tundra, and only the willow in bud.

But some primordial timetable that discounts depth of snow and scarceness of food has called her out of hibernation to begin the work of her species. The arctic summer is brief; her span of time short. She must begin the work of building a crude nest or "hive" in which she can lay her eggs. Honey and pollen must be stored in the waxen cells she will construct for the eggs to hatch and be nurtured in. By late summer, the eggs will have passed from egg to larvae to young bees to adult, some of whom will also be laying eggs. But in autumn she and her colony of several hundred daughters will die. Only one bumblebee will survive, an impregnated female who will hibernate through the long arctic winter to make her lonely reappearance in the sun-warmed days of late March or early April, to begin the cycle of life again.

ROOFING

Now that the roof beams are in place, Sam begins to lay on the roof logs. The cabin roof is pitched to allow for spring thaw runoff and to better support the weight of winter snows. Roof logs or poles are therefore laid in two sections, meeting end to end over the center ridge beam. All the roof poles will overhang the cabin wall by a few inches.

As I pass the poles up to Sam, he lays them side by side, rearranging them and switching them about for the tightest, snuggest fit. It is important to avoid spaces and gaps between the poles. I watch my giant tepee of skinned logs diminish to none as the roof begins to take shape. When all my peeled roof poles are in place, barely six feet of one side of open space is covered over! Suddenly the small cabin's roof looks enormous. Back to the sawhorse . . .

ANOTHER SPRINGTIME VISITOR

Returning from the day's work down at the shore, I stoop to enter the dogtrot and back out in a hurry at a barrage of high, sharp little barks. After a second, I stick my head back around the door and am greeted with another shrill chattering. I glimpse a glittering small eye, then a departing wave of a beautiful furry tail. In less than a minute, the visitor returns, scurrying into the dogtrot by way of a small tunnel he's dug under its side wall. Once inside, he sits up on his hind feet, turning his head in swift, short movements to look about, and then he sees me again. Another flick of bushy tail, a burst of scolding barks, are his automatic response. They're a prelude to his hasty reexit through the hole. This little rodent is not as bold as our winter ermine but his appearance means as much trouble. Fat, bright-eyed, wearing a beautiful thick winter coat and full fluffy tail that doubles his length, this is the first parky squirrel out of hibernation.

A glance inside the cabin and we know he's spent the day there. Things knocked off shelves, kitchen supplies turned upside down; he's scurried over every surface, investigated everything. These handsome little rodents can do as much damage to an arctic cabin as a porcupine or grizzly bear! Anything they can "squirrel away" will be carted off. Everything they can get into is left sprinkled with minuscule droppings. Digging inside through log chinking or burrowing in around floorboards, they leave a clear entryway for voles, shrews, ermine and more parky squirrels to follow.

When these ground squirrels emerge in April, by way of tunnels dug up through the deep snows from their underground winter dens, they are in their prime. Just out of hibernation, their meat is fat and tender, their pelts thick and soft. By early May they are breeding. Winter fat is soon lost and fine pelts scarred and scraggly from the many battles that take place at this time. Over the luxuriant easy months of the arctic summer, they again begin to store up fat for the winter, and the pelts again turn smooth and thick. In late September or early October, the parky squirrels enter their dens tunneled down under soft tundra and moss.

Although these small creatures are preyed on by eagles, hawks and all the larger mammals—wolves, grizzlies, wolverines, fox— the ultimate predator, man, finds them choicest eating in April and September. Arctic bush dwellers use both meat and skin of the parky squirrel at these times. Some of the most handsome Eskimo parkys are made from numerous squirrel skins, intricately patterned and fitted together into warm and durable winter parkys. In the Arctic, the name "parky" makes more sense than "ground" squirrel.

With this Koviashuvik squirrel out of hibernation, others will soon follow. Last autumn I saw a great number of burrow entrances in the tundra all around camp. We check the cabin chinking and corners, inside and out. After a short search, the hole is found where our visitor dug out the dry moss to squeeze between two logs and get inside. Rags and cardboard tamped into the hole will have to serve until we can get more moss and turf from under the snow. A trap is set in the dogtrot, somewhat reluctantly on my part, for aside from their general destructiveness, these are winsome, sprightly little animals to have around. They could be tamed to come close enough to feed from one's hand. But not enough tamed to teach them to leave our house alone. Domestication would be a disservice to us all!

Another good day's work at the shore.
Back up the mountain, we find our dinner in the dogtrot.

RECIPE FOR PARKY SQUIRREL

After skinning squirrel, stretch the pelt on a small flat board to be scraped later, or hang on line to dry. Eviscerate squirrel, removing and saving liver, heart and all sweet fat particles around internal organs. Quarter or prepare in pieces as for fried chicken. Dip the parts in lightly seasoned flour; brown in hot caribou fat. Add squirrel fat. Cover and simmer on damped-down Yukon stove for thirty or more minutes, testing for tenderness with fork. Serve with wild cranberries and hot sourdough flatbread.

RECIPE FOR HOT SOURDOUGH FLATBREAD
A Koviashuvik Invention

Mix together:

> ¾ cup whole wheat flour
> ⅓ cup sugar
> ½ teaspoon salt
> ¼ cup dry instant milk
> ½ teaspoon soda

Add:

> ¼ cup melted caribou fat mixed into
> 1 cup sourdough sponge

Stir all ingredients, but do not beat.

Spread batter thinly over a Blazo-tin cookie sheet, and cook in a medium-hot camp oven for about 35 minutes.

Variations: Add to the batter a handful of raisins, wild cranberries, nuts or anything else you have about—even chopped moose, or an egg if you have one.

LATE APRIL

A patch of bare earth in front of the cabin door!

Where the snow has been kept packed down all winter on paths around camp, the tundra begins to show through in spots.

On all the white mountain slopes, other dark patches slowly begin to appear around the bases of spruce trees, on outcroppings of rock most exposed to sun. Once the sun can reach these exposed places, the earth itself will begin to absorb heat and the warmth will spread. The great thaw will then begin *beneath* the snow as well as from above, where sunlight continues its work against winds still chilled and chilling from their long travels across thousands of miles of ice and snow.

There is the smell of damp warm earth at our threshold.

Four parky squirrels frisking about camp today, one trying to get into the cabin via the roof, another rattling around in the dogtrot, knocking over snowshoes and supplies, a third teaching a much smaller one how to climb up into the cache. The small one acts bored with its lessons, darts up the slope and almost onto my boot before either of us remembers to be spooked. Between traps and .22, Sam keeps the squirrel population controlled. But by the time these four pelts are scraped and hung from the ceiling lines for drying, we hear a digging at the cabin corner and a crash of falling cans in the dogtrot!

The winter snow has sunk six to eight inches since the return of the sun. The soft, even hum of its shrinking rings the camp for miles, competing with the hum of the flies on the sunny side of the cabin. A steady murmuring drones across the white cover until sunset, when silence descends, abruptly.

LATE APRIL—EARLY MAY

Reynard-Vixen is a regular visitor now. Once a day, sometimes twice, he comes into camp. While he may visit us for the easy "hunting" our meat scraps supply, it's obvious that he also comes because, in some mysterious way, he simply enjoys our companionship.

Once the ritual of the food offering is complete, the fox is ready for play. Prancing and leaping and rolling about in the snow is a preface to his game of tossing snow off his nose up into the air. There's a curious quality in this sociability. Though the frisky playfulness is reminiscent of the actions of all domesticated pups and cats, in no way has this wild fox become "tamed." These moments of mutuality, of companionship, are always on his terms; we respect those terms.

Today the fox is lured close enough to take a scrap of caribou from Sam's hand. This seems to me a kind of "victory"—proof of "trust" between "wild" creature and "tame."

But something is surrendered in this victory. As he very cautiously approaches and snatches away the meat scrap from Sam's hand, his stance and eyes reflect only an intense wariness—or is it fear? I become acutely aware that human language is merely human projection when I try to record my impressions of wild creatures. I have no words to do more than to describe, out of my own human, therefore circumscribed, vision, the complex and mysterious language of the other species.

Today our fox must be very hungry, hungry enough apparently to take the risk. Either our camp "hunting" does not provide enough real food for him or this is the time when winter fat dissolves away and the creatures thin down to ready for the heat of the long summer days of the Arctic. Our fox looks thin, very lean, these days. His flanks are hollow; his body gaunt. The beautiful red coat, now mottled tan and gray, is shedding, beginning to look worn and threadbare.

It is obvious from the animal's uneasiness that he prefers the scraps to be tossed to him at a safer distance. After the first scrap, we do not attempt to lure him close again. He mouths and gulps down a couple of morsels and sets about burying the rest. Then at once digs them up, carries them a few feet away, reburies them. This is his customary preliminary to play. When the play begins, it always takes place nearby, never more than ten feet from where we stand. He leaps, rolls in the snow, prances, tosses snow high in the air, lunges at clods of snow, digs furiously, and leaps again and again. Yet at the slightest move or sharp sound from us, the carefree romp stops, changing instantly into alertness. He turns watchful, wary, waiting. Reassured when we make no further move and continue to talk softly to him, he resumes his game.

We make no effort to enter into the play. To come too close seems to violate that invisible circle of safety each of us draws around himself. Never knowing the perimeter of the circle, one must enter it only by invitation.

We're not yet sure of our fox's sex. True to our own, Sam calls him Reynard; I call her Vixen. His Eskimo name, *tireganiersiut*, is much too cumbersome for so small and delicate a creature. Sam picks a shorter, easier one that rolls well off the tongue when addressing a fox: "Kia," an Eskimo term, meaning "Whose is it?"

We're now certain the fox den is in a bank of the creek bed, halfway between the cabin and the lake ice. But to avoid spooking Kia or his mate, if he has one, we have not gone near the area.

Red fox as well as the cross phase and the rarer silver or blue fox inhabit the Arctic. The white arctic fox, rarest of all, is very seldom seen in the mountains. His habitat is the region along the Arctic Ocean and north of the Brooks Range. All arctic fox are predators on the snowshoe hare, the ground squirrel, vole and ptarmigan. The fox population in any given year is therefore linked, at least in part, to the snowshoe hare cycle, which reaches a peak in population density approximately every ten years, and then diminishes sharply.

If Kia has a den in the territory, and this is denning season, he may continue to return here on his night hunting forays for some of the food scraps he has cached around camp. Thinking of Kia's wild heritage, I wonder if the frozen caribou scraps we offer him are satisfying to a hunter of live prey. If we could investigate his den, we would surely find a good-sized cache of more appropriate foods, for foxes, according to the old trappers, "stockpile" food. The wolves seem to be aware of this, for they often help themselves to the fox-den cache. And in the equitable ecological arrangement of the shared territory, fox feed on the carrion of wolf kills.

Though small and slight—probably no more than ten to fifteen pounds in weight—Kia holds his own in a territory of fellow predators. There are few predators on the fox, perhaps because he *is* lithe and lean, not good eating for any but the voracious wolverine, but primarily because he is keen and swift. Against the eagle, who may swoop down at him, he can defend himself well. With the wolves, grizzlies, moose and caribou he lives in relative harmony. Man, with traps and guns, is his greatest danger.

KIA

Sitting out in the early May sun scraping squirrel skins while Sam is up in the forest cutting trees, I catch a blur of motion down along the creek bed. Kia trots into clear view, heading up toward me.

We haven't seen him for three or four days, and for a moment I'm not sure that this is Kia. His fine auburn coat has lost all its redness now, darkened to a drab grayish tan and brown. The soft, long-furred pelt looks mangy, moth-eaten, as his coat thins to a cooler one for spring.

He stops suddenly, sniffs a spot in the snow, cocks his head to listen to whatever it is that he hears down there, suddenly rears, then pounces, digging furiously down, down, down, disappearing in a spray of white as he sends snow crystals flying in all directions. All I can see of him is his rump sticking up out of the snow. Then he emerges, his nose, head and chest covered with white. As he stares down into the hole, he looks perplexed or perhaps annoyed. He must be hunting a parky squirrel or a vole. Heard it moving around in its underground burrow beneath the snow and tundra. Or perhaps he saw it as it started to dart out of its den. The hunt is obviously not successful. Standing squarely on all fours and studying the snow around him, Kia moves his head in quick darting turns, cocking his ears to listen. The underground creature is either playing possum or has traveled on to some safer part of the underworld network of tunnels. After a pause, Kia looks up at me as if he had forgotten all about his prey, breaks into his characteristic trot, and continues on up the slope.

Only a few feet away, he stops, staring fixedly at me while I ask, in the soft, even tone we always use with Kia, how he is and how his day has been. He yawns, turns away indifferently and, passing within three feet of where I sit, trots over to the slops dump. On his way past the open dogtrot door, he pauses, looks intently inside, but does not go near. Nosing among the slop scraps, he seems to find little of merit.

As distant ringing blows of Sam's ax begin, Kia lifts his head, ears taut, stares up toward the forest above camp. But after a moment, he loses interest and returns to sniffing about among the slops. The continuing sound of the ax intrigues him once more. Curiosity and appetite vie with each other; curiosity wins. He trots off in the direction of the chopping sounds. Every thirty to forty feet, he stops, looks all around, his gaze pausing to rest on me before he looks up again toward the forest, listens, then moves on.

Sam is working upwind of the cabin and Kia must pick up his scent. Whatever it is that intrigues him—scent, sound, Sam's presence, or all of these—Kia is on his way to investigate. He crosses the white tundra to Sam's snowshoed trail. But he doesn't step onto the trail, or cross it. He trots along beside it, and when the trail curves and he *must* cross it, he leaps over it to the other side to continue on, leaving his own trail of small delicate prints beside the one of the man.

SPRING WILLOW BUD SALAD

Willow buds are best picked and eaten right off the branch. Between the two common species of willow which grow in the Arctic, the smooth-leafed variety is better eating than the fuzzy-leafed. The tender new leaves and buds of the former, though still minuscule in size, are faintly crunchy in texture, delicate in taste. Like the marrow of caribou, spring willow is indescribable. Eating spring willow is eating essence—the essence of new green life. That the new willow have no fragrance that we can detect is surprising. This may be because cold apparently lessens the sense of smell, or freezes more subtle and delicate aromas. Only pungent odors, like those of spruce smoke and moving game, strong penetrating odors which do not lose their strength as they travel on the wind, seem to survive cold to stir the human sense of smell.

But taste, and texture, and satisfaction of that third dimension for which we have no name but can only describe as an atavistic hunger—hunger shared by moose and ptarmigan—for something green and fresh and of spring sun, these are abundant in willow buds. All these dimensions are lessened in the "hothouse" willows we brought inside last week. By comparison to those picked freshly from along the trail, these forced new bud growths sprouted in the cabin are mealy and insipid in taste.

As the sun warmth opens more and more of the buds, enough can be gathered to make salads to eat with roasted moose or caribou steaks. Although best eaten as they come from the branch, a Koviashuvik salad dressing on willow buds is an interesting change.

RECIPE FOR WILLOW BUD SALAD DRESSING

Gather a small bowlful of willow buds, removing outer husks from buds.

Mix together equal parts of melted caribou fat and leftover pickle juice (wine, vinegar or lemon juice may be substituted if they are in the cache). Add salt and pepper to taste, a pinch of dill seed crushed between the fingers, and a teaspoonful of dehydrated onion. Let set for five minutes so onions will have time to be reconstituted. Mix again, pour over willow buds, and toss.

Willow buds may also be boiled in a little salted water and, when cooked, mixed with melted caribou fat. But much of the taste of spring is lost in cooking. Drink the broth or use in soups.

Some Eskimos also eat the scraped inner bark of willow, but these scrapings are too bitter for my taste.

Wherever Sam goes along the trails, Kia also seems to go. But not at the same time. When he follows along, he keeps well out of Sam's sight. Later, when we find his tracks running along parallel to every trail, it is clear that he keeps a close check on human travels.

We now know Kia is male. Wherever Sam stops on the trail, Kia stops, too. Beside each yellow human stain on the snow, there is a smaller fox one.

If Kia has a mate in his den, pups may be born at Koviashuvik by late this month, May, or early June. Although we know the approximate location of the den, there is no way to get close enough to it down in the creek bed to observe the family without spooking them.

We live with them on their terms. Some of the old-timers say fox can be easily tamed. But why should they be? It will be a lesser universe when all the wild has been domesticated. . . .

Thousands of flies surround the cabin.

If there is a dominant sound of spring moving in, it is now in the steady, unbroken hum of the flies, a single note of the same pitch, buzzed in unison, but counterpointed by the higher-pitched note of copulating pairs.

Plants begin to sprout as the snows melt. Cotton grass shoots emerge from the round, newly exposed tops of tussocks, at first as fuzzy black-headed new grass, quickly turning golden with spring pollen.

The creeks break free from their long frozen stillness and the new sound of rushing water merges with the humming of flies and sweet bird songs.

Before moving down to our "summer camp," we spruce up winter camp, spring-houseclean the winter cabin. Our winter water supply is now gone. The snow closest to the cabin vanished. But with spring thaw sending small rivulets everywhere down the mountainsides, we discover that what appears to be a new trickle only thirty feet from the cabin is actually a spring now bubbling out of the exposed tundra. Serendipity, to find this close-by source of water, saving us many quarter-mile treks down to the creek. With this abundant new supply of "running water," compulsion takes over: I launder everything in sight— all those things accumulated over the winter when laundry was not the easiest chore, everything now given a quick freshening in melted snow waters. Flour-sack dish towels, long johns, sweaters, jeans, wool socks—I soak and scrub everything wash-able in this unlimited supply of water and sun.

Spring cleaning in the Arctic differs little from that elsewhere in the world, a ritual of transition provoked by the new season's quickening of life, a sense of another new beginning—an excuse to sun and air and freshen and renew our den and ourselves. The cabin windows cleaned, polished, turning the hand-blown glass defects into bright glass jewels, with new appreciation of their very quality of glassness. The whipsawed spruce planks on the floor scrubbed and rescrubbed. Table and shelf surfaces, too. Cartons from under bunks unpacked, sorted, repacked. Bedding, caribou furs, sleeping bags sunned and aired. Odds and ends of winter's dogtrot accumulation rearranged into different ac-cumulations. Around the cabin, odds and ends rediscovered and rescued when revealed after the snow's disappearance. Books and supplies and clothes to go down the mountain to the summer camp packed on the sled, which is parked 250 feet down the trail, where snow still remains.

Winter mukluks exchanged for less heavy summer boot pacs, leather-topped boots with rubber bottoms. However, as the tundra even where free of snow is still frozen, and feet are soon numb with the cold, we switch back to winter mukluks.

Hands numb, too, from the washing done at the ice-water spring. But by late afternoon, the last of the sun-dried, wind-freshened laundry is taken down, sweet-smelling clean, and put away.

Everything left clean and neat, cabin and dogtrot doors carefully braced against predators, we at last set off with the overloaded sled. Now only a thin crust of snow is left on the mountain trail. In many places the trail is awash and rutted with fast channels of melt.

Near the bottom of the mountain trail, the torrents merge, increase in size and force, deepening ruts. The heavy sled balks, tilts and skids about, jamming onto exposed tussocks and boulders, and we lift and shove and haul the last sledload over the trail until, exhausted and panting, we finally pull up in front of the shore cabin door with our worldly goods.

Out in the middle of the lake ice, two caribou and a fawn stand and stare at our antics. We stare back, they spook, trot on to the north and out of sight.

The runoff which has turned the mountain trail behind the shore camp into a rushing stream now floods the low area just behind the cabin. Unless we keep the water moving, drain it off somehow, we soon will have a mosquito hatchery in our wilderness backyard. Sam spends the morning chopping down willow and alder brush along two channels dug to keep the melt moving out onto the lake ice.

At midday, all work stops while we watch a large herd of caribou traveling northward on the ice. These keep to the far side of the frozen lake, as if they sense man's presence on this side of the shore. The deer are strung out, moving steadily but in no visibly ordered fashion. The ice's snow cover has shrunk, turned to slush.

Most of the caribou are cows and yearlings, but even at this distance, I can spot a few handsome two-year-old bucks. My mind's eye imposes one of those butchering diagrams on a particularly fine fat buck. The caribou ribs, loin, rump, steaks become magically visible under the smooth tawny skin. I glance at Sam, wondering if his thoughts are as mine, wondering if he will turn and head for the rifle. But he seems totally caught up in watching the migration. This is the largest herd we've seen, numbering over two hundred. When Sam turns away, it is only to gather up the cut willows and alders in order to use them as a crude bridge to fill in a ford across our backyard bog of melt water.

An hour later, stragglers in the herd are still passing. They are even more spread out now. Some travel the far shore; a few are crossing the lake ice on a diagonal path. A small band of about a dozen seems to be heading directly toward us. But three-quarters of the way across the lake, they sight or scent us, stop, stare for a long minute or two, then the leader turns northward and they move on.

If they continue in that direction, they will come ashore just beyond Koviashuvik Point, north of the cabin.

Sam moves quickly to the cabin, comes out with the rifle. Without any words but "Keep low and out of sight," we set off at a near run through the thickets of willow and alder, toward Koviashuvik Point. Now I understand Sam's delay—rather, I understand the surface clues, if not that complex, mysterious set of instincts that guides the hunter in his hunt. But hurrying silently through the brush, bent low, avoiding hummocks, fallen limbs, the densest tangles, I sense that now the wind is right, the brush screen behind which we can get close enough to the deer is right, the odds are in the hunter's favor as they have not been up to now.

Sam sprints on ahead of me through the thick growth, parallel to the shore, moving swiftly but noiselessly. Then he makes an abrupt right turn across a patch of clearing and bounds over the tussocks for the shore. I cannot yet see the caribou through the willows, but I can see Sam ahead of me raise his rifle, brace himself against a spruce tree, sight carefully and fire. The crack of the rifle, an explosion in stillness. At my feet, a sudden noise as startling as the rifle shot. A ptarmigan hen clucks frantically from almost under me. We veer sharply around each other; hurry on in our opposite directions. When I rush up behind Sam, the open view of the lake ice reveals the caribou about three hundred yards offshore.

Like a tapestry of the hunt, nothing moves. All the caribou, unmoving as if frozen midaction, stare in our direction. The shot must have missed—no caribou is downed. I wonder why, if Sam missed his target, he doesn't fire again. When the caribou stand motionless this way, the hunter can drop several if he chooses.

Then one deer begins to run, hesitates, changes direction, stops to stare again, runs off. All the others seem suddenly to take the cue, begin to mill about, some heading back across the ice, others toward the north. The last to run moves only a few faltering feet, then drops to the ice.

A few of the others turn back—look as if puzzled at the fallen deer, then at the shore. We move out onto the ice. The caribou, circling, backing nervously, turn away from the wounded one, to run off in scattered directions.

We walk out to the deer. A prime young buck. The *coup de grace*. A reassuring feeling to know this fresh meat will get us through until the lake ice has thawed and we can fish for food. But as I look down at the fallen deer, alone on the vast ice plain except for the tiny figures of the other caribou of his band, now distant, resuming their journey northward, I glimpse for a finite second the fragile thread that connects us all, one to another.

As the dwellers of the Arctic say, we have "taken our spring caribou" today. But in the "taking" is a rediscovery of a truth that is seldom any longer revealed in the illusions of man-created environments. The eternal lesson of wilderness, learned and re-learned in this dailiness, is the reminder that, in survival, we must admit to our biological necessity as predator. In that admission, however, is an end to human arrogance, to any act of irresponsible predation. To live with the full knowledge that we are the ultimate predators might invest our responsibility with not profane, but sacred, meaning.

I hurry back for the big sled; we hoist the heavy carcass onto it. Sam pushes; I put the harness rope around my shoulders and pull.

At the cabin, we remove the deer's head with its still immature spring-furred antlers. Then the tongue, which at once goes into a pot to boil for supper. Hoisting the deer to hang from the spruce log rafter over the door of the dogtrot, we start the skinning.

The caribou skin is poorest quality in spring, at its thinnest, mangiest, already shedding and riddled with holes caused by warble flies. As we work we can feel the warble fly cysts as hard knots along the buck's back. In July and August, the large stinging flies burrow down through the hair of the caribou to lay their eggs. By spring, hundreds of larvae, up to an inch in length, are maturing in their sacs attached under the hide of the caribou. To make use of the hide, after skinning this buck each cyst must be cut open and the larvae removed along with the thick liquid contained in the sac.

These actively pulsating larvae must be torturous to the live caribou. Badly infested deer, crazed by the wriggling parasites from which they can find no respite, at times break into wild, racing, erratic flights as if trying to escape the apparently painful irritation.

Like the far north's human inhabitants, the caribou may find the winter, even though food is harder come by, the best season of the arctic year. For even when the warble larvae mature in late spring, bore through the caribou's hide and fall to the ground, relief is short-lived. The plague of the warble flies is at once replaced by another: tenacious, biting, irritating, swarming clouds of mosquitoes—the most ferocious beast among the wild creatures of the far north!

Though this new caribou hide is thin, shedding and marred with holes, we can make good use of it once it is scraped and the hair removed.

Until we have had time to build a cache at the shore cabin, we store most of our spring meat in Big Jim's old cache, sledding over to it the quarters of caribou wrapped well against the flies. The lake ice, now visible under its thin layer of slush snow, is pockmarked all the way from fresh caribou droppings.

Sam sleds the entrails and head out onto the ice and leaves them there for passing wolves, fox, wolverine and birds. The other predators will have their share.

First blizzards of winter, time for trailmaking

Grizzly bear hide

Kia

Billie and her biggest catch

An example of the food chain—
one trout caught, three fish
brought in

Young bull moose, his antlers covered with velvet in summer

Route to the tree-planting site on the top of the Range

Spring caribou

Picking new willow buds for
salad for lunch

Young cow moose

Ptarmigan cock in his spring
plumage, perched on woodpile

Gathering cloudberries on
Caribou Island

Building a chair for the cabin

Tern on her nest after driving
Sam away

Scraping weasel skin while Girl
watches

Hanging laundry to dry on
spruce-pole line

Cleaning grizzly skull for Fish
and Game Department, which
conducts studies on the Brooks
Range grizzly

Staking down and stretching a moose hide on the lake shore

Preparing for winter in August. The trout will be smoked. Billie is sorting berries.

Smoking the fish in the smoker made from scraps

Koviashuktok—" being fully and pleasantly in the present moment . . ."

Moose totem over the cabin door

Dark billowing stormclouds. Hail, sleet, rain, snow. Gusty winds. "Spring showers."

Filling the pollen baskets on the upper segments of her legs with willow catkin pollen, the bee remains in our territory.

She favors the blue hairband Sam borrows from me to keep his hair out of his eyes. Hovering over it, if Sam stands still, she lights on the blue ribbon and buzzes excitedly.

A spring richness in the bright new cones heavy on the topmost branches of the spruce trees.

Additional streams of melt now cascading down the mountain slopes, carrying brown tundra-colored water out over the lake ice at the shore, every rivulet at once detectable by the rusty stains it leaves along the shoreline. Sam's winter trails crisscrossing the lake ice stand out clearly against the slush snow surrounding them, the hard-packed snow of his snowshoe journeys raised like a bas-relief above the level of the ice.

A facility erected near camp. Behind a screen of three young spruce. Two spruce poles braced out over a Blazo can honey bucket. The roll of paper secure from nest-makers in an upsidedown coffee can. Incomparable view.

A pair of pintail ducks arrive, circle and land on brown melt water covering the edge of the lake ice. They may have arrived too soon. No open water. They peck here and there, stand and look curiously about, then the male, with a white throat and a dark head, squawks and takes wing. The female close behind, he heads for the north end of the lake, the major Koviashuvik nesting grounds, on tundra dotted by many thaw ponds from which the ice has already disappeared.

Spring comes to the Arctic as motion—a quickening of pace, of movement, a rapid succession of spring events. One day, quite unexpectedly, the first tiny star flowers have arrived beside the old mining cut—so delicate among winter's dry strawlike grasses and fireweed stalks and spring's fresh new green shoots pushing up from the velvet mosses of the tundra. Delicate and somehow exceedingly precious are these first small five-petaled white blossoms. Everywhere newness stirs, on every light spring-touched breeze: tips of new green growth on spruce branches, bud and leaf on willow, the first greening hints on alder, on tacamahac. Across the lake ice, a black ribbon along the shoreline is a narrow open lead of water. Breakup.

White-crowned sparrows, robins, more jays, a thrush, others I do not recognize—all are in a state of constant joyful motion around the camp. They seem to sing nonstop these fine clear days.

In between spring storms, days of brilliant blue sky with snow-white puffs of cloud scudding swiftly along.

A raging all-day sleet and hail storm turns into a gentle spring shower as warm air moves in from the south. Winter-spring interchange in an hour. A mighty roar comes suddenly from the source of the largest creek at Koviashuvik. Broken free of the last of the ice jam at its mouth, the creek waters rush out on the lake ice, hurling pebbles, rocks and slabs of ice before them. The rotting lake ice begins to crack open, break apart, pile up on itself, and a great dark circle of open water appears at the mouth of the creek.

The Anaktuvuk hunters say caribou are not so smart. If the hunter acts like a caribou, they say, and holds a caribou rack in front of him, he can often fool the caribou into letting him get close enough for a shot. After several days with no caribou passing through Koviashuvik, a band of five strolls across the lake ice, heading directly for our cabin.

We watch them, wondering at what point they will discover us and spook. I have been hoping to get some photographs of the arctic deer, but there seems to be no way to creep up on them without being sensed or sighted well in advance.

We are downwind of this band, and we have caribou antlers. Sam raises the hefty rack in front of his head and hunches low. I get behind Sam, my camera ready. We move out onto the ice toward the approaching caribou. Within a minute or so, the leader has seen us. He stops, we stop; he stares, we wait. He continues on toward us. The others follow. We all move slowly toward each other. The distance between us and the deer is now only a couple of hundred yards. The leader seems to have forgotten our existence. Then a large cow behind the leader stops. She stares intently in our direction; we continue moving slowly forward. I try to imitate the hind end of a caribou, staying right behind Sam, trying to walk hunched low in his same steps and pace. The cow is not fooled. She wheels about, moves out from the band a few feet, turns to stare again in our direction. Now the others stop, mill about uneasily, look toward us and then toward the cow. They now know something is wrong. The leader, suddenly alert, spooks, turns, runs a few feet, stops, again looks fixedly at the familiar rack on the strange creature approaching, then heads diagonally off at a rapid trot as the entire band scatters in five different directions away from us.

A great circle of caribou hair carpeting the tundra. The snow is gone. The wolves made a winter kill.

All rhythms quicken as spring takes over.

Everything is in motion, growing, heightening, appearing, greening—a time of "firsts." The first butterfly, small, gold-black, markings reminiscent of a monarch's, but very small in size. The first grayling swimming in the creek waters which merge with the first open water of the lake, a good place to feed as bits and morsels of insect larvae and debris from the runoff catch among the riffles. Arctic grayling, sleek and handsome, distinctive with its high dorsal fin, but too well fed by spring's bounty right now to pay attention to our fishing lure. The first mosquitoes—a new note in the spring song; the first arrivals seem exceptionally large in size. The first itching welts. We add a new scratching rhythm to spring.

It is good to be eating fresh foods again. Caribou liver, steaks, ribs—the fresh meat diet makes us feel healthy, strong. We find other spring bounty as well. At Koviashuvik Creek we gather more spruce poles to finish covering the cabin roof. While Sam takes his trees, I pick the last of the autumn's cranberries from the creek bank. These have already been well harvested by the birds who found them first. The ringing sound of the ax stops; the crack of the .22, a sudden whir of wings. We hike home with our bounty—a quart of berries, seven roof poles, a ptarmigan for supper.

Where do you get your water? friends ask in their letters. By now, I would have to ask in return, In what season, what month, under what conditions? We have been able to take pails of water from a fast-rushing creek to either side of our shore camp—but no longer. As the snow level diminishes, the rushing waters pick up tannin and surface soil from the thawing tundra and are now too brown and thick with ooze for clear drinking water. And the narrow open lead at the shore, churned constantly by the wind-shifted lake ice floe, offers no answer. Sam chops a hole in the lake ice, some thirty feet from shore, far enough out to escape the silt and debris of the shore melt. The lake ice is now only about three feet thick. The hole is like a well into which Sam lowers the bucket.

The mosquitoes increase. This crop is smaller in size but much more numerous; more persistent as well. They find their way into the cabin through the open door, and even around the edges of the tarp. Although the cabin turns close and hot, we must keep the door closed, day and night, against the swarms. After waking a dozen times in the night to buzzing songs and itching bites, we race now to finish the roof and get the cabin mosquito-proofed.

Overnight, it seems, the fireweed shoots are two inches high, the best size for eating. They taste less nutlike than the new willow, but they're equally good—crisp and fresh. We eat them right from the ground—and I add a handful to our lunch's willow salad.

The open lead in front of the cabin is several feet wider today. Sam wears his hip boots out to the edge of the ice floe, crawls up onto it to get water through the hole. Comes back, steps on a rotten spot and falls through. Fortunately, it's at a shallow place and he gets only a little of the ice water inside his hip boots.

Breakup dictates our chores. We had hoped to work more on the cabin roof today. Instead we ready the boat, which we will now need to cross the widening lead. While we are scraping and repainting the boat bottom, the sparrows and robins join us, investigating, calling and singing, like mischievous children trying to get attention. Around the corner of the cabin comes a deep squawking. A ptarmigan cock appears, his snow-white plumage now deep velvet brown on head, neck and the upper part of his body, making the lower half, which is still snow white, like a white skirt above white feathered boots.

The vivid red comb over each eye looks like a ruby set into the brownness. He eyes us, still clucking in the deep voice—but he is not afraid. From somewhere behind him, we hear the softer, higher cluck of his hen, but she stays hidden. He takes a short flight onto the woodpile and remains there, watching us, and answering each time we squawk back at him.

The sound of an airplane! Daryl's white Cessna flies over the mountains, buzzes the cabin, then circles to fly very low over the lake ice. It is obvious that he is checking it out with great care before he sets down this time. We can only watch helplessly; any signal we give might be misread. After several circling runs which barely skim the ice surface, he pulls up. We watch him head south, away from us. He has decided not to land. There go our summer supplies. We will very soon run out of staples— flour, sugar, coffee, tea, tobacco. Well, we shall make do with what the land provides or do without. We get back to work on the cabin roof.

Again the sound of a plane, Daryl's plane, returning. Has he changed his mind? decided to take the risk? But as he comes in low, heading directly toward the cabin, we know he plans to make a drop.

The plane zooms overhead so low I could reach up and touch the wheels were I on the cabin roof; it passes on and up, and a small white object thuds to the ground at my feet. Rushing to open the packet in case some signal back is required from us, we find the white object is an airsickness bag, weighted with a metal nut, bound with a strip of fluorescent red tape, and with a note printed on the paper. Daryl's message, which he must have been writing as he flew away to the south and back again, reads:

And it came to pass that in the days of the majestic sun the Man of Koviashuvik and the Woman of Wisdom were to be without fresh supplies until such time as the white eagle could transform its appearance to that of a swan and land on the unhindered waters of the big lake that was the home of the Man of Koviashuvik and the Woman of Wisdom. Those that look after these matters could do no more.

At 3:30 A.M., sunrise. The sun flaming suddenly over the mountain, funneling the bright rays into the cabin window, into our eyes, jolting us awake.

Once awake, we are up into the morning. The brighter the daylight of these nights, the less the habit of sleeping through the illusion of "night" seems to apply.

In less than a month we will reach the longest day of the year—the summer equinox, June 21. From that day on, we will begin to lose the light again, and by mid to late August, the night skies and stars will have returned. I love these dramatic changes of the arctic seasons. Each scene of the drama demands an adaptation. One must change with the changes, not resist them.

The birds sing as we stand outside and watch the bright day come in. The sun picks out the greening birch groves from the smooth brown slopes of mountains across the lake. A lovely serenity marks the time of dawn. But still, the lake ice covers the waters, and the spring breeze sweeping across the ice plain is chill.

We hurry back inside to have a cup of hot chocolate, to read, to talk, to watch from our spruce-pole bunk the sun rise, pass on and up beyond the confines of the window.

From across the lake, a strange yet vaguely familiar cry—a wistful sound, evoking memories of our first days here, just before freeze-up.

A loon has returned to Koviashuvik.

The last of the water birds to leave, suddenly gone one day, when the ice had covered almost all of the lake, now he has returned, with ice still covering most of the waters. He swims in an open lead. His laughing call, only one of many different songs, today sounding thin and somewhat lonely. If others have come with him to these northern waters, they do not answer. But his arrival is welcomed by us. No "visitor." He's here to find his mate and raise his fledglings. Koviashuvik also belongs to him.

Awake today to a golden morning filled with even more new cries and calls. Added to the peeps and honks, clucks, squawks, trills and melodies, this one, a shrill, high, single-noted "keer, keer." Circling and soaring out over the center of the lake ice, in which a wide lead has appeared since last night, are a half-dozen graceful white birds. Like an aerial acrobatic group, they seem to dance with the air, gliding downward to touch the water lightly with their beaks, then sweeping on upward to circle and glide again and again, calling to each other or perhaps to no one in particular but only out of sheer joy at effortless motion in space.

These are the arctic terns, the most beautiful birds of the summer north, the birds of light. These are the birds who, at Koviashuvik, have just ended their spring migration flight from Antarctica, traveling eleven thousand miles from the other end of the world to mate, to nest, to raise their young in the long days of light in the arctic summer. In late summer, when night begins to return, the terns will begin again their flight toward the light, taking their one or two near-grown chicks back with them to their wintering grounds in Antarctica.

As the melting ice moves steadily back from the shores each day, the first rings break the taut dark surface of the open water lead. A perfect circle, two and a half to three feet across, is suddenly there, without visible cause. Another appears twenty feet away; still another. In the last, a flash of silver breaks the surface. The rings speak at once to an instinct older than anything learned. The big arctic lake trout are up from the deeps where they have spent the long winter. They are coming up to the warmer surface waters near shore to feed on new insect larvae, small snails and tiny herring. Sam promptly climbs down from the roof where he is working, gets into his hip boots, takes his pole from its niche at the side of the cabin, casts out from shore into shallow water. Unlike the fishermen who decide to go fishing according to their own timetables, we follow those of the fish. Their signals today won't be ignored!

Three casts later, the line snaps taut; the pole arcs; the reel growls from the pressure on its line. The contest has begun. It may take one minute or fifteen. Or, if the trout is one of those doughty, wise old monarchs of the deeps, the contest may be over before it's begun. He will be the one who got away. If he is securely hooked, it will take time to bring in a large arctic lake trout. There is not any shortcut, no way to rush this process of subtle communication between the two ends of the line. There is no substitute, no sublimated or synthetic experience, to duplicate this relationship between the two creatures in this ancient contest, linked only by a thread that connects one to the other.

Not until the fish has been played out by the fisherman's skill and brought into shore to be freed of the hook does either know which is to be the victor.

This arctic trout weighs ten to twelve pounds, and is about two and a half feet long—one of the great ones, twenty or more years old. The rate of growth of these lake trout of the northern waters, like the growth of the far northern timber, is exceedingly slow.

Warm summer winds and rain from the south turn the remaining ice into a dark gray slush. The free-floating pan still fills the center of the lake, but all the shoreline is open water.

A tern flies around the point, following the shore lead, hunting. He stops midflight, ten or so feet above the water, hovering in the air in one place with rapid beating of wings—then dives, plummets like a falling stone, beak first. Hits the water, misses his prey—soars upward and on a few yards, stops, held fixed in air by the quivering wings, plunges head downward once more—misses—and again swoops up, flies on, his eye intent on the water below.

Something below catches his eye. He brakes midair, as if an invisible lasso has jerked him to a stop, half turns, twists, hovers, dives once again.

What he is diving for we cannot see. There are small fishlike creatures, sculpin, perhaps baby herring, in the shallow, warm shore waters. The tern's luck is not good today. He sweeps on following the shoreline, in the exquisite hunting flight pattern, his streamlined body graceful, light, the perfect design for maneuvering in air. Though the tern's sleek feathers glisten white in the morning sun, on closer view they are a pale and delicate gray. The sharp-pointed bill, a fiery red; on the finely modeled head, a sleek black cap.

A second tern rounds the point from the north—and a third. All are hunting now. The last to appear has better luck. His dives hit the water with a resounding thud. He soars up from the last plunge a little more slowly this time. His beak part open, fixed on some edible thing he has secured, he wheels round and heads back, the near-translucent wings propelling him swiftly northward. His bounty may be for himself or it may be a courtship gift to offer to a potential mate. For though the

terns now congregate, sun, bathe and roost in social community, already the preparation for choosing a mate from the
flock begins.

So far the legend that the fiercest animal in the Arctic is the
mosquito remains folklore. But perhaps our tolerance increases
as the hordes increase. Certainly they are plentiful. Repellent
in liberal amounts keeps them at bay during the day. At night,
when the bright sun sets behind the peaks at around eleven-
thirty, the air cools and the mosquitoes, drawn by the warmth
of the cabin, find their way in around the still-open places
along the roof logs. And since we are even warmer than the
cabin, they soon find their way to us. Then not even repellent
helps. There is nothing to do but swear, slap and suffer!

Sam makes a screen door, a miracle of construction of sluice-
box boards, patched ancient screening, spruce poles, moosehide hinges—and all trimmed round with overlapping strips
of caribou fur to compensate for the strange fit around the
crudely adzed doorjamb. Soon we will be mosquito-proofed.

The roof logs are all on! The last one fitted into place. Flattened cardboard cartons laid over the logs keep the turf from
falling through between them and down into the cabin.

Next, we take two-by-three-foot sections of tundra. These
slabs of natural roofing material must be gathered from many
different sites since the recovery time required for tundra
regrowth is many years. Tractor tracks across tundra still remain
as swampy barren strips twenty-five years later. The slighter
the scar the faster it will heal.

Carrying the cool, moist rectangles of moss, plants, grasses
over the shoulder, we bring them in from scattered areas, some
far from camp. Sam gets halfway up the ladder and I hoist a
slab of the heavy turf up to him. He lays the turf slab over
roof poles, fitting and overlapping each to provide tight, protective cover.

We will have the best insulation available anywhere against arctic rain, snow and cold. With its reddish cranberry plants and blossoming blueberry plants, my roof looks like a bright penthouse garden.

Hot, earthy work, though, in the blazing spring sun. After a few hours of turfing, we decide we need to go fishing. The rings in the water are calling.

Only a few more sessions of roofing and then some chinking in and around the corner roof logs, and we will be absolutely mosquito-proofed in at least one small refuge at Koviashuvik!

SUMMER

June 12, and the lake is free of the last of its winter cover. It looks bigger, bluer—more lovely than I remembered.

The greening of the brown mountain slopes and tundra meadows continues. Leafing birch and new bottle-brush grass are vivid slashes of yellow-green down the mountainsides, where fast-running creeklets of melt provide the most moisture.

In this telescoped season of light, the rate of budding, leafing, growing, change becomes intense, frenetic. The spruce already show a half foot of new growth at their tips. Thick clusters of chestnut-brown spruce cones ring the upper branches of even the smallest trees. The sparrows feed on the spruce seeds, clinging to the cones upside down to pry out the kernels.

If birds and squirrels enjoy these fruits, why shouldn't we be able to eat them? Someday I must grind some kernels and see what kind of flour they may provide.

Two days after the ice has gone, a familiar buzz over the mountains and Daryl's plane, now converted, with floats, into the species "White Swan," circles and lands, barely ruffling the lake waters as it taxis in to shore.

He has brought our supplies, and a moose steak from his own larder. We, in turn, have a fine fresh-caught lake trout to send back with him.

We sit in the sun over coffee, cookies, talk—and catch up on the latest news of our neighbors in the Koyukuk. In the mail, the most important communication is that our friends Jan and Don will arrive at the end of this month for a visit. Exciting news, but the source of some unexpected, vaguely formed questions and doubts in my own mind. Though city people, our friends are "nature lovers," a shorthand term, I suddenly realize, for a thousand different varieties of possible relationships to the world of nature, from those who enjoy strolling down the city street where boxed trees are set along the sidewalk to mountain climbers. But the nature of wilderness? Will our friends merely tolerate—or will they truly enjoy—our world? Will they really be able to move into Koviashuvik as it is, or will they try to remake Koviashuvik to fit themselves? Will others being here in our dailiness change our own relationship to Koviashuvik? Two more persons here will double our population, and doubling a population overnight anywhere is a radical shift in the ecology.

Rereading their letter, I suddenly realize that all our exchange of correspondence about their impending visit has not represented a reality for me. It has been an abstraction on paper. In a way, that insight pleases me. It means that I have moved a step closer to the reality of Koviashuvik. With their arrival Koviashuvik will change. I wonder how?

Black clouds building all morning, narrowing the horizons, curtaining the mountains—all the world gray and heavy with moisture, centered over the lake. Winds begin, then the rains, building within minutes from fine sprinkles of scattered drops to heavy drumming, cascades beating down on lake and tundra, and quickly intensifying in sound and wildness as rain turns to pellets of hard-driving hail, covering the land with a solid coat of white ice stones.

Sound and wind and hail stop as suddenly as they began. Left behind, a water landscape, like a delicate blue-tinted Japanese print, of low-hanging wisps of clouds caught and anchored to mountainsides, the storm like a living thing, wrapped in a dark rippling cloak, moving on, northward, pushed along by the golden sunlight streaming in from the south.

The storm past, we go out into a freshly cleansed world, using the boat to round the point into the next bay to fish for the great northern pike.

Fishing in natural places where man has not yet tampered with fish species or their habitat is pure adventure. Fishing for the feisty great northern pike, which in our arctic inland waters often reaches a length of more than three feet, has drama, suspense, humor, challenge. Sam says the pike is the dumbest fish he knows, with not even a teaspoonful of brains, but that this also may be why he has survived, unchanged for eons. Dishu wrinkles her nose in distaste at talk of eating pike, although many northerners eat the white flaky flesh, as we do, with great pleasure. A carnivore, the pike has a ruthless appetite for baby birds and ducks—perhaps this is what troubles Dishu.

We take the boat close into the protected bay where the pike inhabit the murky, warm waters among the sedge grasses growing along the shore. Sediment from rotting underwater vegetation, algae-covered "moose" moss and fallen spruce cloud the clear waters when an oar touches the lake bottom or a sluggish pike stirs. Casting for pike must be exact. The lure must land just short of the edge of grasses but miss catching onto them. Until I get the feel of casting, I spend most of my time hauling the boat into the grasses to release my lure, and rowing offshore again.

When one of Sam's casts finally catches the attention of a thirty-eight-inch pike, our first awareness of it is in the torpedo-like wake that shoots from the grasses to race after the lure. The charge is so sudden and so exactly honed in on the lure that one expects immediate success. But anything may distract the fast-moving fish from his chase—he can be spooked off when the boat looms in his attention or by the shadow of a bird flying over the water, by a passing water beetle, by a dip of the oar. And once spooked, he seems to forget completely that he was after something. Only if the lure is cast to land again directly in front of his eyes will he bother to pick up the chase.

Once caught, the great northern pike is a furious fighter, thrashing and struggling without letup, and putting the amateur or unwary fisherman into danger of being stabbed or bitten by those long, needle-sharp teeth before the fish is in the bottom of the boat and safely stunned. Sam lands the big fellow, and I raise my boots up out of the way to avoid those teeth!

Several smaller pike streak after my lure, only to become indifferent when I slow down the reeling in or speed it up too much. But at last, one takes the lure, a younger pike than the thirty-eight-incher, but still a good five-pounder.

Once the two fish are in the boat, I see another reason for Dishu's distaste. Unlike the silvery trout, the pike is not so handsome a creature. Its powerfully muscled body is sleek, graceful, but the flattish head tapers into a long, snoutish mouth, with its ring of efficient teeth.

Nevertheless, lunch is a gourmet meal, with pike steaks dipped in seasoned flour and fried a golden brown in caribou fat, eaten with willow leaf salad. The pike flesh is sweet and flaky, not even as strong in taste as the delicate flavor of the trout. Only the task of removing the large, numerous "Y" bones keeps one from feeling the glutton!

Today, in the moist dark places far back under the largest willow where the birds do not go, I find the last of autumn's crop of cranberries.

And still the birds come in from the south!

The sky over the lake filled with a live white cloud, soaring, dipping, diving, circling, bathing, swimming—a great chorus that trills, cries, calls, chirps, sings. Too many to count today. A guess of around seventy-five terns, fifty gulls, eight parasitic jaegers—these latter, fortunately, few, for they are the most blatantly predacious of the bird population, living by stealing the eggs from the nests of terns and gulls, attacking the terns in midair to steal the food from their beaks.

There are several hundred of the tiny phalaropes here today. An exclusive colony, forming their own separate cloud, river, wave— apart from the aerobatics of the large birds. Yellowlegs and peeps, too, are here, but these avoid the milling flights to hug the shore while adding their voices to the melodious cacophony.

The loons, several pairs, seemingly oblivious of the whirling activity, also have their own community, which is busily diving, drifting, laughing, calling, racing over the water.

Twenty geese fly in neat formation across the lake, by-passing the crowded sky but honking excitedly. Ducks, mergansers, pintails, others I do not know crisscross the air, announcing their presences, too.

Three ravens watch the action from the tops of three spruce, then fly down to strut along the shore, as if patrolling the beach, and add their own raucous voices. The white-crowned sparrows and robins sing nonstop, more sweetly than ever, as if in response to the fantastic sounds of the world today.

The winter melt runoff complete, the moist tundra begins to dry except for the perennial thaw ponds and bogs, which seem never to dry up. Warm rains fall from great billows of dark clouds that race in from over the mountains to meet above Koviashuvik. Heavy showers fall on us, while the sun shines brightly in brilliant blue sky to the south and north.

The showers pass quickly, blazing sun emerges to steam the tundra. In this close, tropiclike moist heat, the legendary arctic mosquitoes really arrive. In clouds, waves, swarms. When they descend over the land of the arctic tundra, all other creatures lose stature; the mighty bull moose, the fearsome grizzly, and even competent, creative, aggressive, destructive man is relegated to a subservient role. The mosquito, the most vicious creature to be found in the Arctic, now dominates the world.

Humans, dogs, caribou are harassed beyond belief by this tiny, tenacious, ruthless female. Though both male and female have the famed beak or proboscis, only the female has within it that crucial apparatus of six tiny needle-fine and sharp lancets that bite into flesh, not to let go until she is gorged with your blood.

In these early summer days, unfiltered northern sun beats unrelentingly down and not a breath of air stirs. Or if a feeble wind does rustle through willow and spruce, it only seems to excite the mosquitoes even more, for on these days when body heat increases and there is no wind to lower the temperature or to dry perspiration, we become beacons for every mosquito around. No effective way exists to cope with this plague. There is no protection against the demons but a blind, internal determination to survive. Even atheists pray for wind.

We stay bathed in repellent. Every exposed patch of skin is covered with it—hands, face, and after a week or so of the experience, even the rims of ears, fingertips, eyebrows and hair. Clothes, too, are constantly sprayed, for shirts and jeans offer little protection from the arctic mosquito. In spite of temperatures that are up in the high eighties, the long johns go back on again.

Today a lightweight parky is added. I now understand why in Anaktuvuk, in midsummer, many of the villagers continue to wear fur-trimmed parkas. My own three thick layers of clothing finally help put a stop to the ruthless stingers. But I soon find out that the added clothing's boost in body heat attracts even denser swarms, which thickly cover our clothes, hover incessantly and noisily against our repellent-and-sweat-drenched faces, dance excitedly on our warm breath. Despite the clothing and repellent, many land, bite; others are breathed in.

Few caribou, moose, bear or men travel at the lower elevations during these days. The high slopes and ridges, where there is some wind to stir the air, are favored routes. Best, now, to avoid the lowlands, marshes, creek beds and willow thickets, where nothing stirs but clouds of the biting insects.

If one is forced to make a siwash camp in the low-lying spots in these times, various protective devices are tried, but none very successfully. Gloves and head nets offer a little extra protection, but they add to one's own sweaty heat; the nets also cut down on visibility. Smudge fires may rout the mosquitoes somewhat, but the side effects, mainly smoke suffocation, are as obnoxious. If one is packing a mosquito-proof tent to sleep in during the day, the cooler and bright nights are often a better time to hike.

Before modern insect repellents, the early arctic summer

travelers, in addition to wearing their thickest wool underwear under heavy shirts and pants, sometimes resorted to a home-made repellent concocted of a few drops of creolin mixed into moose tallow or lard. If one could tolerate the smell, the remedy apparently helped to some extent. Smearing it on dogs was also commonplace, but less effective, for they would soon lick off the grease. Dogs sometimes went mad or died from the bites of thousands of the arctic mosquitoes. Caribou have been observed in mosquito season to run themselves to exhaustion trying to escape the swarms. Bands will sometimes take to the water just for respite.

As for humans in these days of plague, they try heavy, protective clothing, frequent, plentiful applications of repellent and a certain invincible patience or transcendence, punctuated by uncontrollable eruptions of symbolic violent acts. These otherwise senseless gestures are useful only for their therapeutic value: like striking out at a suffocating swarm with one's shovel; or giving vent to nonstop barrages of epithets so fierce as to be tolerable only to someone else in the same predicament; or counting, with maniacal glee, the number of critters murdered by slapping an open palm against any part of one's anatomy. A heady satisfaction, this act of mayhem: I've counted twenty-one mosquitoes done in at one such blow.

Small comfort there is in the more rational acknowledgment that without these tiny pests, the ecological food chain of the Arctic might collapse. As each fresh hatch of mosquitoes become breeding adults, their eggs are deposited on the surfaces of the abundant arctic waters—lake shallows and still bays, thaw ponds, the quiet crannies and sloughs of streams and creeks, among the swampy tussocks. Quickly hatching to larvae that feed voraciously on algae, bacteria, infinitesimal aquatic creatures, they in turn are fed on by birds, the grayling, pike, trout —and we, in turn, feed on the fish. Processed mosquito. The billions of larvae that escape being eaten evolve into a pupa stage from which they rapidly emerge as winged, six-legged, beaked, mating, blood-feeding, egg-laying propagators of the legend that is no legend.

On these early summer days when the sun blazes down as on a desert, and the wind seems to stir only on the far mountain peaks, we have no choice but to become stoics. And so we adapt. Live with the demonic creatures in some semblance of tolerance, if never harmony.

Meanwhile, escaping periodically into the mosquito-proofed cabin is a nerve and carcass saver. This season of the arctic mosquito . . . this too shall pass, we mutter, from the refuge behind the crude screen door.

June 21, the longest day of the year.

The earth tilts back toward winter, and summer only just begun. From today on, we begin to lose the light, a little more each day. At midnight the sun seems to ride along the rim of the mountains, not to disappear from view until Truth, the tallest peak at Koviashuvik, passes briefly over its face.

As we stand outside, watching the constant play of salmon-pink and gray clouds shifting in the dawn-colored sky, the ptarmigan cock struts out from the willows, clucking softly, eyes us curiously but matter-of-factly, flies up onto the rooftop on the moose-antler totem above our heads, and with comfortable little bassy mutterings, settles down to roost.

We have barely gotten to sleep again when a roaring crescendo of sound jolts us awake. It sounds like a tidal wave rushing toward the cabin. Dashing outside, we see a huge cow moose racing furiously toward us in the shallow waters. She passes right in front of us, heading south. At her heels is her almost newborn calf. Both are running as if for their lives.

Two hundred feet down the shore, they stop and look back, but not at us. The cow is staring fixedly at some point beyond us back along the shore.

Whatever she sees or senses that so threatens as to make the moose oblivious of the danger we and our camp would otherwise represent sets the cow in desperate flight again, with the baby still following right on her heels. His thin, spindly legs seem to fly through the air in the spray from his mother's pounding hoofs. Even after they have rounded the next point, we can hear the churning, splashing sounds of their racing feet.

Only wolves could have spooked the mother to such flight. We scan the tundra and shore for signs of motion. All is still. But there is a mood of danger in the night.

This morning, fresh tracks of three large running wolves on the shore in front of the cabin. They, too, were headed south.

A golden eagle passes over, circles back to fly low over camp, flies on to catch a thermal and rises, soaring higher and higher until our eyes can no longer follow the infinite speck on the edge of the cloud.

The single loon who lives in our bay has a pair of visitors this morning. They swim into the bay to join him in diving, drifting, calling, racing and running over the water.

While I do the washing at the lakeshore, and Sam sharpens his saws, we sing. The three loons come closer, swimming over to the waters in front of the cabin, where they remain, drifting, listening. Then one pushes his head forward, the neck stretched out, and calls the three-noted call. Sam, putting his hands to his mouth, blows a whistling similar call, answering. All the loons reply excitedly. Sam calls again and the loons swim closer, answering. Another call; they come still closer. Like a Pied Piper, Sam pipes them in until they are only a few feet from shore.

Four terns come shrieking around the point, scolding among themselves. And the loons turn bottoms up, one, two, three, and dive. They come up a long minute later, far out in the lake. The terns have sailed on by, their scolding cries receding into silence. But the conversation with the loons is over, the moment past. They and we go on about our business.

Sam calls me over into the willows near the cabin, with a warning to stand very still. I obey without question. Turning my head very slowly, I look all around, find nothing unusual. I listen hard, trying to hear beyond the slight rustle of gentle wind stirring willows, the familiar bird calls. And then I hear the tiny peepings of newborn chicks.

Mixing in with the chicks' voices come soft reassuring clucks of ptarmigan hen and answering bassy squawks of the cock. Moving slowly and easily toward the sounds, I can still see nothing but the browns and beiges and greens of tundra. Then, motion. A tiny chick rounds a tussock three feet away. Then another—and more, all scampering by as if we are not there. Eight—ten—fourteen chicks in the clutch, each downy brown-beige baby scurrying along, peeping merrily. The hen follows the last chick. She freezes at the sight of us, begins to draw herself in, sinking closer to the ground, alert, poised, tense. Her cluck is louder, higher, sharper—a warning, a signal? The cock rushes in from the other direction, hunches to a low, menacing crouch, hisses fiercely. The hen then scurries after the chicks, turning once to hiss at us before she runs on to circle about the clutch as if trying to herd them into a tight, safe little corral.

I take a step closer for a better look at the babies. The cock leaps between them and me as if to cut me off. His neck drawn back sharply, his head flat against his body, he looks at me warningly, hissing rapidly. One chick darts from its mother's side and heads for Sam, running right across the toe of his boot. Sam lifts the chick and holds it out for me to see. The hen and cock at once run at Sam, flying up as if to strike him, hissing furiously. Sam puts the baby back down on the tundra and off it runs. The hen turns and hurries along behind it, as if to shoo it out of harm's way. The cock in his low, threatening stance faces Sam and waits, head flat against his body, raised beak opened wide, combs erect and rigid.

We move gently off, stopping only when the willow screen separates us from the ptarmigan family, then listen once more. The thicket is again filled with merry peepings, the hen's quiet reassurances and the cock's bassy answers.

The last week of June. All the birds seem to be nesting. Across the lake at Billy Glen Creek bay, we find a tern's nest—an indentation in the sand, six feet back from the water's edge, roughly lined with bits of dry grass. The two eggs are dark olive drab with blackish-gray mottlings. Each is as large as the circle formed by Sam's thumb and forefinger touching tips.

We have barely had time to look at the nest when the mother tern swoops in from over the tops of the spruce in a screeching attack. In a frenzy of fluttering wings and open-beaked cries, she dives again and again at Sam's head. I rush back to the boat and, expecting her mate to respond to her cries and to join the assault at any minute, upend an oar in the air to divert his dives from my head. But no mate appears. The single tern is on her own, and she does not let up. The fierceness of her attack on Sam may in fact be because she is alone in trying to protect the nest.

Attempting to photograph the nest, Sam throws his parky over his head, ignoring the tern's attack. I can hear the sharp crack of her beak striking cloth in each plummeting dive. Sam finishes filming, and talks softly, reassuringly, to the bird. But nothing will divert her. He returns to the boat. She follows him, still diving and "screeing," until we have pushed well off from shore. Finally, circling back to her nest, she hovers above it, suspended in space, wings fluttering, before dropping slowly, wings outstretched; lifting her wings skyward, she then folds them close as she settles on the nest.

As we are leaving the bay, three other terns race in from the north, soar over the nesting area, calling excitedly. But she does not answer them or leave the nest. The others do not follow the boat. They light on the spruce trees near the nest, to silently watch us row away.

Around the bend, we head once more for shore. No terns greet us with warning cries. But a small agitated "peep," a rock sandpiper, darts out from behind a low willow on the sand beach and runs up onto the tundra, out of view.

Under the willow in a small depression in the gravelly sand is her nest. This, too, is lined with dry grass. In the nest are four buff–olive-green eggs with black mottlings. These are half the size of the tern eggs, but surprisingly large for so small a bird.

The nesting grounds to the north of the lake are alive with birds—gulls, ducks, terns, sandpipers, and a large pair of white birds, perhaps snow geese or swans.

The few jaegers who were here earlier seem to have moved on. Whether it is because other predators have moved in or the jaegers were too few to win their way against so many terns and gulls, I do not know. Perhaps their stay was only a rest stop on their migration northward. But all seem to be gone now.

A strange new bird rounds the point, follows the shoreline and heads into camp, winging in at a fantastic speed and flying right toward me, as if I were his target. Speckled gray and white, this stranger has an exceedingly large head for the size of his body, and a large, wide bill. He continues coming straight at me until only a few feet away; just as I duck back, he veers sharply to race on along the shore, making a loud, trilling, one-noted sound.

This is the first kingfisher we've seen at Koviashuvik. Here to stay, or just passing through?

Alone at Koviashuvik. But no feeling of "aloneness" without Sam here. Picked up yesterday by Daryl, he has gone to Fairbanks on business. I had wondered how I would feel in this great wilderness, without another human around. If anything differs in being the only human critter about, it is that the sense of being *in* the universe intensifies, sharpens. All those small chores I promised myself I would catch up on in Sam's absence are still waiting—the books unread, letters unwritten, work undone. I find myself even more preoccupied with *this* world than usual. Much of my time goes in looking, observing, sky-watching. The drama of summer mountain storms is all-absorbing—the constant shift of clouds, of light and shadow; dark falling curtains of rain to the south, turning the mountains to deep blue silhouettes; the brilliant arctic blue sky and billowy white clouds to the north, sun goldening the new green of mountain slopes. The sunlit lake, reflecting back twin images of the universe at play.

Awakening to the bright daylight of middle-of-the-night, I

watch the sky again, now flaming with red and orange sunset-sunrise, and like a flame, ever in motion, moving, alive.

This time alone races—different without Sam, but never lonely. Meals are minor celebrations shared with a book instead of major ones shared with mate and partner. The most noticeable difference is in traveling around the territory without Sam. Leaving camp for a hike, I carry the rifle. But on the trails, now thickly overgrown with willow and alder, blocking visibility ahead and around curves and turns, I also carry a "bear protector." I made this noisy apparatus from two empty coffee cans tied together with a two-foot string. Grizzly sows roam with their cubs this time of year. I've seen no sign of bear in the immediate vicinity, except, perhaps, for the fresh digging for roots done by some creature along the trail, the tracks too blurred by the rain for me to decipher them. If bear are about, this metal clacker should give them fair warning. Unfortunately, it's an awful sound for me to have to listen to; it scares off all other game as well. Coming down the trail with some supplies I needed from the upper camp, I find fresh wolf tracks traveling next to those I made going up. But my noisy approach has surely spooked the curious wolf miles away by now. The jays and robins, though, do not fly away at my bear-scare racket. They only scold furiously at the clanking apparition until I pass.

Sam returns to a joyful welcome and bears unexpected gifts!

Among his treasures, a new camp stove to replace the wired-together ancient Yukon stove; a large bag of store-bought cookies; two heads of lettuce and a box of petunia seedlings sent by our gardening friends in Fairbanks. An even greater surprise, when I row out to Daryl's float plane to get Sam. He hands down a wriggling handful of warmth, about which he quips, "Brought you some fresh meat, too." The warm, baby-fat-soft quivering creature he hands me is a two-month-old beagle pup. I lift her to rub my cheek against her smooth warmth, and her little pointed tail vibrates like an arrow quivering in its mark, her pink tongue dabs at my face.

When we set her down ashore, she is off like a firecracker, racing about camp, sniffing, exploring, looking, licking, investigating. Perpetual motion, and every motion, every gesture, as with all cubs, adorable and winning. We wonder what to call her. Observe she is a wild girl indeed, to let loose in the arctic wilderness. "Wild Girl" gets no response from her. But "Girl!" seems to get her attention.

We have often talked about having at least one dog at Koviashuvik, but the outcome has always been left in ambivalence. Some in the far north say it is good to have a dog because you will always be forewarned of a bear on the trail. Others swear that a dog can be more of a danger than the bear because a dog may well provoke an encounter which might otherwise be avoided. We remember reading somewhere that the beagle's heritage includes the role of "bear dog," as beagles were used in Europe in olden times to flush and hold a bear at bay for bear hunters. However, this round fat ball of pup does not look much like a budding warrior.

My image, when we've spoken of a dog at Koviashuvik, was always of a large, strong, intelligent, thick-furred dog of the north, the malamute—perhaps a malamute sired by a wolf, as some of the Anaktuvuk dogs had been fathered by wolves who came into camp when a malamute bitch was in heat. Fantasy adjusts itself, with some effort, to this tiny, sleek-haired, frolicsome beagle pup. No husky arctic dog, she at least may come to resemble her ancestors and eventually become a mighty hunter. Looking for a "sign" to prove my theory, I try calling her "Diana," but she acts deaf. Only "Girl!" can make her stop long enough for an inquiring glance before she is on her investigative, sniffing romp through camp again.

Her coat is so smooth and thin that her fat belly glows pink through it. Come winter, I have visions of having to make miniature parky and mukluks for this thin-coated little creature. But friends in Fairbanks have sent her to us; one look and Sam couldn't refuse her; neither can I. Now we are three, at Koviashuvik, for better or for worse.

Koviashuvik ecology is changed radically by one small pup entering the scene. I am never unaware of her presence. While she may someday develop into that "mighty hunter," at present she is wolf, wolverine, bear, eagle bait. I'm not sure she would have the good sense to avoid a porcupine, either. We take her everywhere with us, even into the boat, where she cries until I allow her to climb into my lap. Caught in this dilemma of my need to treat her as a pet and my knowledge that she will need strong discipline even to survive here in the wilderness, I think of the dogs at Anaktuvuk, who were given extremely matter-of-fact, no-nonsense treatment, including kicks and cuffs when they got unruly or howled too long or just on general principle. Little attention was given the pups except by the children. No affection was expressed to the adult dogs, who seemed to be looked upon only as work dogs, never as pets.

The jays are fascinated with the pup. She "woofs" at them; they scold back. But neither seems to view the other as a serious threat. The ravens who often land on the beach just below the cabin can't quite compute what kind of critter has been added to their world. They swoop low over the pup, squawking, looking. Girl waits until they land, then charges them with fierce barks until they fly up into the safety of the spruce trees.

To preserve the last of the caribou, we turn it into jerky. Sam builds a smoker over a fire pit dug into the tundra near camp. A spruce "tripod" or tepee is covered round with canvas scraps and flattened carton cardboard. In this raggle-taggle but efficient enclosure, thin strips of lightly salted caribou meat are hung from spruce branch crossbars. The meat is then smoked all day over a slow-smoldering fire which is kept from flaming up by a loose cover of still moist spruce bark peelings and tundra moss laid over the willow coals.

The smoked jerky has an excellent flavor. I am reminded, as I admire our invented smoker, that it looks like nothing ever suggested in any "How to . . ." material I've ever seen. One of the best rewards of the simplified existence we live here is the opportunity—the necessity—to create and invent. Discovery is always in that unique first-time experience of one's very own!

Our friends arrive tonight, close to midnight. The sun will still be up, of course, when they charter in from Bettles.

All chores done here, our day will be a waiting one. Any "work" will seem merely "busy work." Therefore, we move with the holiday mood, and explore around the lake for more birds' nests, see what game is moving about.

While I gather together the Thermos and smoked fish for picnic lunch, the cameras, rifles, fishing gear, repellent, Sam and Girl hike over to the point to pick up a weathered log Sam has earmarked for his wood carving. Putting the gear into the boat, I hear a bark from close by. But not Girl's bark.

Scanning the tundra around camp, my eyes come to rest on a white fluffy brush moving along just above the top of a thicket of low willow, a little distance behind the cabin. It looks at first like Kia's erect white banner of a tail. But as the moving white patch comes closer, and at last emerges from out of the willow, it is the thick ruff of the white wolf.

Seeing me, the wolf stops midstep. Half crouched, staring straight at me, he remains absolutely motionless. Exquisite creature! Large, powerful, beautiful—with a thick pure-white coat except for the gray, almost salt-and-pepper stretch of fur along his back, still darker rings of fur around his eyes and a shining black muzzle. I do not move, even hold my breath, in a wish to prolong this moment that seems so miraculous. He does not move. I am not afraid. He does not appear to wish to leave. I wish him to stay. Time arrested. Details of a moment imprinted indelibly on memory, like a blaze on a tree, carved deep, a mark of permanence. Sun-whiteness of fur. Golden eyes, not wary— but no word for what is in his eyes or mine. Can "trust" even hint at it?

A faint yip in the distance. We both hear it, are aware of what it means. But as if we do not wish to acknowledge it, for when we do we must break the spell to deal with some other reality beyond this moment, we slowly, reluctantly, turn to look toward the sound. It is Girl, with Sam, coming back to camp along the trail. As slowly, the wolf and I turn back to each other. A sense that what has been is now ended. We do not look back toward the dog and man coming toward us, but only at each other. And then the wolf turns, and is gone.

Not even the trembling of a willow leaf marks his passage.

We have just returned from across the lake when a moving blur on the waters, heading for the point, catches our eye. The blur becomes a pair of antlers! A single caribou . . .

We are back in the boat and on our way in less than thirty seconds. The caribou becomes aware of us, switches direction, swims toward a farther point of land. Once he reaches shore, he will disappear into the tundra faster than we can follow. Though we race after him, keeping the binoculars trained on the swimming deer, he has too much distance on us already to offer good odds that we will have fresh meat for the next few weeks.

We are still several hundred feet away when he reaches land and climbs ashore, this fine, fat buck, and disappears in among the spruce. Sam is out of the boat before it hits shore, racing up the three-foot rise from beach to tundra and out of sight.

With one arm I hang onto Girl, who wriggles furiously to get free and join the hunt; with the other, tie up the boat. I stay on shore, holding the quivering pup, waiting, stooping low to stay out of range should the caribou double back and get *between* Sam and me. Seconds later, the crack of the rifle says that at least the deer is sighted. I wait for another shot; hear Sam's call instead.

A hundred yards in from shore lies the answer to our food problem, the answer to feeding our guests. Serendipity? Grace? But even our delight at our good fortune does not remove our acknowledgment and gratitude to the creature of our successful hunt. The religion of hunting peoples is reality-based. No symbols stand between.

The pup is not allowed to run free until Sam has completed the *coup de grace*, but it takes all my strength to hold on to her. Once down, she races instantly toward the kill, a bundle—a force—of quivering instincts as she nears it, her tiny tail stiffly extended, her hackles up, growling low in the throat, sniffing excitedly, rearing up onto hind legs to leap into the air, coming down to earth into a low crouch, growling, growling. . . . I need not worry about her being "taught" to be beagle. Her instincts are instructing her well!

Our friends will be here in only a few hours. We can rush the preparing of the meat, finish the job before they arrive. Or we can wait, include them in this part of our lives, share with them, involve them in, the profound firsthand experience of preparing the meat that will feed us all for the next month. Sam cuts the jugular vein and we maneuver the carcass head down onto a sloping knoll of tundra, to bleed, be gutted and left to cool until Don and Jan can take part in the butchering.

Though the pup still quivers and growls as we work with the caribou, she gradually quiets. Periodically the smell and proximity of the carcass retriggers her excitement and she races in close, growling and barking, hackles up, tail erect. Sam orders her back, using this experience to train her to sit obediently near the kill, quiet, self-controlled. She understands, though her great effort to comply sends waves of trembling spasms through her fat, pink little frame. But when caribou gonads, heart and liver are placed in a pile on the mossy tundra near her, it is suddenly a demand beyond her grasp, this having to endure such a conflict in desires. She rushes at the meat, grabs up a gonad, plops down with it held between her paws, starts to tear hungrily at the raw meat with her sharp little teeth.

Sam reaches her and snatches away her prize before she can even get down one bite. This quick action, the sharp words that go with it, send her slinking off, head and tail dragging, brown eyes soulful, looking guilty and miserable. A few feet away from the pile of meat, she sits on her haunches, eyes the meat longingly, sighs, gets up, circles round a dozen or more times as she does in her box when arranging her caribou furs for the night, and finally settles into her "nest" in the tundra. Curled close to a sun-warmed tussock, she falls asleep.

Finished at last with the eviscerating, we rig a spruce-stick brace in the carcass to keep it open to the air for cooling, take the delicacies, call the pup and head for camp, hoping the wolves will be traveling paths other than through these parts until we return tonight after our friends have arrived.

Our friends are here. It's pleasant but strange to have others "living" here at Koviashuvik.

Though Jan and Don were exhausted from their long journey, they were eager to help with the caribou butchering, astonished to find themselves preparing their own food in daylight midnight. We left head and offal for the other critters, ferried back the caribou quarters in the boat. Have been eating fresh boiled tongue, heart, fried liver, steaks and ribs, eating like gourmets on sweet fat caribou meat, and feeling the particular good health that comes when a fish diet is replaced by one of meat.

Though enjoying that sense of good health, at the same time I also feel an increasing exhaustion, particularly after our non-stop sessions of talk. I think I have already forgotten the forms, the style, of social communications of the "outside" world. We find ourselves now talking a great deal about things Sam and I never feel we have to say. Jan and Don have many questions, quite naturally, about everything here—what they see, the way we live, our things, cabin, tools. The questions are sometimes surprisingly difficult to answer because their assumptions have very little to do with the reality of *here*. To give a precise answer to a precise question doesn't really say anything. It's almost as if there is no mutual frame of reference from which to begin.

How to answer questions about this cabin, for example—why it is built the way it is—unless one knows about the timber here, the transporting of logs and firewood, tools available, arctic winter nights, a philosophy that is reality, not theory, of living within an environment while disturbing it as little as possible. How can we speak of arctic summer if one knows nothing of arctic winter? Summer is not a "time" but only one face of "timelessness."

A certain frustration in conversation continues, making little undercurrents of tension in our mutual affection. Like Eskimo and white, communicating across an almost unbridgeable void between two radically differing life perspectives. Questions framed as if everything questioned were reducible to objects. Our answers nonanswers, because they refuse to deal with life and world as data, fact, object. The hunter does not teach his young son how to hunt by "telling" him how. He does not even try. He takes his son on the hunt, many hunts, then sends him to hunt alone. Eventually, if the son has the outer gifts of seeing and hearing, of true learning, and the inner gift of whatever must already exist within to be made perfectible as "hunter," he knows. Knows not "how to hunt," but knows wind, light, signs, scent, tracks, patterns; not the prey, but this particular prey; knows not his own eye and steady hand on rifle, but his eye, ear, sensings, timing, rifle, steady hand on this particular day, this hunt, at this moment; he knows the instant for and of the kill, and he knows sacredness, acknowledgment, the interchangeability of himself and his prey.

Can this be taught? Only if the gift is there to begin with, then to be polished, refined, perfected. The Eskimo hunter's son does not "ask" how to hunt. He observes, listens, interprets, learns, hunts. Questions/answers? Where to begin?

Better than to "talk" anymore of "how" we live, we try to shift the verbal to the doing, involve Jan and Don *in* our living. With us, they gather dead trees, haul them to camp. Chop wood for the stove. Fish. Don helps Sam build a small temporary cache, screened against the flies, to store the caribou in. Jan washes dishes in cold lake water. They spend long hot hours helping to find, haul and lay more slabs of turf on the cabin roof. Jan and I scrape the caribou skin. We are "busy" now, but there is no way to avoid a certain quality of "busyness," for their involvement in Koviashuvik living still carries a playing-at, a game, "how to do," "try everything" overtone, because it is not their reality.

I soon find that while they are busy, I prefer to sit in my wheelbarrow "lawn chair" and watch the sky, wind on water and leaves, the hunting terns, the curious loons, the mischievous jays. There is not enough work, really, to busy four people. In this decision to sit on the sidelines, I learn more of myself. I am watching our friends as I watch the gulls, Kia, the wind in sprucetops, floating clouds. In the good-natured charging into the tasks I see Jan and Don involved in, I look at still another facet of the overtones of "busyness." They approach each task as if there were a deadline, an urgency, to finish the chore, to reach a goal. The *goal* is to be finished. A race with time.

It is the way of the "outside." Calendared, clocked. Here there is no separation between work and nonwork. Building, fishing, hiking, cooking, bird watching, cloud dreaming—which is work and which nonwork? All are living, goalless, process, connectedness. The universe will not run away. And being without a goal is not being in a vacuum. It is being.

Yet I feel I must explain away my "laziness," or they may think I have turned antisocial, unfriendly. For in the present need for "groupness" among "outsiders," to choose to step away from the "group" implies a rejection or negation of those in the group. But how to communicate my real reasons for preferring to sit in my wheelbarrow while they are busy? I can't. They must discover it for themselves. When they can sit quietly they will, perhaps, know why I choose to be in the wheelbarrow instead of in the midst of all this activity. Even to watch this present busyness is wearing. I turn back to the soaring gulls, the diving terns, the handsome red-eyed loon, the wind on his ruffled feathers and on my cheek.

Our friends are here—but not yet. They are still running by the clocks of "outside." If *koviashuktok* can just begin to make itself known to them, with luck they may yet during this brief visit discover its meaning. With luck . . .

Jan and Don show signs of restlessness. It was predictable. Like so many travelers, they have come less to experience wilderness than to have experiences in wilderness.

Having reached Koviashuvik, their destination, they now need another. Another goal, another fixed objective. It is the way of the city dweller. He cannot be somewhere unless he goes through the action of moving from here to there. That's how he knows he is somewhere else.

We plan a hike. They must discover firsthand that the mountain slopes, which from a distance look so invitingly velvet smooth, like rolling green lawn, are in fact thick tangles of willow and alder brush through which trails must often be hacked. And that the vast black thaw ponds, looking from afar so interesting and pleasant a place to hike, are in fact a no man's land of endless bogs filled with slippery, ankle-breaking tussocks and deep mire; and they must know firsthand that the swarms of mosquitoes they abhor here near camp are as a gentle summer breeze compared to the hurricane assault of the plague of bog mosquitoes. That the creeks which from a distance look like clear passage through the slope growth, suggesting the best unobstructed natural trail up a mountainside, are in fact so tightly bordered by impenetrable brush, so choked with rough-edged, multisized boulders and rocks, so dense with waiting armies of the fiendish mosquitoes, that arctic foot travelers hurry to cross them or drink from them, but blaze new trails or seek out game trails to follow.

Knowing the style of so many backpackers (which is to cover the territory as if a race to get out of it were under way), I decide to stay at camp while Sam takes our *cheechakos* (Alaskan greenhorns) out on a training session which we are calling a hike. In fact, I long for some aloneness. I use the excuse that having already explored the small lake which is to serve as the "goal," the "destination," I will stay here, catch up on my journals.

Packs are packed, rifle checked, cameras and film readied for the overnight hike. I know Sam will give them a good hike. They will return having had the kind of "experience" they are searching for.

This morning I boat everyone over to the north end of the lake, where they will start their hike up and over the mountains to a small lake nestled among the peaks.

The hikers depart, and I return home to revel in my aloneness,

which seems today to encompass all the universe and all its
creatures. I talk with the birds, and with a scolding summer brown
weasel who unexpectedly turns up. Kia passes through camp,
barely pausing for a brief stare at me and then at the cabin door,
through which come excited yips as Girl sees the fox from the
window. Kia looks more scraggly than ever in his summer-shed-
ding coat. A parky squirrel sits on the woodpile and barks fero-
ciously until a jay, chattering equally fiercely, lights near him.
Squirrel streaks off in one direction; jay in another. The loon in
the bay calls, and I answer, but in my own voice, for I cannot
seem to master the loon's voice Sam talks to them in. And then
the white-crowned sparrow joins our talk in his sweetest call.

The day is filled with sun and motion and uninterrupted serenity until a harsh, clattering sound of another kind of bird comes
in from the south. A helicopter circles low over the camp.
Through the transparent cockpit bubble I can see three figures.
We exchange waves. The chopper lands on the narrow shelf of
sand beach a hundred yards from the cabin.

More visitors.

The strident whine that seems to fill all space slowly ceases as
the great spinning blades come slowly to a stop.

Three young men step from the chopper. Though curious, I'm
not particularly glad to see them, for their way of arrival is an
abomination, a kind of defilement of a holy place. There is no
more obtrusive, abrasive sound to invade the wilderness than
the screaming whine of the helicopter. And several of them have
been heard this summer, sighted at a distance, for the oil and
mining companies are now moving into this last great wilderness,
and the chopper is their new transport answer to invading and
conquering the wilds.

I soon learn this is an oil-company-leased chopper; its crew,
part of a team assigned to do an "ecological" study on the proposed oil pipeline route. Two of this crew are "fish men," ichthy-
ologists, who ask to borrow our boat to make temperature and
depth checks of the lake. While they are out on the water,
the young pilot and I sit on the sand, joined by Girl, who is

ecstatic over having someone new who will play with her. My "guest" and I are soon talking like old acquaintances. There was surprise in him at first to find anyone living here. But understanding of why we have chosen to live in the wilderness soon comes out of the discovery that we share a similar perspective on the dilemma of the "outside," on its dehumanizing obsessions with goal and with things, with status, efficiency, massness. We talk of the changes that are taking place, their promise and their risk, and are both surprised that the fish men return so quickly, two hours later.

The two return with many questions, not only about the fish at Koviashuvik, but also about climate, small mammals, plants, etc., the "specialties" of other members of the team. I find I do not enjoy talking about Koviashuvik in terms of data, facts, objects. I realize they are interested primarily in doing their job.

I invite them to return and talk with Sam tomorrow night, for he will, out of his scientific base, give them all the biological and ecological data they require, as well as a perspective in which to view it—*if* they can hear.

They say they would find it helpful; we say our good-byes.

The chopper revs up, the whine building like a slow scream into a hideous clatter, the wind from the whirling prop blasting the camp spruce and willow halfway to the ground.

I wonder how the birds, hiding their young in tundra and grasses, react to this holocaust of a disturbance. The chopper swings up and away, like some giant superbird, strangely graceful in its own soaring flight, and the three men wave as the helicopter makes a last pass overhead and flies on to the north, where their camp is located.

Long after the sound of the chopper has faded, my hearing retains the imprint of the piercing, droning whine of rotor blades.

I have enjoyed this meeting with these three. I must remind myself that they are not to be confused with their detestable machine. The machine is only a symbol of human choices. Technology, in symbol, comes today to Koviashuvik. It is not this sophisticated flying machine, or the ugly sound it leaves stamped on my mind, that troubles me. It is the values guiding those who decide what use to make of this superaircraft, this symbol of the incredible power and accomplishment of our technology, that disturbs me, leaving me with this vague feeling of anxiety, of concern, that clouds an otherwise delightful meeting with the young pilot and the two fish men. I wonder if they became specialists on fish because they really loved something about the miraculous world of fish as I have come to love it, or whether it was a choice based on love of data gathering, applicable to any object—or was the decision made in that nameless laboratory where jobs and job benefits, status, money, prestige are the primary goals?

Only now, when quietness and serenity return to camp, do I become aware that the birds are also returning. Now they come out of hiding, back from their flights of fear, returning to their homes, to their territory. But not with their usual songs. They are as subdued as am I. I am thinking not of these men or of their great mechanical bird but of beginnings. For every end, including the end of wilderness, has its beginnings. . . .

Late this afternoon the hikers return.

I listen to the accounts of tussock-filled swamps, of cool, sparkling mountain lake waters, of near-drownings in waves of mosquitoes, of Sam's sighting a grizzly, of great vistas of mountains and high valleys, of a new sense of where they are and what the land is like for foot travelers. A good hike!

The men fish for dinner, and while the trout is frying, the chopper arrives. I have by now recounted my own adventure in meeting the crew, and based on my report, the usual "feeling out" time needed for new acquaintances in the Arctic is soon dispensed with. The chief of the group has come, too.

They are invited to share our supper. Jan and I quickly eke out the fare for company with pots of instant apples and instant potatoes on to cook, and our trout dinner has the overtones of a feast—a celebration.

Over coffee, we talk of their "study." It is very clear that these scientists are caught in a dilemma. This ecological study, at best, is a token, a gesture being made by the oil pipeline companies to try to appease the increasing concern and protest of militant conservation groups and the ecologically aware public. No ecologist, no scientist, of merit would pretend otherwise. This quick examination of three widely separate areas, made only in summer in a winter-dominant environment, only a brief period spent at each site? All of our guests reject this project as a valid scientific study. They are openly cynical. They shrug off the fact that the study is obviously being made for public relations reasons, and that they themselves will have no control over what use is made of their token findings. But, the two young cynics laugh, it's a paid "vacation" in the Alaskan Arctic, which they've always wanted to see.

And so our evening passes around the old stove. The crew leaves at midnight, in a sky that seems on fire with the crimson of the low summer night sun. The sound of the superbird receding into the red night makes me think of the last lone loon before freeze-up.

Awake to the good smell of fresh-perked coffee and the sound of Sam and our loon laughing at each other.

At midmorning, a raven, screeching incessantly, circles a tall spruce tree along the shore. From out of nowhere an even larger bird streaks at the raven, drives him off, then alights on the top of the same tree. A newcomer, this huge bird. The largest ever seen at Koviashuvik. Dark body, white head. Through the binoculars we see it is a bald eagle, not quite mature. He sits motionless, in perfect balance on the slender tip of the spruce tree. He has his eye on the camp, on us—and it is a little unnerving to know how well he can see every detail of us with his incredible vision while our own poor sight must use binoculars to even remotely approximate his.

He seems to enjoy his view of our territory, for he stays on his delicate perch without shifting his weight for ten minutes, twenty, a half hour. Two terns flying along the shore sound increasingly agitated as they race past him, but they do not fly in to challenge him. A gull soon follows, swooping in just over the eagle's perch, not remaining to circle round for a good look but racing on past with harsh cries. A small peep scolds shrilly and tirelessly from a nearby nest on the shore. But the eagle seems oblivious of them all, not moving so much as a feather for what is now almost forty-five minutes.

We take off in the boat to see if we can get closer by water for a better view of our visitor. Still nothing moves but his head as it swivels to watch us. As we circle round and in toward shore again, the eagle shifts his weight once, twice, spreads his great wings and lifts to sweep out over the lake, making one circling flight high and wide of the boat to look us over, then soaring on along the lakeshore to settle down on still another, much more distant, spruce. Unless he remains for a while in the territory, he is not likely to ever let us get close to him. But it is enough to have met at a distance this exquisite monarch of the birds.

Rowing into the placid water of the bay near Rooney's grave, we come upon a bull moose, haunch deep in the waters, feeding on underwater mosses and plants. His head is completely submerged. Only the rounded tips of his immense rack show above water. The antlers are still covered with velvet; his coat is now a rich, glossy brown. He looks sleek and fat, prime winter meat, but not quite yet. When he lifts his dripping head, a long green mossy tendril still hanging from his dark muzzle, he is not startled at seeing us. He slowly turns and climbs ashore through the marshy tussocks and green sedge grasses, turns his head to watch us for another few seconds, then moves off into the willow thicket along the creek. Where he stood in the mossy shallows his huge hoofs have left depressions in the muck half a foot deep.

Jan and Don decide to try a three-day hike up into the mountains across the lake. We row them to the opposite shore, wish them well and watch them take off at a near running pace across the tussocks toward the stream which they plan to follow up the mountain. It is the hardest route they could have chosen, this narrow creek, thickly brushy with high willow and alder. Better to fight the tussocks on the lower slopes and to rim up to the pass over open tundra of the heights than to battle those strangling, scratching, stubborn willows. But they must find out for themselves.

For bear protection, Don is wearing a heavy .44-magnum pistol in a holster. He chose it after reading some magazine articles which recommended it for use in "big game" country. I doubt if anyone in the whole Koyukuk owns such a firearm. For hunting or grizzly protection in these parts the rifle is considered the only reliable firearm.

After dinner, our ecology "study" group drops by in their chopper to take in the nets they've put out for fish samples. After their work they join us for a while. They have been feeling frustrated, they report, almost claustrophobic, a curious word to hear in this vast free space. Not all the crew are congenial, it seems. Equipment ordered for the study has not yet arrived. No one feels he can do an adequate job in the limited time they have been given.

The hot coffee, the roaring old stove under the crimson evening sky, the circle of friendship and quiet talk shift the spirits of the gloomy crew, and when later they climb aboard their mechanical bird, they seem in better cheer than when they arrived.

Jan and Don trudge into camp at lunchtime, returning two days early after only one night out. An overnight. They must have kept up their usual fast trail run to have covered the territory they describe. But watching them ease back into the dailiness of camp life, aware that they sit with more of a sense of stillness, talk less as if they have stopped fearing that all must be said at once or there will be no saying, unconsciously lift their faces to the sun or wind, catch the flash of a white wing, eyes following it, without spoken question or commentary, I think they are moving back now toward what we all still carry in our genes of ten thousand years ago, unacknowledged, unrecognized, but perhaps sensed. . . .

They are beginning—just beginning—to know. Just beginning to recognize the source out of which they were created. They are showing signs of rediscovering the universe as their home.

On the trail. First night out.
On a mossy clearing beside a swift-running, sparkling clear creek, we camp for the night with our friends. Early-evening red sky. Spruce blackly silhouetted against craggy skyline. Ahead of us, across the creek, a long hard climb tomorrow, up to the high peaks of the mountain chain we must cross to reach our destination, Mirror Lake, thirty miles on foot from Koviashuvik. . . .

We set out this morning in the boat, which rode deep in the water with four passengers and four heavy backpacks containing two two-man mountain tents, ammunition, a set of dry clothes each, fishing gear, cameras, food. Since Don carries his bear protection in the form of his mighty pistol, Sam carries only the .22 rifle. We are packing food supplies for seven days, most of it dried, instant, dehydrated trail foods, the kind backpackers buy ready-packaged in stores that cater to the industry. We could travel with nothing more than dried fish or caribou jerky, a little sourdough sponge and flour, to be supplemented with fresh fish, ptarmigan and berries. But our friends have brought the store-bought trail foods with them, and so we use them.

Rimming up to the higher slopes, we see three Dall sheep grazing. Sam, in the lead, picks up the game trail. The wind dies down, making our progress under the blazing arctic sun hot going at times. The wind stilled, mosquitoes join us in force. Moving east and climbing steadily. The terrain subtly changes. The last of the sparse spruce groves disappear, the landscape becomes more stark, wind-swept. For a brief part of the climb, we walk in a dry, rock-strewn creek bed. As we ascend still higher, snowbanks in the deeper cuts block our way and we have to return to the mountainside.

This is Girl's first major hike, and though she starts out at her customary frisky canter, by early afternoon she has lost her exuberance and begun to whine softly. Every little while she runs up to Sam or to me and yips half-heartedly, as if asking to be picked up and carried. We reassure her but do not pick her up.

Our afternoon is spent breaking trail through waist-high willow and alder cover on the slope. The wild tangle spills over the whole mountainside. Sam hacks through the worst of it with a machete. We break through the rest. Hundreds of feet below is a fast-moving stream. After three or four hours on the steeply slanting pitched ground, feet ache from walking on their sides instead of bottoms. This part of the journey is even more wearing for Girl, who must try to find passage through the impenetrable mess of thick branches and twisted roots. Periodically she gets caught in them, crying frantically, until one of us sets her free.

The trail journal entry for the first day concludes:

By the time we reach this clearing we are exhausted. Looking at the climb ahead of us, we decide to stay here for the night. Build a fine fragrant fire of willow, bask in its warmth, for the evening has turned bitter cold after the baking heat of the sun. Pitch our tents on the thick moss cover while our instant dinner is cooking. After supper, savor the steaming hot coffee, sit quietly, listen to stillness, saying little, turn in early to make journal notes and to fall into the good sleep such days always bring, with Girl, weary but well fed and content, curled up in a warm ball at the foot of our sleeping bag. The deep luxuriant moss of the tundra is the finest mattress ever designed!

An excellent breakfast in the crisp, bright morning air, and we have quickly struck camp, hoisted our packs, and are ready to move on. The climb up offers two alternatives. One is to rim around and up to the ridge, which means making our way through

more of yesterday's nearly impassable scrub cover. The other is
to head straight up, via an ancient dry creek bed or cut which
is clear of scrub but choked with boulders and rocks. Jan and Don
rim around. Sam and I take the direct route. We arrive almost
simultaneously at the jagged outcroppings of rock that erupt
from the peaks.

The high places of the universe are a special world unto themselves, especially this world of arctic mountain peaks. No tree
or bush breaks the horizon. There is little to divert the eye from
the vast unbroken sweep of mountain and valley and shining
ribbons of streams far below. A few boulders and piles of ava-
lanched rock dot the barren landscape. Lichens and scrubby
clumps of grass cover the rock faces. Here the wind never
ceases. Only the continual arctic sun warms us against the hint
of ice that is carried on this wind.

After the climb, Sam and I take shelter from the wind in a
curved depression of rock, rest, eat a few raisins, share a smoke.
Resuming the hike, we are no longer traveling as a group, but
are spread out over the vast rolling top of the world, seeing each
other in the far distance only as bright specks of color against
the brown-green scape.

We all lunch together in a high meadow, stretching out on the
soft grasses not only to rest our pack-sore backs and legs, but
to get below the constant, singing winds. Girl circles round and
round, clearing a little flat place for her nest. Before we can
get her food out of the pack, she has collapsed into a tight
curl of warm, exhausted sleep.

By midafternoon, we have gradually descended into a high
valley to cross a tussock bog where bright red mushrooms and
fat purplish blueberries dot the marshy place. For part of the
way across the bog Sam finds a well-traveled game trail—and
though our boots sink ankle deep with each step in the wet
ooze, for a while at least we do not have to jump and balance on
tussocks.

Leaving the swampy plateau, we descend more, passing
through a spare stand of white spruce to an outcropping several

hundred feet above and a half mile from our destination, Mirror Lake.

The difference between our own lake, only thirty miles distant, and this body of water is striking—like the difference between soft- and sharp-focus photographs. Here there are no softened gentling lines to the landscape. Only a few hundred feet higher in elevation than Koviashuvik, we are beyond that marginal arctic timber line here. And except for the lone stand passed and one equally small grove of spruce on the far side of the lake, no trees grow on these barren mountain slopes ringing the water. The lake itself is divided into almost equal halves by a flat land bridge a half-mile wide. The bridge of land is itself halved by a line of dark-green willows, telling us that a sizable stream must connect the two lake bodies.

We know, too, that the final leg of our journey will be the hardest one. Our destination is the far side of the lake, and to get there, we must cross the land bridge, which is predictably an endless tussock bog. As we stand for a moment looking out over the stark, lonely scene, braced outwardly against the wind and inwardly for the crossing to come, even the pup is caught in the eerie mood of this wild and desolate place. Girl stares eastward, then, beginning to whine softly, uneasily, retreats behind Sam's boot to wait, exhausted, flat on her belly, her head resting on two outstretched paws.

The muskeg is no better or worse than we anticipated, only greater in distance to cross. Wading the creek where it is spread out shallowly, we cross very slowly, cautiously, for the water level is a bare quarter inch below the tops of our boots. We rest briefly on the other side, sitting on huge tussocks and eating the blueberries which are everywhere around us. Girl noses in wherever a hand is busily picking the tart little berries, and watching us eat what we pick, she, too, begins to pick her own, biting each berry smartly off the low bush and gulping it down.

Beyond the muskeg, we head up the slope of the lake's far side to the spruce grove. And in the sun-slanted shadows inside the grove, set up our tents and start the fire. After the desolate immensity of the vistas we have traveled through all day, our camp within the grove seems intimate, cozy, secure.

Next morning, I write in my notebook:

Slept as if dead last night. Only once did I awaken. Sometime in the night, the sound of something large crashing through the brush only a few feet from our tent made me lift my head and open an eye. I vaguely remember Sam bounding up and out of the tent, reaching for the rifle, which at night stands just outside the tent door. Whether it was my exhaustion, or trust that Sam would handle whatever needed handling, I was asleep again before he even returned to the sleeping bag!

We spend several days exploring. The creek is abundant with grayling. We broil them over the campfire for breakfast, for dinner. Sam flushes a ptarmigan, and though one is not enough for a meal for four, we each have a taste, and our friends enjoy the sweet wild flavor. Sam and I are surprised at how few birds, compared to Koviashuvik, seem to be nesting here; few game tracks, by comparison, are to be seen in this territory. We come across one set of wolf tracks, one of moose (our visitor to camp in the night).

Then Sam hikes along the lower lake and comes upon grizzly tracks on the shore. Curious, he follows the bear tracks until he comes upon a pile of scat so fresh that it is still steaming. Only then does it occur to him, he tells us on his return, that he has only two cartridges in the .22 rifle, which, *fully* loaded, is not the best bear protection in treeless country. He decides to call off his stalk for bear pictures.

By the time we leave, the little camp in the grove has become a place of special meaning, a forest home in the wilderness, like an ancient sacred grove where, inside its circle of safety and at-homeness, are our fire, our small shelters, our songs shared with white-crowned sparrow and thrush, our sharings of feasts, adventures, wonders seen, meanings discovered.

The first leg of our homeward journey uneventful. Packs a

little lighter, our food having been well consumed. We are all by now more toughened up physically, Girl as well. We cross the muskeg at a good clip, relieved to have the worst one behind us so early in the trip. Girl, fully recovered, eager to go, leaps most of the tussocks like a graceful young caribou, only occasionally misjudging a height to land straddle-legged, marooned flat on her belly, atop them. She gets behind only when she stops now and then to munch on blueberries.

The morning has come in bright; we start off in warm sunshine. By midday we are traveling under an overcast, pleased, at least, to have the chill wind that's come up at our backs. But by evening the weather has rapidly deteriorated. To escape the freezing winds, we stop early and set up camp in the bottom of a sandy creek bed beside a narrow little stream. Dead willow along the banks is ample for our fire. But even our tents and warm sleeping bags do not keep out the chill of the night. The creek bed, six feet below the surrounding tundra, acts as a funnel through which the night-long winds rush.

Morning is bright again, but so cold and windy that we hurry breakfast and breaking camp to get in motion, for the fire does not warm us. The climb back up the high ridge that separates us from Koviashuvik takes only a few hours and is a fairly gentle ascent. But when we reach the last and highest plateau before the peaks, a fierce wind hits us full blast, head on. The last mile to the crest where we begin the descent is a bone-chilling trek. At the very summit, we stop briefly to rest. To escape the battering gale, the four of us lie flat on our backs on the turf, close side by side, in the lee of a scant two-foot rise of rock. Huddled together, we fortify ourselves with a few nuts and raisins; at once give up trying to shout to each other above the shriek of the winds. Girl crawls in between us, making herself into a compact warm ball, falls asleep.

Readying for the descent, which will be by a different, steeper route than that of our ascent, we pause for a moment on the wind-blasted summit. From it we can look down upon Koviashuvik in the far, far distance. After the starkness of the land where we have spent these last few days, and from the barren craggy peak of shrieking, buffeting icy winds where we now stand, the land of Koviashuvik looks verdant, near junglelike, with its stand of green spruce, tacamahac, birch and lush growth of willow and alder. But even from here we can see that the blue lake far below is patterned with white lines—whitecaps. The blow is not just here at the heights today.

We start down. Sam in the lead sets a very fast pace. The steep descent becomes an exercise in resisting gravity and momentum. Wind and our own weight complicate the endeavor. In motion, the only control the body seems naturally to exert is a braking tension against the breakneck race downward that becomes its own force propelling us. Body leans backward, legs move independently, toes never touch the ground, heels dig in on each step to brake the speed.

Halfway down, we cross timber line, move in among scattered spruce, which help to break the wind a little. Rest briefly in the lee of a boulder; continue on down, at the same rapid pace. The tussocks at the bottom of the slope barely slow our speed. And reaching more level ground, I realize that the pace of the descent was due not only to the natural downhill pull of gravity; in our hurry there is something we're responding to of the urgency in the very mood of this day—the feel of the winds, the whitecaps that cover this inland lake.

As we reach the beached boat, the challenging cry of a tern overhead makes me brace myself for a diving assault. But the tern is not concerned with us this time. A gull twice his size has wandered into his territory. The slower-moving, less maneuverable invader is no match for the tern's outraged attack. The smaller bird, repeatedly diving and screaming, with all the furious energy of the wind on the heights, finally drives the gull off. The sky is empty again.

We load the packs into the boats and head out into the choppy water. Away from the lee of the land, exposed, we move into winds that hint of those on the ridge. The skies leaden; the first heavy, drumming raindrops begin to fall. The overloaded boat rides so low in the water that each wave sets us awash, threatening to capsize us. To reach camp, we are in for a three- to four-mile ride northward into increasing winds and roiling waters as we move farther out into the lake. But the opposite shore is only a mile away. If we can get to that shore, we can always beach the boat and hike the miles back to camp.

We aim for the sandy beach directly across the lake. Reach it, though there are moments when I think we may well become statistics in the annual numbers report on accidental drownings in far northern waters. Drenched from the waves and rain and thoroughly chilled, we go ashore and wait to see if the storm will play itself out before we decide to move on, on foot.

Meanwhile, making a fire on the beach, we get soup and instant dinner cooking, gather blueberries for dessert. Though we've added our ponchos, only for wind protection since parkys are already soaked, the wind still cuts through and chills the bones. Taking our supper in tin plates and cups back onto the tundra, we huddle down in a mossy hollow to eat our meal.

An hour later, Sam and I, with the four packs, try the boat again. But the prow of the old wooden craft crashes down so hard on each high wave that I expect to hear wood splinter and give way. Each wave breaks with a spray so high and dense that we seem to be awash in a perpetual ice-cold shower bath. We turn back. Even in the middle of this struggle, I have a sense of something defining our actions that lies beyond the storm itself.

The reality of the here and now—the Storm—enforces waiting, serenely or restlessly, easily or uneasily. The difference lies in *koviashuktok*, the way Sam and I live. The impatience we are caught in, this mood of trying to defy the reality of the storm, is the subtle effect of our awareness of what our friends are feeling. The ecology of our usual attitudes at Koviashuvik undergoes a change because of their presence.

Reminded of this, I move back fully into the life of now while we wait out the storm, coexist without resistance or anticipation, accept the storm, enjoy it. The others find their ways of "passing time"; I harvest blueberries, delighting in the harvesting in wind

and rain, unthinking of what is to come next, no longer concerned about when we will get "home." I *am* home.

A bright, still morning after the storm, with a hint of change in
the fresh-washed sparkling air. Autumn? The last week of July,
and the teakettle on the cold outdoor stove clanks with a layer
of ice when I pick it up this morning.

The mood of Koviashuvik is quieter now, as if the feverish
business of spring and summer, having reached and passed its
crescendo, is now prepared to stand still for a moment, enjoy the
fruits of its frantic activity. Greening has ceased; all growth,
having reached its apex, seems content to rest, to be. The full-
leafed willow turn their silver side to the wind, and in the distance, sunlit, look like newly arrived silver-white shadows among
the dark spruce. Flaming fireweed at the summit of their blossoming time are at their most riotous.

Our friends will be leaving soon.

They have been with us almost a month. During this month
I've become sharply aware of how friendship is assumed in the
thin, surface connections we make with others in most places
today. Though I called Jan and Don "friends," they were more
acquaintances, surface persons to me. What has happened here
this month, though, has not to do with "friendship" but with community. Our concept of community today warps its meaning, has
little to do with its reality. Living fragmented lives, we try to
build "community" out of the various worlds of the job, school,
the family, the club, church—all separate from each other, all
fragments of the whole of our lives. The binding strength, the
totality, of community requires a commonality, a shared base that
makes the acknowledgment of "other," the survival of "other," as
necessary, as sacred, as one's own. Sam and I have this. We are
a community. I have seen a faint glimmer of this same commonality emerge out of this brief time of our shared life with our
friends. It has taken a month, but I sense its beginnings. I do not
know why this intimate, daily connection with the universe with

which we live here at Koviashuvik creates—demands—harmonious, affirming interrelationships, but it does. To live in harmony with others, including spruce, willow, grass, water, cloud, wind, sun, rock, the birds, animals, is essential, and still possible here if not elsewhere.

As for Jan and Don, when they arrived with their city-quickened talk and gestures, their restlessness born of anxiety and dis-ease at the sudden removal of calendars and clocks and systems too long in charge, I wondered if I could weather this invasion of tranquillity and inner ease. But we have weathered it. In the experience, it is they, not we, who have changed—have been changed by Koviashuvik. They seem to run and move and talk and think less feverishly. Quieter inside themselves, perhaps they've learned to hear a little more of the abundant sound of the universe around them. They have learned, perhaps, to take the time, the necessary time, to look, to sense, to feel and to be, a little more.

I can see subtle changes in the small details of our being together.

As we prepare supper tonight, Jan and I move in harmony as a team, comfortable in our "work," savoring the doing of the necessaries. She no longer chatters as she did when she first arrived, when chores were still mechanical, little pleasure taken in their doing but only in their being done.

As I prepare the last of the caribou in a stew, adding a backpack package of dehydrated vegetables and some rice, Jan makes our dessert, a pudding mix thick with blueberries she has picked earlier from Koviashuvik Point. As I watch her slicing the loaf of sourdough bread for supper, I know she has forgotten for the moment her large efficient mechanical kitchen at home, stocked with all the packaged superabundance of the marketplace that someone has labeled the American Cinderella's glass slipper come to life. I sense in her some of my own profound pleasure and delight in the preparations we make for this feast.

Whether a month of wilderness will have given them enough to hold to when our friends return to the synthetic environment they live in, I don't know. Perhaps the gift will remain, some-where in the soul, a faint reminder in the small memories like the memory of bread broken here among us where bread still has worth and meaning, where this simple act is something of the sacred that can still be found.

Sam sights a grizzly bear today roaming the slopes. Now is the time for the bears to come down from the higher places to feed on the blueberries, which are fat, ripe and everywhere!

The day of departure is wild and stormy, the lake pounding like a surf against the shore, the sky dark, Koviashuvik socked in.

Even so, our friends are packed and ready early, for no amount of weather-predicting and guessing can say whether Daryl will be able to get in for them or when he will arrive.

From Jan and Don's tentative and distracted air, I guess that they have already departed Koviashuvik, are already moving back into their own busy world, immersed in future, not in pres-ent. We all need to bridge our departures and arrivals, I suppose; project ourselves into a safer time realm than the uncertain, changing now. I sense that they are putting on their psychological armor, readying themselves, shifting into the high gear in which they must run in the whirling, cluttered, cacophonous, competi-tive world to which they are returning. The gentle quietness they have known here will not protect them where they are going, no more than the *koviashuktok* of the Nunamiut serves them in the world of cities. I have an answer to my wonder at whether this quality our friends have lived with for a month could be carried with them as sustainer, nourisher, as I watch Don and Jan. They are already in transition, on their way whirling into a rootless future.

Daryl's plane comes in just under the thick soup of overcast. His flying partner is piloting today. Joining us for a quick tea and cookies, but with an eye never off the weather, which is socking in even more solidly, he is soon ready for takeoff.

Whatever deep feelings we hold about our friends' leave-taking are diffused by the drama of the storm, by the icy, hard-driving needle spray of rain, by the chilling wind as Sam ferries Jan and Don and their belongings by boat to the bobbing aircraft twenty-five feet out from shore.

The engine revs up, the plane turns, and with a mighty thrust plows into the white-capped waves, racing forward, skimming their crested white peaks, finally lifts. We watch the small craft disappear into thick grayness; hear the last note of its hum enveloped in mist and low-hanging clouds before we rush back into the cabin.

There, no sound left but the crackling of the fire.

For some reason I do not understand, as I stand silent in the warmth of the Yukon stove, listening to the singing of the flaming spruce logs, it is as if I am hearing the fire song for the first time. I look around the cabin, see *it* as if for the first time, caribou furs on bunk, ceiling logs I skinned only a little time— or was it a long time—ago? The windows frame familiar and beloved scapes of mountains, tundra, spruce trees, water, all now wreathed in gray mist and softly darkening clouds of summer storm—all old, and all new.

Our friends have left, left just as they had begun, barely begun, to be taught by timelessness, solitude, by the rhythms of other creatures' lives, by the universe, to know that existence is a relational cohesiveness of many parts, of which they are only two. Hopefully, they leave wiser, more wholly human, even though in leave-taking they, as do most of us, resorted to habit, to what is longest known, safest.

Has the experience here touched them deeply enough, spoken clearly enough the secret language only the heart can understand and hold to? I do not know. I question, wonder still, doubt—but I do not know.

AUTUMN

INDIAN—OR ESKIMO—SUMMER

The rainy season carries us into August, bringing thick, leaden skies, cold north winds, more snow to the mountains. Overnight, tundra and slopes are splashed with brilliant golds and reds as willow and alder and birch react to the cold of the Arctic's autumning.

Today we awaken to a glaringly bright sunlit world after the past week of grayness. The sky intense and cloudless blue; the earth white and dazzling with a new six-inch-deep blanket of snow.

Girl races out into the morning and goes berserk. Running, leaping straight up into the air with all four feet leaving the ground at once, burrowing her nose down under the white stuff, pouncing on it, sniffing it, rolling in it, barking, growling, whimpering at it. She has never before met snow, this pup born of a springtime litter.

Six loons pass by, flying together, something I have not seen here before. Has the early August snow hurried them south prematurely? are they passers-by from the north or some of our own, readying for the approaching migration southward?

Sam, too, heads out into the snow, climbing to the peaks to check fresh tracks, to hunt for Dall sheep. Few of these wild sheep are ever sighted in our mountains here; they prefer the higher, craggier peaks to the north. But the snows always bring a small band or two of stragglers into our territory. This early forecast of winter heightens our craving for meat. Fresh Dall sheep is a rare and succulent meat, well worth the hunt in the high places, so the caribou hunters of Anaktuvuk say.

I stay at camp for the mail drop. The raw, buffeting winds from the north are so strong today that three passes over camp are necessary before Daryl can make the drop close enough to avoid my having to hike a distance for the wind-blown mail sack.

By bedtime, when Sam returns, sheepless—not even any tracks, so they have not yet begun traveling this way—a wild kaleidoscopic sunset of reds and oranges and slate-gray streaks has taken over the sky. Tonight the thermometer reads twenty degrees.

The moon returned last night.

"Night" has returned so gradually that we almost missed its coming. But night is still twilight, a dusky blue, not yet dark.

In the southern sky last evening, a high cloud descended slowly, a soft cover sliding down to reveal, for the first time in all these months of constant light, the great golden moon. An astonishing sight, this near-forgotten glowing moon, a sudden glimpse, a comprehension, of the immensity of the universe— our own planet spinning in space, connected by invisible threads to that golden anchor on which men have now walked, have lived out their clamorous dreams of newer, bolder conquest, have acted like men acting like gods, to leave their mark on still another world along with their debris and their tribal flag.

Here, at Koviashuvik, the full golden world up there is still ancient beauty, wonder, the herald of one more spin of the eternal clockworks men live by. But that man has walked there has changed it, if only in the mind. If we continue engineering ourselves into adaptive man merely to survive this cluttered, complex present for that dubious future we may or may not possess, I make a wish on this moon that we program mysteries into our efficiencies. But I somehow doubt that adaptive man, whom we have already become, will think to program a thread of wisdom, a touch of the poetic, into his attempt at survival.

I whisper a wish into the still night air. "Leave it alone, man. You've done enough damage for these few centuries. Wait a little while until you know better why you are compelled to walk on that mysterious golden world. . . ."

But only a young gull hears. He answers uneasily in his mewing cry, already grown more piercing, bassier. I am aware that I do not understand his kind any better than I understand my own kind. I only dimly sense that he, as we, wears golden threads that irrevocably connect him with that round full world of light in the new nighttime sky above Koviashuvik, and that to bind threads too tightly may snap them. . . .

Bright autumn days of late August, marked by the sense of life moving quickly toward winter.

The construction of a permanent cache at the shore camp begins. Four holes dug, four sturdy spruce logs upended into them, braced. A tall ladder made next. A platform of spruce poles built atop the four poles, then on the platform the cache walls begin to rise. A miniature log cabin up in the air—high enough to keep bears and wolves from getting into our supplies. The top portion of each leg of the cache is sheathed in scrap metal from tin cans to keep smaller varmints from climbing up them.

Sam sighted a caribou a few days ago but, upwind of it and too far away, could not circle round in time to get close enough for a shot. So we fish some more, trolling the deeps, but with increasingly poor luck. The trout are just not biting. Then across the lake off Rooney's Point we discover why we've had little luck.

A rocky reef, two to three feet below the surface of the clear sunlit waters, is suddenly teeming with trout. We cast out and can see several trout at once streak after the same lure. Some spook off as they near the boat; others take the hook right next to the boat. Sam catches a male so huge that reaching out and gaffing it almost yanks him overboard as gaff takes the full weight of fish. The female trout caught are leaking eggs. And in the busy reef waters, other females are depositing bright orange roe. This must be the spawning season of the arctic lake trout.

The trout we catch on the reef have never been fatter, in more prime condition. We fry up some of the dense oily roe, but it is so rich that a few spoonsful are my limit. And still, with all this rich, fat fish and roe, we hunger for caribou.

A lone wolf singing on the mountain just above camp. Awakened in the middle of the night, we light the kerosene lamp, stoke the fire, make hot chocolate. Step outside to admire the night. This night would seem a very dark one, I suppose, were we to come to it after the glowing brightness of night in the city. But though night has returned to the Arctic, it is far from "black" yet. We can see every detail of rock, willow, spruce, mountain contour across the lake in this light, even though the clouds cover the moon.

Scanning the heavens through breaks in those clouds, we see a faint single point of brilliance, a shimmering dot of light, and then another—and still another! The stars have returned—rather, we have returned to the stars. Not yet the dazzling jeweled beacons of our long winter night, but they are more welcome than we have words to say.

With our hot chocolate, we toast our old companions, whose presence is made known to us this night because the lone wolf sang and called us awake.

The loons are flying more now than they have all summer.

Today a pair flying side by side. A little behind them, a third loon, smaller and not so graceful or skillful a flyer, following persistently along, flapping his wings awkwardly but getting farther and farther behind—and squawking in a peculiar, non-loon-sounding voice with each beat of wing. At the call, the other two loons separate to veer around, take up a position to either side of the smaller one, who does not stop crying, and all three continue on in formation on this training flight session, preparing, practicing, for the long journey southward which is soon to come.

Sun lower in the sky each day. Autumnal golden light casting longer, more softened shadows against the incredible colorscape the land has become. Meadows of blueberry turned scarlet; willow and alder thickets a hundred hues of red and gold. Cold air moving in from the north keeps Koviashuvik sparkling clear, the color in motion, clears the mind's cobwebs, anticipates winter. Something happens to us these days that makes us heady, holds us at a high peak of intense aliveness, intoxicated on sweet crisp autumn air, the perfume of winter moving on the wind.

We cross the lake to gather the last of the overripe berries. A strange and astonishing sound interrupts our picking, makes us stop, look about, startled, confused. Like a great pack of wolves —or dogs—in trouble; baying at some creature caught in a trap? Impossible! Indecipherable cacophony of voices. I search the terrain, but only wind moves over slopes and tundra. Then look skyward. High overhead we see them. Hundreds of geese, flying in a perfect V. Honking without letup, the wave of birds passes overhead, the southward migration journeying from the far north. Before their honking chorus has faded away, another begins, and a new wave is sighted. Another high-flying flock in V formation—this one less neatly, less precisely, formed, the V wavering, scraggly-lined—flies over, and all the sky echoes with a sound I've never before heard firsthand but shall never forget as long as I live, this sound of the geese's migration song, heard by centuries of earthbound listeners like me over eons of autumns. . . .

A smaller flock of only thirty or forty passes overhead. And though their chorus makes a much thinner sound, they, too, are compelled to honk and honk and honk. All afternoon, flocks wing over Koviashuvik on their southward journey, each band announcing its passage in a fresh and glorious round of goose migration song!

The caribou are moving south.

Today a band of fourteen passes. While Sam is skinning poles for the cache, I step out of the cabin to get some wood and see on the mountain crest above the cabin a small band of bucks, cows and calves. My sudden motion has startled them. They stare for a moment, then scatter, disappear over the mountain. Sam continues on with his pole skinning. I say nothing despite my increasing yearning for meat. Whatever combination of factors of wind, instinct, timing, the hunter's own ecology, is required, obviously the right combination does not exist today. But at least we know the caribou are beginning to move down from the north. Soon we will have meat!

This morning, we find fresh tracks of three caribou in the sandy beach right in front of the cabin. By the fish pond, fresh grizzly tracks lead off into the tundra beside the outhouse. More geese fly over. Of the migrating fowl, only a few gulls, ducks and loons remain at Koviashuvik. Most of these are waiting for their young to become strong enough for the long flight south.

After a late dinner of fried pike, we step outside to have a look at the flaming sunset sky. A small band of caribou rounds Koviashuvik Point. We at once melt back into the blind shelter of the dogtrot. I pick up Girl; close my hand around her muzzle to keep her quiet. She has not even seen the approaching caribou but she senses something, and quivers violently. Sam reaches for the 30/06; steps back outside; braces himself against the work-table in front of the cabin. The caribou move slowly along the shore toward camp. Sam, rifle ready, holds his fire; waits until the six deer sight the camp. When that first one sees the cabin, the whole band will stop, stand stock still, staring, then spook and disperse into the willows. Perhaps because we are downwind and they get no scent of us or of the spruce smoke, they remain unaware for a surprisingly long time. At this range, and with luck, we may be able to take two deer from this band—half our needed supply of winter meat.

The deer amble slowly along, the click of their hoofs on the shore pebbles sounding faintly above the lap of the waves. Sam still holds his fire. Then at two hundred yards, the lead caribou halts. He has seen the cabin, become aware of our presence. All the caribou stop. Stare. In the dimming light, I can't tell cows from bulls; both are antlered. Sam can. He fires. To my surprise, no deer drops. The rifle scope must be off. Sam fires again; still none drops. Sam looks puzzled; quickly moves away from the worktable and closer to the shore; fires again. The band scatters, heading into the willow thickets—except for one who stands rooted to the spot, as if frozen.

Sam says, "That's the first one I fired at. He *must* be wounded!"

As he starts down the beach toward the deer, its knees suddenly buckle, it falls, lies still. I have heard the Eskimo hunters speak of this occurrence, of how a caribou may stay upright many long minutes after taking a mortal shot. But Sam is still concerned, for now that he knows the rifle scope is not off, he is certain that the second deer he aimed for was also hit. But if so, it has disappeared with the rest of the band. Now Sam feels he must go after it to see whether it was wounded or not.

Examining the spoor along the beach, he is convinced that a second caribou has been wounded. He makes his way through the willow thickets and up onto the tundra, checking the various tracks left by the fleeing band. After an hour's fruitless search across the tundra, he finds no further signs of the wounded animal.

Meanwhile, the light is fading fast, and we have at least one caribou to skin and dress out before it gets too dark to see. We work quickly against the approaching darkness. The buck is young and prime, of average weight, not one of the bigger males. The excellent pelt, free from blemishes and holes of the warble-larvae-infested spring skin, peels away easily from the layer of fat underneath. The skinning knives are hardly necessary at all.

Girl watches from the sidelines, quivering at first with excitement, but after a while, as the chill night air moves swiftly in on us, she curls up in a nest beside a tussock to sleep. We finish the quartering just as that black time between twilight and moonlight settles over us.

Hauling the meat over to hang from the poles beneath the cache to cool and season, we congratulate ourselves on our good fortune that we do not have to pack this first part of our winter meat more than the few hundred feet to the camp.

The first of the winter meat is in!

Sam awakens with bright-red swollen itching hands and wrists.

The line of this severe inflammation stops just below the elbows. It is obviously some kind of allergic reaction to the caribou blood or hide—perhaps a reaction to some form of parasite carried in the caribou skin. Studies made on caribou have found more than a hundred types of parasites living in the host animal.

Returning to the caribou remains to pick up the lower legs for skinning—four caribou shins provide the necessary skins for a pair of mukluks—we find the source of Sam's allergic reaction. Swarms of minuscule biting gnatlike insects hover over the offal. Apparently they are attracted to the caribou blood, and to Sam's hands, as he works on the caribou remains.

When we look for the caribou head in order to saw off the antlers for making implements, we find it has been dragged several hundred yards away into the willows.

Wolves. Fresh prints show at least two adults have already found the kill.

Though the winter meat is "seasoning" as it hangs under the cache, we do not wait. Our meat hunger is too great. The cabin is filled with the fragrance of caribou tongue and heart boiling on the Yukon stove. We have fresh-fried caribou liver and gonads for lunch. Girl licks her chops and watches every bite we take, even though her fat round belly is already taut and bulging with her own good scraps. She has a particular fondness for the rich, crispy cracklings from the sweet caribou fat I've been rendering all day on the stove. So have we.

A strange, somewhat troubling, night.

The frosty moonlight is so beautiful that just before bedtime we take a stroll along the narrow beach to Koviashuvik Point.

Girl, frisking along in front of us, suddenly stops and begins to bark wildly at the willow thickets along the beach. Nothing moves in the willows—no animal or bird answers the pup's frantic barks. But even as we walk on, calling her, she refuses to be quiet or to leave the spot.

We come back for her; make our way cautiously into the dark of the willow. A few feet inside the thicket, there is a large, rounded shape silhouetted in the filtered moonlight. The dark form fills a bare hollow in the brush.

The pup's frenzied yelps and the strange stillness of the form in the night make me suck in my breath, for a second frightened of the unknown. But what it is soon becomes clear. This is the second of the deer Sam took two days ago. Mortally wounded from one shot, it moved so quickly into the shelter of these willows, falling at once and at once hidden from our eye level, no wonder its spoor could not be picked up on the tundra.

This discovery is difficult in a number of ways. Sam is distressed at the possibility that the animal may have suffered unnecessarily after being hit, although the shoulder-neck wound must have quickly ended its life. Secondly, what are we to do with the carcass after it has lain here, uneviscerated, for two days? We will salvage what we can, but already there is a powerfully strong and gamy smell to the carcass. We debate getting out the lantern to try to skin and dress the deer tonight, then decide against it. The cool night air will slow further deterioration. We can get to the job early in the morning. We wonder that the wolves have not yet found the caribou. Perhaps they were diverted by the offal and head of the first kill.

After dragging the carcass out onto the beach where we can get right to it in the morning, Sam has second thoughts about the wolves—or they give us second thoughts when we hear a clear, familiar song, not quite a quarter mile away. As a precaution against them getting to the carcass before we can, Sam sets a wolf trap at either end of it. Since our competitor hunters in the territory are adults, and, therefore, cautious, they may be warned off by the traps.

Girl is still spooked, will not stop her shrill barking. We pick her up and carry her home to her caribou-fur-lined bed, into which she curls without a murmur. We, too, crawl into our caribou furs.

It seems only minutes later that Sam sits up in the bunk, tense and listening. The cabin is dark; it is still night. What is it? I whisper. Listen, Sam says.

From somewhere outside comes the sound of clanking metal. It makes no sense. Nothing in camp could make such a sound even were the wind blowing hard. And if the wind were blowing, I would hear it in the sound of waves breaking on shore. The clanking continues, sporadic, uneven. Then Sam is out of bed and rushing breakneck into his clothes.

Something is in the wolf trap. Something large enough to strain the chain that anchors each trap to thick willow roots. I rush into my things. We close Girl in the cabin behind us.

With the .22 rifle and the torch, we head for the caribou carcass. The night is black, the moon a ghost glow behind a bank of thin, low-hanging mists. The clanking grows louder as we near the carcass. In the dim light of the torch, a very faint outline of a creature moves, then hurls itself forward into space, falls to earth again—and the clang of the chain is like a crack of a whip. We can barely make out the shadow form, suddenly still, suddenly aware of our presence and of the small circle of light seeking it out. Two hot gold spots of light catch the light and reflect it back at us. The golden slanted eyes of a wolf. The wolf lunges toward us, then backs, teeth bared in a low, deep-throated growl. Lunges again, and the clash of metal chain fills the night. Sam moves in closer; hands me the torch; raises the .22—then lowers it. We move in still closer. But the torch is too dim for him to sight the rifle. The animal must be killed with a brain shot. Sighting must be accurate enough for one shot to do it. The poor light from the small flashlight is useless. I hurry back to the cabin, light the lantern. Girl is in a frenzy to go with me, but the pup could be a menace to herself and to us as well. I lock her in again, walk away from her howls of protest from behind the closed door.

The lantern is an improvement, but its circle of light drops off abruptly only a few feet from the source. I take a deep breath; move in until I am only a few feet from the wolf, swinging the lantern high to cast its brightest light onto the trapped creature. She is a young adult, a gray—and as I come near, her thrashing grows more frenzied. Sam moves in even closer; fires into the wolf's brain. The wolf drops. Sam moves closer. The wolf drags itself up onto its feet, wavering, the gold eyes fixed on Sam, the teeth bared. All the laws of nature say that life should have ceased at that first shot.

Sam mutters something which I cannot hear, but suspect is a sound of sorrow; sighs; walks up to the wolf; fires again. It drops and is still. We both stare down at the beautiful creature, slowly let out our breaths. Sam hands me the rifle and bends down to release the trap from the wolf's leg. There is a spasm of sound and sudden motion as the carcass seems to draw a deep shuddering breath. The wolf is dead, its brain shattered by the terrible impact of the bullets. But the totality of living tissue, cells, muscles, organs dies more slowly.

There is nothing we can say to each other. In this small circle of light on the dark edge of the night-still lake of Koviashuvik, here is all the miraculousness of life and death, of the universal struggle of the life force against death. It might as easily be Sam —or me—there, gasping at the breath of night, with wolf watching, uncomprehending or vaguely sensing in her way, her golden eyes turned on us as ours are now fixed on her. There is nothing to be said of this kind of experience, this knowledge. Compassion, humility, wonder, kinship, mercy, the eternal circle for each of us, all of us, predator and predator, brother and brother— there are no words that can tell of it.

I lower the lantern. We wait, silent, while the shudderings, the occasional gaspings, continue. The wolf is dead, but the wolf is dying. We do not wish to leave her here for a wolverine or other wolves to find. Sam releases the trap, hoists the carcass on his back. Walking close beside him, I hold the lantern high; we step carefully over the boulders, cross the runoff creeks and follow the beach back to the cabin.

By lantern light, Sam rigs a pulley onto the doorframe of the dogtrot, and hangs the carcass from the spruce beam. No marauders will come this close to the cabin. Tomorrow we have much work to do.

A faint perfume of frosted tundra and spruce smoke from our chimney is on the sweet night air. But over it all lies the pungent wilderness smell that is the smell of the wild wolf.

With the first light of dawn, we are up and at work.

I do not know what is triggered in our little "bear" dog when she sniffs frantically at the door, whines, barks, claws at the doorjamb. Let out, and encountering the hanging carcass just outside the door, she seems berserk with fear or excitement or something older and unknown. Sam drives her away from the carcass. She watches the skinning from a distance, but her neck hairs stay stiff and bristling.

After the wolf is skinned and the carcass taken off onto the tundra, where it will be found and used by others, we start to work on the caribou. For our use, the meat is already over the borderline in decomposition. Had we a dog team to feed, the meat would be usable. Or, if we were near starving, we would chance it ourselves. We salvage a ham, just in case, and the pelt, the leg bones for marrow and the leg skins for mukluks. The wolves are welcome to the remains.

Many hours each day scraping skins. When the sun is highest, I work outside. But now the sun rides lower in the sky each day. Its warmth is subdued; its light, the light of the arctic autumn, golden and haunting. When the mountains tip up to hide the great globe, turning wind sharp and chill, I bring the skins inside and continue scraping, sitting on the floor, my back to the stove warmth. The wolf pelt requires great care in working it. A careless thrust of the sharp-edged scraper will cut the fine skin through.

Two days of blustery winds and rain have faded the bright colors of autumn. Red and gold leaves swept from their branches by the storm soften the tundra to brown.

Each day is shorter by seven to eight minutes as we spin back toward the long arctic night.

Labor Day. Down to ten degrees!

By noon, a raging blizzard; six inches of snow in less than an hour. With ice below the tundra, snow and cold north winds above, the earth's summer sun warmth will soon be gone. Snow falling on the mountains deepens, holds.

Snowshoe repair. Some small rascals—weasels, parky squirrels, voles, shrew—have been eating on the leather thongs this summer!

No caribou offal or remains left at the site of the kill.

Even some of the tundra itself has been devoured. The grass and moss where blood and bits of flesh spilled are now close-cropped. Fresh wolf scat and tracks surround the site; smaller tracks, too, perhaps Kia's.

Today the sense of game on the move is very strong.

Again and again we scan the distance with binoculars. A flash of white across the lake near Rooney's cross catches my eye. In the glasses is an immense bull moose with a stunning rack. We watch him feed in the shallows, amble up onto shore, lower his head to scrape the magnificent antlers up and down against the trunk of a spruce tree, then move on along the shore. I wait for Sam to say the word; this is the time, if we are to take a moose for our winter meat. But Sam goes back to working on the cache; I return to my skin scraping on the outside worktable.

Minutes later, the awareness of other or others returns, this time so strongly that I turn again to scan shore and slopes. A slight motion on the tip of Caribou Island—a small band, perhaps a dozen, of caribou, milling about the narrow beach.

With rifle and cameras, we are in the boat and on our way toward them in seconds. To our left, on the mainland shore, the bull moose has settled down in a thicket, watching our approach; to our right, the caribou have not yet sighted our approach. Circling wide to avoid the attention of the deer, we head for a point midway the island's length, and downwind of the caribou. We may drift in close enough toward them, with luck, and film the band before they take flight. But the minute we reach the shallows, we are sighted, smelled, sensed. The entire band turn to statues, all eyes fixed on us. Now that they are aware of us, we have no choice but to head right for them, as fast as possible, hoping to catch them on film at least from a distance.

In the band are several cows, with bucks, yearlings, two calves. However, the central figure, the caribou that commands our attention, is a large buck perhaps four years old, prime and sleek—a tremendous caribou compared to the other bucks we have seen. No question but that he is the leader, the dominant one, the one the band will follow. We keep our eyes fixed on him as he stands immobile, at the water's edge, watching our approach. Alert, taut, he is poised to move instantly. When he does, we expect him to lead the band inland. Instead he suddenly bounds forward into the water. The others follow at once as he begins swimming out into the lake, toward the opposite shore. We speed after them. Gain on them. Sam takes the boat in closer and closer.

When we are only a few feet behind them, the swimming band spooks, changes direction. But not the buck. He continues moving away from us. The others, panicking, forget or ignore the leader; disperse, regroup; and in their coming together again, head straight at the boat. Abreast of the prow, the furiously swimming band divides itself in half. Break formation to swim around the boat. And suddenly we are caught in the middle of the band. Sharp-pronged antlers rake the sides of the boat, curve over the sides.

Camera is completely forgotten as the boat rocks violently from side to side, tipped over one way and then the other as the milling caribou bump against its sides. Still caught in the center of the swimming herd, locked in by the caribou's herding together around us, we are swept along with them; cannot get free of the tangle.

Fixed in this moment of half-adventure, half-nightmare, I know that if I have any trust that we will get out of it without capsizing or drowning, it is probably greatly dependent on Sam. But one look at Sam and trust is badly shaken, for he seems to have gone as berserk as the situation. While I have been ducking antlers and hanging onto Girl, he has been busily working over a coil of rope.

Sam jumps to his feet and, with a wild whoop, swings the looped rope round and round over his head and out into space past the twisted prongs of the deer surrounding us, and toward the head of the mighty buck. Using the boat like a rodeo horse, he tries again and again to lasso the buck. When the rope falls short each time, stopped by the wind, he tries to maneuver the boat round to get closer to the leader. Jockeying, spinning us in and around the swimming deer, he then tries to separate out the buck from the rest. At last he succeeds.

The buck strikes off in a different direction. Once the buck has left the band, Sam holds the boat between them, keeping the buck and the others apart until the leader is clearly heading back toward the island—alone. But we do not follow him. Instead Sam takes the boat in close, right behind the caribou band, whooping, hollering, nudging the backside closest to us with the prow of the boat, herding them forward, driving the whole band toward the shore.

Finding myself in the middle of a roundup in the Arctic requires some adjustment in my perception of what is happening. Having long accepted the fact that Sam may be the only Renaissance man of my acquaintance—theologian, hunter, log cabin builder, biologist, fisherman, philosopher, survival expert, ecologist, artist-writer, explorer, cartographer, maker of fires and of arrowheads—I know that he is a many-faceted and skilled creature, the kind of creature with possibly the best odds of any for surviving that unknown future that is so rapidly closing in on the planet. But this new facet of Sam's survival skills, discovered here in the unlikely middle of an arctic lake, comes as something of a shock. Sam's cowpunching days were before my time.

Even so, I am too wise a woman to ask questions in the middle of a roundup. I know he wants that prime buck for our winter meat, but I guess that he also wants to get that spooked band safely ashore before the cows head out into deep water again and the calves become too exhausted to make it to shore. We herd them on in like a bunch of swimming cattle until they hit the shallows and go bounding ashore and off over the tundra.

We race back toward the island. Cruising parallel along the island shore, we see a flash of white antler inland. It is moving parallel to us and in the same direction. Almost simultaneously, we and the buck reach the end of the island where a three-hundred-yard channel of shallows separates the island from the shore of the mainland. The buck bounds into the channel, starts to swim across. We round the end of the island, turn into the channel, attempt to converge on the same spot of beach on the mainland.

But the buck has the advantage at the moment. He will reach that shore point much faster than can we, for we are still several hundred yards distant from it. When the buck rises dripping and sleek from the shallows to step ashore, we are still over two hundred yards away. One leap, one great bound, will take him inland, behind the shore screen of scrub brush, to disappear, out of range.

But the hunter has counted on the predictability of caribou behavior. Before that bound occurs, even as the caribou buck is contracting his muscles to the tautness of a coiled spring about to be released in a single mighty leap beyond our reach, he turns his head to stare at us. In that single, predicted second of the stare, I know what is to happen; slide forward; hunch down flat in the boat bottom clutching Girl under me and sense Sam quickly raise the rifle.

A deafening crash explodes over my head. I do not move. Hear the thud of rifle being set down in the boat, feel the boat move forward before I raise my head. By the time we reach the buck where he has fallen back in the shallows, little of him shows above water except for the great antlers. The shoulder-neck shot was clean and immediate.

By the time we haul the carcass ashore, dress it out and get back to camp across the lake, dark will have come. Easier to rope it onto the stern of the boat and float it back to camp, where we can work by lantern light if necessary. Sam uses the lasso rope to tie on our winter meat, and we head back for camp.

Getting the carcass ashore requires all our strength and more. This is the biggest, heaviest caribou I've ever seen. With night coming on quickly, we eviscerate and skin the deer on a patch of soft moss away from the cabin, then maneuver the carcass into the wheelbarrow to hang it from a temporary cache in the nearby spruce trees to be quartered in the morning light.

The evening is cold. We rush to finish our task, to get back into the warm cabin where our supper of a panful of marrow bones that have been roasting all afternoon is awaiting us. As we finish stringing up the meat, wolf songs begin on the mountain behind camp. They, too, were aware today of caribou on the move. Their song tonight may well be a song about *our* winter meat. As a precaution, Sam sets wolf traps to either side of the fresh meat cache, and we go home to our marrow bones and rest.

This morning at about 2 A.M., Sam stepped outside; returned and shook me out of my warm sleep to come and see the return of the aurora borealis filling the heavens, dancing in rippling waves from east to west, to focus, finally, just overhead. Welcome back, old friend!

Up early to get to our chore of quartering the caribou and hanging it to season. Another perfect fall morning, crisp at about fifteen above zero, sky swept cloud-free by the fresh north wind.

Our excellent breakfast of sourdough hotcakes and caribou steak is interrupted—screams, howls—impossible to describe. An unearthly bedlam of wild shrieking cries.

Outside, nothing can be seen, but Sam races at once for the wolf traps. It is Girl, not a wolf. I wait outside the cabin, half expecting Sam to call for the rifle, ready to bring it quickly if it is needed. The agonized cries continue; I hear beneath their shrill persistence only low murmurs from Sam, can see only his outline, vaguely in motion, everything shrouded by the brush, Sam's form bent over where the traps were set last night. He straightens, moves out from the willows onto the beach and comes toward me, holding Girl locked under one arm. Blood covers the pup; Sam's hands and arms are also crimson.

Not knowing what damage the pup has suffered, whether bandages or rifle are to be requested, I ask no questions but am ready for either. Sam says by way of reassurance, "The blood isn't hers—it's mine. She bit me while I was trying to get her out of the trap. She didn't want to; she couldn't help herself."

I fill the basin with warm water; get out the whiskey bottle. Sam puts Girl down on the floor. She cries out, begins to whimper. But when he nudges her, forces her to move, she does move, moves painfully, dragging her hind leg and hip, crying. Sam feels the limb for breaks. Girl lets him touch it, but cries out as he does, bares her teeth, puts her mouth to his hand as if to bite, then licks the hand instead.

There seems to be no actual break, though the pup's leg and hip are still swelling, are darkly discolored. All cubs, including puppies, have strong healing powers. Girl may be left with a game leg, but the odds look so much better than I had feared that our relief makes us almost joyous. Sam puts her in her box. This time she does not circle about to make her nest but sinks down at once, nosing the furs and whimpering softly.

Next we care for Sam; bathe his hands and forearms. When the blood is washed off, a half-dozen bites, two deep, ragged ones, are visible. We pour whiskey over and into the wounds; leave them uncovered for the arctic wind and sun to heal.

We finish our cold breakfast, but eating now seems a secondary thing. Girl's whining stops; she falls into the deep sleep of an exhausted cub.

I have made a mistake with this beagle pup. The Eskimo people are right not to make pets of their dogs. Survival here is too marginal to confuse a dog by treating him as a pet one minute and expecting him to be survival oriented the next. Girl has been warned away from the traps every time a trap has been set. Yesterday's accident was caused by her own disobedience or willfulness. If we had *kicked* her away very hard the first few times she went near the traps, as would the Eskimo dog owners, she would have learned without question not to go near them.

Sam would have been able to train her to obedience and survival if I had not immediately loved and treated her as a pet.

If she had had to be destroyed yesterday, I would not want another dog here in the wilderness. It is a place for wildness, not domesticity.

The feel of game about remains strong.

Late afternoon, a spot of gold moving on the water catches my eye. Something swimming toward the island from the south. Glassing the motion, we see a creature swimming along, but cannot tell what it is. It has the look of a swimming porcupine, like one sighted in early summer, late sun goldening the hairs on its back. We watch it swim for more than a mile in deep water. Reaching the island, it climbs ashore, then rounds the point and trots on along the sandy beach toward the far end of the island, apparently heading for the mainland. From its size and loping gait on land, we decide it must be either a small black bear or a wolverine. And with that decision, Sam reaches for the .22 rifle, I reach for the camera, and in less than a minute, we are in the boat and on our way across the lake. We can make excellent use of bear meat or a wolverine hide for ruffs.

As we near the island and begin to parallel its shore, in the distance we can see the animal reach the end of the island and plunge into the channel waters to swim over to the mainland. Although I've never seen wolverine or black bear in water, there is something about the look of the creature we are rapidly approaching that makes me certain it is neither of the animals we've assumed it is. The closer we come to it and the more I study it, the more certain I am that the brown fur showing above the water surface is not, as I had assumed, the back of an animal, but its head. And that massive brown dome can belong to nothing smaller than a grizzly bear.

From my seat in the prow of the boat, I focus the camera in on the bear just as he reaches the shallows. He lumbers ashore. Turns. Faces us. I throw the zoom-lens lever to close-up. The great grizzly fills the frame. His small, glittering eyes are fixed steadily on us; lips pulled back to reveal sharp teeth, broad black snout lifted, sniffing our approach.

The head in the viewfinder grows larger and larger. But the bear is not moving toward us. We are heading straight for the grizzly, who is only a hundred feet away. The boat does not slow or change its course. That grizzlies do not care for the water, as I have been told, is obviously a myth. This one has just swum more than a mile and looks as if he is poised for another dip— in our direction.

I glance quickly over my shoulder at Sam to see why he hasn't changed course. He has that same wild-eyed look of joyous anticipation that he wore all through the caribou roundup. I glance quickly at the bear, who, now only about fifty feet away, is the largest, most powerful creature I've ever seen, planted as solidly as a huge boulder, waiting, looking, ready and alert for that instant when the boat will land right at his feet.

Taking rapid stock of the situation, I realize that in the prow of the boat I will be the first thing to hit the shore. And should Sam even now have to use the rifle, I completely block his range. This insight tells me how irrational my thinking or the situation has turned, for no paltry .22 rifle will be able to stop a charging grizzly bear. It occurs to me that I may appear, in the grizzly's eyes, to be charging *him*. One leap takes me from the prow of the boat to the stern. Sam and his wisdom are now between me and the grizzly. But in that one blind, survival-motivated gesture of mine, I also give up some film wildlife

photographers dream of. In the second my back is to the beautiful beast, the magnificent, golden-humped wild grizzly bear
silently turns and pads off into the brush.

Sam readies to beach the boat and follow the bear. He wishes
to observe the bear close up. And he is also thinking of winter
meat, of sweet bear fat and of a fine bearskin. He also assumes
I want more pictures. I do. But I scan the shore where the grizzly
has just disappeared, and note the thick willow and alder brush
with not a climbable tree anywhere. To enter that blind tangle
of thickets with only a .22 rifle, even with the best of hunters,
is something I cannot bring myself to do. I shake my head,
firmly negative, reminding myself that the women of Anaktuvuk
are certainly no cowards, but they, too, avoid grizzlies.

Sam turns the boat and we head back to camp. Nothing more
is said about the encounter. My chagrin at having spoiled the
hunt and missed some great photographs is bothersome. But with
it, I know that one of my certainties about grizzlies, one of my
survival plans about grizzlies, has now been thoroughly destroyed: grizzlies *do* swim.

Ten degrees above zero this morning. The world cloaked
in ice frost, sparkling in early slanting sunlight. Remember the
rich tundra greens of summer, the hot reds and golds of autumn.
Now tall grasses dry and goldened, willow and alder branches
stripped bare and stark—all glisten like fine polished crystal in
their ice sheaths this morning. The lake, steaming thickly at
sunrise, later turns tranquil and still.

Sam takes off to cut trees for the cache. He goes prepared to
hunt as well, taking the 30/06. Through the binoculars, we
have seen the grizzly bear feeding in the open meadow across
the lake.

This day goes slowly for some reason, perhaps because I know
Sam is surely on the trail of the grizzly. I can see the boat, a
pinpoint of color, beached across the lake. That it stays there
long beyond the time Sam needs to harvest trees makes me
certain that he has gone after the grizzly. There is nothing to

worry about, I know, and yet I remain vaguely uneasy, go frequently to see if the boat has moved from its mooring.

Not until almost dusk does the boat leave. Even with it still halfway across the lake, dimly outlined in near dark, I know Sam has taken the bear—the mound that mars the familiar shape of the old boat is surely the grizzly pelt.

Reaching camp, Sam wearily ties up the boat. I reach for the massive pelt, which is rolled and tied to a packboard, to lift it ashore. But it weighs almost a hundred pounds. Sam spreads it out on the tundra for me to see. The hide stretches nearly three yards in length. The back fur is honey-colored; the grizzly hump, golden white. The rest of the pelt is of a darker brown, except for the leg fur, which is black and very glossy. The curved talons extending from the leathery foot pads are two inches long. And the head huge, beyond what I ever could have imagined. Sam has also brought back the skull, to meet the requirements of the state's game laws. All grizzly skulls are measured as part of the data gathering and study done by the Fish and Game Department. Even more astonishing than the size of the great skull are its powerful jaws and the size of the tusklike canines.

We roll up the pelt, carry it inside the cabin to keep it from freezing. To scrape this huge skin will take days and much care. When we maneuver it under the table, where it barely fits, Girl leaps about snarling at the fur, nape hairs stiff and bristling. No commands cut through her frenzy. A smart slap finally brings her round, makes her sit nervous and quivering across the room, still eying the pelt, the whites of her eyes showing like those of a skittish horse.

Over tea, Sam tells me of the hunt—of sighting the grizzly a mile away feeding in the meadow, of moving round downwind and of the stalk to get within range. Of the bear becoming aware of the hunter, turning to meet him head on, of one shot fired, of the bear hit but not dropped, rearing up, snorting, blowing, growling, swiping at its muzzle as if the shot had hit him there, rocking from side to side as if preparing to charge. Then of the bear turning, running, Sam following, but losing sight of the great bear as he raced up the slopes, toward the creek and into its dense tangle of willow. Of Sam then moving cautiously to the edge of the willow screen, of trying to rim up high enough to look down from above into the thicket to see if the injured grizzly might be below him. Of hearing snorting and blowing in the nearby brush, of wheeling round to see the bear, eyes fixed on the hunter, and only a few yards away. Of two quick shots fired, the second a breast shot, instantly dropping the bear. Of the *coup de grace,* and the quiet moments of stillness in the thicket as Sam squatted beside the great creature, thinking, wondering. Of beginning the skinning job, taking head and pelt, and being suddenly shockingly aware that the white-fleshed carcass without its fur coat resembled with surprising likeness that of a human. Of dressing out the carcass and leaving it on the tundra overnight to cool, for dark was coming on, and trees to cache the meat in were too distant. Of our mutual prayer that wolves and wolverines would keep their distance until tomorrow, when the job of caring for our winter bear meat can be finished.

Up very early today to get across the lake and take care of the bear. But the weather is not cooperative. Twelve degrees this morning—blowy, cold, sleeting. And the lake roils and churns, breaking up the shore ice that already extends out several feet. While waiting for a break in the weather, Sam works on the grizzly skull.

There is enough flesh on the huge skull to feed several people; it must all be cleaned off to preserve the skull for the Fish and Game men.

It is now snowing heavily to the north; Sam is concerned about the meat. The minute the wind dies down a little, he takes off with Girl for across the lake. When he returns a few hours later, it is with a leg of bear, the internal organs and a great sack of fat. The ham is so heavy I cannot lift it—the foot disturbingly human in shape with its five toes. Bear fat, pure, sweet-smelling enough to eat raw. But bear, like pork, is a host for trichinosis, and all bear meat must be thoroughly cooked. Fat, cut into small cubes, goes onto the stove for rendering. Bear tongue, heart and gonads go into the pot to boil for dinner, and several more meals as well.

At supper, I try some of everything, for bear meat is new to me. The tongue is excellent, very similar to that of caribou except for its coarser texture. The gonads are stronger-tasting than caribou or moose. And to eat the heart of grizzly bear is to understand in one blinding insight the sacred connotation of our ancestors' identification with the wild.

Many trips will be necessary to pack the rest of the meat down the long slope and into the boat to be ferried to our camp cache. Today Sam returns to finish the butchering of the bear. He then packs all the meat over to the nearest stand of tall spruce, where, improvising a temporary cache, he hangs the bear quarters. It should be fairly safe there as it seasons, hung high enough to keep it from the wolves. We can transfer it to camp at our leisure.

I begin scraping the fine pelt. The skin side is so greasy from the bear's thick layer of fat along the back just under the skin that I exchange my clogged-up, slippery scrapers for my skinning knife and ulu. Working with them, I slice away the ridges and chunks of fat, taking great care not to cut through the fine, thin skin of the underbelly. After several hours of work, no more than a quarter of the huge pelt has been defatted.

The first ermine joins us today. He seems to have moved in for the winter. His smooth pelt is now pure white but for the black nose and a small brownish patch on the cheek and the immense saucers of black eyes that fill his little face. We smell his musk before we see him. His arrival is abrupt, a sudden dash from out of the woodpile into the dogtrot. He wants the fresh meat, of course. Climbs right to it on the high shelf. When I appear in the cabin door, he rears up beside the meat as if declaring his ownership rights. I scold him. He barks fiercely back at me, but when I start for him with my skin scraper, he skitters off fast enough.

An hour later, I hear him arguing with Sam at the cache. When Sam comes back into the cabin, the young ermine follows him right to the door, barking and scolding as if demanding he be invited in!

Another sound of winter in the night. Tiny teeth chomping on something in the kitchen corner. Shrew sounds.

Wintry overcasts, snow falling, mountains whitening.
When the sun breaks through briefly, its warmth is muted, feeble.

We have never been busier! A caribou leg, almost completely frozen, must be butchered into roasts, stew meat, chopped caribouburger. Cranberries reaching their peak must be harvested; I have already picked many quarts to take us through winter. Skin scraping fills every extra hour; wood gathering and fish harvesting and smoking must go on. And all done with a feeling of great anticipation, of excitement, that winter is so close at hand!

A break in the weather; overcast swept away during the night by cold winds from the north. It is still, and the sun, without wind, seems almost brilliant. Wanting to savor each moment of its remaining warmth, I work on the skins outside. Sam takes off across the lake for more poles, more firewood, more fish.

An hour later, I hear a faint echo of a rifle shot waft across the water. I wonder if Sam has encountered a grizzly, or taken a caribou, although with two caribou *and* a bear in the cache, we probably have enough winter meat to take us through.

Immediately following the shot, the thin distant sound of the wash of waters drifts across. Glassing the opposite shore, I see three moose in the shallows. One, a great bull, is standing, antlered head lifted, looking at the shore. The other two, cows, are moving away from him, heading south through the shallows. Then, from a spot along the shore a few hundred yards above where the bull moose stands, I see a tiny, light-colored speck that is the boat pull out into the water, pass around the bull and disappear from view into the channel behind the island. What is going on over there? Sam is not after one of the moose. Bulls are in rut, our moose season closed, enough winter meat. But what does the rifle shot mean?

When Sam returns, I find out. Crossing the lake, he saw the handsome bull and his two cows in the shore shallows. Hoping to get some film on the courtship rituals of moose, he beached the boat several hundred yards downwind and crept through the brush toward the three moose. Just as he reached a spot a few feet inland from the trio, set down the rifle and readied the camera, he heard a loud snort behind him.

. . . He wheels about to discover a second bull moose, barely twenty feet away. Snorting and huffing, the young bull sways his mighty rack from side to side, swoops the massive head down, swings it up, catches up a five-foot-tall spruce tree in the carved prongs, uprooting tree and tundra and flinging it high into the air, lowers the great head, paws the tundra and glowers at Sam. A second series of snorts is heard now, behind Sam. The bull in the shallows, thirty feet away, has heard the challenge.

At some point during this moment of confrontation, front and back, Sam says that he is certain he must have made some conscious decisions. All he can remember is that it was one of those moments containing a kaleidoscopic vision of an entire lifetime. Yet during this insight, he automatically dropped the camera, reached for and readied the rifle, and at the exact instant of the young bull's charge, fired. No head-on shot will stop such a charge at such close range. With the cool logic that the survival imperative seems to create, he fired over the moose's head. Without a break in speed, at the thunderous clap of the rifle shot, the moose veered off to the side, whirled around and vanished in the brush.

By now it is clear, Sam reports, that he accidentally had joined in a competition for a moose harem. With the young challenger momentarily departed from the battlefield, Sam himself now had the full challenging attention of the old bull in the shallows. The two cows under dispute splashed away from the scene of gunfire, along the shore shallows toward the quiet of the island. This was the moment I witnessed through the binoculars.

Sam decided to forget pictures; to leave the territory while the leaving was good. He raced back to the boat, passed the old bull by with a respectful wave of the hand, and went fishing.

A glorious late autumn–early winter day: clear, with a fine open sky.

Late in the day, the wolves begin to sing. A hunting pack? or our old friends, returned home to Koviashuvik for the winter? No more than a half mile away to the north, two begin a duet. A third, and then a fourth, join in from the mountain slope behind the cabin. We fall asleep to wolf song. Wake up at four in the morning to wolf song, but this chorus comes from no mountaintop or away to the north. This many-voiced choir rings our camp.

Listening in the dark night, we hear two voices that seem to be coming from the other side of the wall. Three more add their caroling from right behind the cabin. Another three begin to sing their own eerie night song on the third side of the cabin, from somewhere between the privy and the woodpile. A dozen wolves can sound like a hundred-voice chorale.

Something in this wild chorus makes one's own blood sing in answer. I feel no fear, only a great excitement, wonder, that they have come so close to give us this greeting—or so I choose to believe. That their full-throated message is a hymn of praise to our campful of fresh winter meat is more likely!

We lie awake in the darkness, listening to the wild song, reveling in the presence of the wolves as, one by one, a voice drops away, another quiets, until at last a pair finds itself singing a lone duet—and then they, too, are quiet. The song is over. The pack has moved on.

The scent of something more easily attainable than our meat has crossed their awareness. Or the hunger in them drives them on to more promising hunting grounds. But they will be back, will return, as winter returns, to Koviashuvik.

Last night's chorus spurs Sam to bring in more of the bear meat cached in the spruce across the lake. He takes off with Girl, to begin packing the bear meat to the boat.

When he returns a few hours later, it is without any meat at all.

He sensed something was wrong, he reports, when Girl began to act up.

The pup delights in these hikes with Sam. She charges over the tundra, sniffing into every hollow and hole, leaping tussocks, but always keeping Sam in sight or scent though not close by his side unless he calls. Today, about a half mile up the slope to the cached meat, Girl's scampering race came to a sudden stop. Guard hairs rising, she began to growl. Fifty feet in front of her was a large gray wolf. As Girl began to bark at the wolf, the wolf turned suddenly toward the dog, teeth bared, growling low and warning in the back of its throat.

At this response, the pup's furious barks cut off abruptly. She wheeled about and streaked down toward the shore. The wolf melted away into the brush. Cussing dog and wolf, Sam raced after the pup to make sure she was not to be wolf bait. He found her cowering and whimpering in the back corner of the boat. On their next try up the slope, the nervous dog kept close by Sam's heels. Halfway up to the meat in the grove, they heard the wolf pack begin to sing.

At the cache, nothing remained of the several hundred pounds of bear meat. Under the spot where it had hung, a wide circle of snow and tundra was packed down hard by the feet of many wolves. Was this the pack that serenaded us last night? Having filled their bellies on cached bear meat, did they then circle the lake, come upon the familiar scent of the man and bear meat at our camp—and gather round to sing to us?

The news is depressing on two accounts. Not only is there a sense of terrible waste and of regret that the fine grizzly went to our chief competitors, the other primary predators of our territory. But now our winter meat cache is again on the lean side for the long cold months ahead. Two caribou will not see us through winter.

We will hope for more caribou bands to come through. Hope for a good ptarmigan crop. Perhaps it will be less difficult to eat our camp ptarmigan family when they become unrecognizable in their white winter dress. And though the fish we have smoked is not substantial winter fare, as an emergency filler it may turn out to be very helpful. Fortunately, too, one ham and most of the many pounds of fine bear fat were brought to camp before the wolves made their assault.

Still, Sam is puzzled about how the wolves brought down the hanging bear meat, for the meat was strung higher than the tallest, most powerful wolf could jump. So how did they reach the bear meat?

Today Sam returns to the scene of the stolen meat. Carefully examines the spoor, the ropes, the bits of flesh still clinging to the ropes, the bark and branches of the two trees that held the spruce-pole bar from which the meat was hung. Before he leaves, there is a snare for wolverine set in the branches of one of those trees that held the pole cache.

Minus six degrees at dawn.

The lake almost obscured by whirling cloud mists of steam. Mountains, water and mist, a sepia-colored world of stillness, of waiting, of expectation. Around the shore, a wide shelf of ice now several inches thick edges farther and farther out into the lake.

When the sun rises to dissipate the cloud vapors, we head out for cranberrying and wood gathering. Rooney's knoll carpeted ruby red with the tiny, fat, round berries. I spend hours squatting on the cold tundra, raking in the rich harvest. Sam works elsewhere on the mainland shore, cutting and hauling dead trees. We rope the logs into rafts, haul them behind the boat. Every trip away from camp these days is involved with winter harvest.

At the small island where in a shaded grove the cranberries grow almost as densely as at Rooney's though they are only two-thirds the size, we find a dead and mutilated loon. The wolves? or an encounter with a pike?

Glassing the peaks, we see motion halfway up a slope. Three grizzlies, ambling across the face of the mountain. One has the blond streak across its shoulders and back, the golden-haired grizzly hump of the adult. The other two, darker-colored and with no light patch reflecting back sun gold, move erratically, without seeming purpose or destination, up and down and across the slope, running a few steps one way, then galloping off in another direction. The blond-humped grizzly moves steadily along at a much more sedate gait than her rambunctious two-year-old cubs.

Sam leaves off his wood gathering to join me for lunch. We stretch out next to the cranberry patch on thick moss where the sun strikes fullest and warmest, and eat our lunch of bear tongue and sourdough bread. It is a fine thing to be able to recognize contentment when one holds it, however briefly, in the hand of one's life. To be able to recognize the look and feel and smell of paradise when one arrives there, to pause, savoring place and moment, is surely the answer at the heart of all mysteries.

Late afternoon, when we leave the little island to return to camp with our booty of cranberries, rose hips and wood, we pass by patch after patch of floating thin silver sheets of newly frozen ice.

Four loons lift off open water to pass overhead. They are all the same size now. They are the last ones here, I think.

Sam returns to check the site of the stolen grizzly cache. Coming upon the spot, Girl breaks into a frenzied barking. And an equally furious commotion erupts in the tree where the snare has been set. A wolverine struggles wildly in the snare. The loop of wire has caught it just above its hindquarters. The creature has already gnawed off part of its own leg to get free. Sam uses the .22, then takes the carcass from the snare.

Sam was right in reading the signs. No wolf pulled down the hanging meat. The wolverine climbed up the spruce tree and out on the pole to chew through the ropes and let the meat fall to earth. He must have been frightened off from his windfall by the arrival of the pack of hungry wolves. He might have stayed and fought off one or even two wolves, but not the pack. Sam knew the wolverine would be back. The memory of such a prize cache would bring him back, even though the wolves had left nothing for him. And the wolverine returned by his original route, but this time he climbed into the hidden snare.

When Sam returns to camp with the wolverine lashed to his packboard, the stench of its musk is overpowering. Feeling the thick, soft pelt, I am reminded of why the fur is so prized for parky ruffs. A golden band patterns the sides and shoulders of the rich brown pelt.

At first glance, the wolverine looks something like a small bear. Belonging to the weasel family, its body is longer, slimmer, more strung out than a black bear's. When Sam removes the skull for a specimen, I can see where the wolverine's massive strength is centered. The jaws and teeth, though small by comparison, look as powerful as those of the grizzly.

While Sam finishes skinning the wolverine, I put in more work on the grizzly hide. The bearskin will make a warm cover for our bunk this winter. The wolverine pelt will make us warm, ice-free parky ruffs. But still I think about caribou and winter meat. . . .

Minus eight this morning.

In our bay, a floating pan of ice a hundred feet across, with diamond specks that are ice flowers beginning to form. The morning is filled with the tinkling bell sounds of wind and wave playing against the ice sheet. A hard, metallic-edged sound is also heard somewhere beneath the high bell-like notes as wind-churned waves wash over the shore ice and strike the frozen earth of the shore.

Freeze-up has begun!

Time now has a quality of swiftness about it that is especially evident at this season just as freeze-up begins. Each moment lived at a peak of aliveness, awareness, expectancy. Any morning now, we will get up and find the lake hidden, covered over with its winter ice dress. The cover will thicken each day. And for a while, we will be land-bound, tied to shore until the lake ice is a safe four inches thick. But as long as there is open water, we feel an urgency to travel by it; continue to berry, wood gather, hunt.

Heading out into open water today, we sight something dark and large in the water off Caribou Island. Hope it is a caribou, swimming. But it appears too dark for that. Watching it as we approach, we are all the more mystified, because it does not appear to move at all. Coming closer, we see first the antler tip of a bull moose, and then a shoulder, showing just above the water line. Approaching it cautiously in case it is an injured bull, we still see no movement. Closing in, we can see the bull is dead, drowned apparently. In the crystalline clear water which is here only four to five feet deep, we can see the whole creature. There is no visible sign of injury, no obvious sign of sickness or disease. This may be one of the bulls of Sam's earlier encounter, wounded in a rut battle and drowned when he tried to swim away to safety.

In our life here together, Sam and I have developed a communication that in situations like this needs few words. I look at him questioningly. He shakes his head. The meat cannot be salvaged; it is rut-tainted. However, it will not go to waste. The fish will feast on the flesh as it disintegrates.

This morning, twelve below zero.

All the bays are frozen over. We can see the ice forming and spreading out, moving toward the lake center.

More ducks pass overhead, winging southward. Our merganser

flock has been gone for several days. The last loons may have gone, too, for I have not heard them call for a couple of days. A few chickadees have returned, and we hear their friendly greeting every time we are on the trail. Our old friends the ubiquitous jays, ready for winter, fluffing up their autumn-sleek coats. And today, a raven heard, its call clearly "Tuk-tu! tuk-tu!"

We hear it from halfway up the mountainside on our way to cut and stack dead trees for winter. Look down to the tussock flats near Last Chance and see the large black bird circling round and round, repeating its call again and again. Something below has its interest. It could be anything, from a saucy jay to a parky squirrel. Whatever it is flashes white. And before that instantaneous flash has disappeared, Sam, with rifle held above his head, is bounding down the mountain and heading for the flats.

The sun where I am is lovely and warm, the tussocks cushioned by dried grasses on top of the frozen tundra. Below me, Sam and the white are hidden by the trees. I might well stumble into range if I follow. I sit down on the tussock to wait, to listen. Ten minutes later, I hear the shot. Know without seeing that we have another caribou for the cache.

From the sound of the shot I can estimate that the deer has been dropped no more than a quarter of a mile from the shore. By breaking our way through shore ice, we can still use the boat to haul the meat back to camp, and save ourselves several miles of backpacking.

By the time I get the boat and find Sam in the grove, he has already gutted and started skinning the fine buck. We work quickly, racing against time to get the boat out before it gets too tightly iced in. In two trips to the shore, we pack out all our meat. Break through the thick shore ice. Take our caribou home to the cache.

Three caribou and one bear ham may see us through. If not, we'll eat arctic doughnuts fried in the sweetest, purest of bear fat. Now I feel ready for winter!

At camp we have to break a path through many feet of ice to reach shore.

After unloading the meat, we bring the boat onto shore and

beach it for winter storage. Now we are landlocked until the ice thickens.

Twenty below zero this morning.

By noon, half the lake is iced over. By nightfall, almost all the lake. Only a few narrow channels are still open in the center. Frost flowers blossom on the field of ice. Tonight a great chorus of wolves sings from across the lake. Perhaps they, too, have had fresh meat today.

Last night, the last of the open leads froze over.

Last night, I heard the last loon call. Today he is gone.

The great plain of ice thickens, shifts, expands, contracts, sings and hums, moans and whispers, calls its ancient message in its ancient voice: "Autumn passed, winter comes. . . ."

POSTSCRIPT

These journals of our first year in the wilderness of the far north have been shared by request. Left to my own choice, I doubt they would ever have been put to print.

While Koviashuvik exists in reality, it is primarily a reality of the interior landscape of my own mind. This journal is less about a place than a way of looking at life in any place.

If the world of my dailiness beyond the Arctic Circle sings to you, do not make the mistake of coming to the arctic wilderness in hope of finding the same song. You must discover your own, not mine. You must discover your own Koviashuvik.

Many have written of the importance of the wild—Thoreau, Muir, Leopold, Marshall, the Indian and Eskimo poets and storytellers. If in sharing this very personal inner-outer world of mine with you I have communicated the urgent necessity to cherish and protect this last remnant of what is and always has been the best of our planet, then it will have been worth the uneasiness I feel in agreeing to publish my journals. My concern is that in writing, lovingly, caringly, of wilderness I may be doing the wilderness, and perhaps you, a great disservice.

The arctic wilderness is not an option for people seeking an alternative life style. Subsistence and survival in any wilderness are a difficult and demanding way of life even for those with the essential skills and experience. Subsistence and survival under the extreme subzero conditions of arctic wilderness are doubly demanding and dangerous. Without Sam's vast experience and knowledge of wilderness survival, as well as his superlative skills in hunting, fishing and living off the land, we could not experience the life written of in these journals. There is no blueprint for these skills; no book ever written that can teach them. And the arctic wilderness is the wrong place to try to learn them. Each arctic winter kills a few more of those without the skills and knowledge.

Another part of my concern is that the delicate ecology of the arctic wilderness cannot sustain many people. Koviashuvik, with its marginal and extremely slow tree growth, has not enough wood available to supply logs for more cabins or heat for more stoves. Heavy fishing in the delicately balanced ecological life of this arctic lake would begin a cycle which would quickly destroy that balance. Game in the wilds of the far north is not abundant enough to survive any heavy hunting.

With the invasion of the oil- and mineral-development technology into the far north (and now there are rumors of a nuclear power enrichment plant, and its attendant "city," to follow), grizzly and polar bear are species in jeopardy. The rapidly increasing number of nonsubsistence trophy hunters, illegal hunting from aircraft and inadequate game-law enforcement are among the most blatant factors responsible.

Few caribou have come through Koviashuvik the past three years. The Eskimos who once hunted here shake their heads in wonder, for many caribou have passed through Koviashuvik for as long as anyone can remember. Some of the old hunters say it is because the "white man's" pipeline camp blocks the migration pass just to the north of Koviashuvik. At any rate, subsistence from the arctic land becomes increasingly difficult as "progress" invades the far north.

What then of Koviashuvik and the Koyukuk?

Not much changes for our resident neighbors in the Koyukuk. Their number remains about the same, give or take a few. Some of us have to spend brief sojourns away from home to make enough money to live at home. Like Anchorage and Fairbanks residents who briefly leave their homes in the Alaskan cities to go work on the north slope, some of us briefly leave the Koyukuk to go work in Fairbanks or Anchorage, but seldom "outside."

At Anaktuvuk, they have new houses now. Old sod huts were

replaced with the plywood boxes. Still newer houses are replacing the plywood boxes, which didn't work very well.

"Progress" comes swiftly to the "Caribou People." Few except the old hunters realize what is being lost in the process. With the native land claims settlement serving as the symbolic ticket to self-determination, the native peoples of Alaska are now joining the line-up at the trough along with the rest of us.

There will be more changes in their villages—as there have been more in our part of the Range.

An oil pipeline construction camp as large as a village is now located some thirty air miles away from Koviashuvik. A second "haul road" was carved through the arctic wilderness along the proposed route of the pipeline. Tons of machines and equipment —earthmovers, trucks, mobile homes and office trailers, bulldozers, power plants, road and airstrip builders, gravel haulers— now reside in several camps along that route. Many environmental studies have by now been made. What they prove is that we still need to know and to understand a great deal more about ourselves, our values, our planet, and what *real* progress means.

From breakup to freeze-up, swarms of helicopters travel these arctic skies. Oilmen, pipeline officials, geologists, survey crews, construction crews—federal and state agency representatives— industrial and academic technicians, scientists, biologists, archaeologists, ecologists—oil and mineral exploration and claims-staking crews.

But when the temperatures slide down to minus thirty degrees Fahrenheit, then minus forty, fifty, sixty, seventy—and, last year, eighty—all the Koyukuk becomes still and quiet once more.

And Koviashuvik?

Timeless, eternal Koviashuvik itself changes almost not at all. Our presence here is as unobtrusive as we can make it. Our tracks upon the land still as faint as we can make them. We fit ourselves into the ecology, live in harmony within the natural cycles of the wild. We have built another cabin because the work of our wilderness education and religious institute requires it. This simple one-room log cabin is also made of logs salvaged from derelict cabins and roof poles from the same selectively harvested slender spruce of the far north. Heated with the same small dead trees, this shelter is identical in size and structure to the "shore cabin" of the journals.

We still choose to have few "things"; we still have no two-way radio contact with the outside world, no generator, no power tools other than a small outboard motor, no all-terrain vehicles, no snowmobile, no sled dogs or pets.

Two months after freeze-up, Girl mistook a wolverine for a playmate. In a single instant, she was ripped wide open. Sam quickly shot her with the .22; she was not allowed to suffer. Her body was used to bait a snare where she was killed. The wolverine returned to the bait. He was killed there. The beagle pup was with us for six of her eight months of life. She had a marvelous life in that brief time of being wild and free. Surely one could say the same for the wolverine. The circle closed.

When it closes for us, where old Rooney and Nakuchluk rest across the lake, on the knoll where the cranberries at Koviashuvik grow the thickest and finest, is where we would like to be. We expect, in turn, to nourish the tundra, and ultimately feed the wolf and the wolverine. . . .

Keep *koviashuktok*, my friends.

74 75 76 77 10 9 8 7 6 5 4 3 2